MICHIGAN: THE PROGRAM

A Curated History of the Wolverines

NICK BAUMGARDNER

TRIUMPH
BOOKS

Copyright © 2025 by Nick Baumgardner

No part of this publication may be reproduced, stored in a retrieval system, or transmitted in any form by any means, electronic, mechanical, photocopying, or otherwise, without the prior written permission of the publisher, Triumph Books LLC, 814 North Franklin Street, Chicago, Illinois 60610.

Library of Congress Cataloging-in-Publication Data available upon request.

This book is available in quantity at special discounts for your group or organization. For further information, contact:
    Triumph Books LLC
    814 North Franklin Street
    Chicago, Illinois 60610
    (312) 337-0747
    www.triumphbooks.com

Printed in U.S.A.
ISBN: 978-1-63727-783-6
Design by Preston Pisellini
Page production by Nord Compo

CONTENTS

Foreword *by Jamie Morris* v

Introduction vii

Part 1: The Coaches

1   Creation and Innovation 3
2   Shifting Sands 18
3   A New Order 33
4   Championships and Challenges 54

Part 2: The Heismans

5   Tom Harmon 81
6   Desmond Howard 93
7   Charles Woodson 109

Part 3: The Family

8   The Quarterback Standard 127
9   Passing through Pressure 145
10   The Runners 168

11	The Pass Catchers	189
12	The Protectors	211
13	Front Seven Belief	232
14	The Wolves	256
	Sources	277

Foreword

IN THE SUMMER OF 1984, I STEPPED OFF A BUS AND ARRIVED in Ann Arbor as a University of Michigan football player for the very first time. I brought two things with me. One was the Army duffle bag my father, Earl Morris—a Green Beret—gifted me before I left home in Massachusetts. That bag held pretty much everything I owned or needed. My father taught me to pack it, exactly how they do it in the military, just before I left. The other thing I brought was my passion. The passion to be great and to be part of something great at what I could figure was the greatest and best-looking (Butch Woolfolk made those winged helmets look so good) college football team in the land.

I could've followed my brothers (Joe, Larry, and Mike) to Syracuse and continued the terrific legacy they built, but I wanted to carve my own path somewhere special. Bo Schembechler's passion for football—and everything about being inside Michigan Stadium—was what I needed. I'd arrived that summer after track season. I weighed 152 pounds. The odds of a player that size becoming part of the greatest rushing tradition in the history of college football weren't great. My passion, however, was. It's what gave me a place at the table.

And while hard work and weights helped, it was passion that kept me at that table.

It was a privilege to run the ball behind men like Jumbo Elliott, John Vitale, Bob Tabachino, Mark Hammerstein, Mike Husar, Clay Miller, Doug James, Art Balourdos, Mike Dames, Tom Dohring, Dean Dingman, and Dave Chester. To be able to share the backfield with the likes of Thomas Wilcher, Bob Perryman, and Gerald White, playing alongside Jim Harbaugh, is something I'll always cherish. My playing days ended in the 1980s, but my passion remains. Watching Michigan head coach Sherrone Moore—nicknamed "Smash"—run the ball 32 consecutive times as an interim (in place of Coach Harbaugh) at Penn State during our 2023 national title run brought a huge smile to my face. I knew our culture, built by those Michigan Men and Women on that sideline, had truly returned to Ann Arbor.

Keep going until they stop ya. *That* is the Michigan culture. What sets us apart.

I'm honored to be included in this book alongside so many great people. I hope you enjoy the ride.

—Jamie Morris
University of Michigan running back, Class of 1987

Introduction

I've been obsessed with football for as long as I can remember. Not "in love with" or "head over heels for," mind you. But specifically and exactly obsessed.

An unhealthy and persistent preoccupation.

I don't remember birthday parties as a kid. I remember playing football games in my head, by myself, in my parents' front yard. I remember simultaneously wanting to puke and cry before my first practice. I also remember feeling like I'd lost part of my soul after the last one. I hated school, but told everyone I wanted to be a teacher—the kind who ignored his students so he could draw plays and practice plans. In my second year of college, I walked out in the middle of a developmental psychology class and called home to tell Mom I was starting over. I wanted to write about football. One of the greatest and most terrifying days I've ever had.

Another where I wanted to puke and cry at the same time.

My life has revolved around a football season in some fashion every fall since I was 12. I'm in my forties now. Every August, when the morning air turns thick and the pollen becomes overwhelming, that painfully happy feeling returns. I hope it never stops.

THE PROGRAM: MICHIGAN

Fortunately for me and my would-be future students, writing stuck. As of this book's publication, I'm a senior writer and NFL draft analyst with The Athletic. Prior to that, I spent a decade covering Michigan's football program at the *Ann Arbor News*, the *Detroit Free Press*, and The Athletic. I co-wrote my first book in 2022, with fellow ex-beat writer Mark Snyder—*Mountaintop: The Inside Story of Michigan's 1997 National Title Climb*.

This book will cover Michigan's historic coaching lineage, from Fielding H. Yost through Jim Harbaugh—their triumphs and their faults. Research for this book comes from my own personal experience covering the program, personal interviews, and several books and newspapers—especially but not limited to the *Detroit Free Press*, *The Detroit News*, *The Michigan Daily*, the *Lansing State Journal*, *The (Cleveland) Plain Dealer*, *The Columbus Dispatch*, *The New York Times*, the *Chicago Tribune*, Michael Rosenberg's *War As They Knew It*, John Behee's *Coach Yost*, Jim Cnockaert's *Michigan: Where Have You Gone?*, and many more. The main scope will focus on people, teams, and dates since 1950. Mainly, though, this book will be about the players who built a family in pursuit of football excellence. One that's withstood two World Wars, multiple global pandemics, the pressure of impossible expectations, the despair of falling short, and the endless grind for perfection.

Michigan's football history is more than fascinating—it's also completely unique, filled with glory garnered by brilliant individuals covering more than a century. It's also a history filled with flaws and failures. Scandals and attempts to cover them up. And, of course, the indefatigable will to keep getting up in an attempt to grow from it all. If I've found one thread that connects the entire thing, it's that Michigan's football program and every person who's ever touched it—no matter the era—operates as a real, honest-to-goodness family. Not a fake one. Real families are flawed. They fight and err. They also come together and achieve the impossible.

One of Lloyd Carr's favorite quotes is a famous one from Rudyard Kipling. And it represents the essence of Michigan's football program better than anything else I've read:

"Now this is the law of the jungle—as old and as true as the sky; and the wolf that shall keep it may prosper, but the wolf that shall break it must die. As the creeper that girdles the tree-trunk the law runneth forward and back. For the strength of the pack is the wolf, and the strength of the wolf is the pack."

I hope you enjoy.

PART 1

THE COACHES

1
Creation and Innovation

ON A FRIGID TUESDAY NIGHT IN DECEMBER 1902, INSIDE AN Ann Arbor banquet hall filled with 150 people drunk on college football, 31-year-old Fielding H. Yost cemented a standard that would outlive every ear that heard it by about seven decades.

His speech, "Why Michigan is Great in Football," came on the heels of his second year at the University of Michigan, two weeks after his second "Point-a-Minute" team finished embarrassing opponents by scores no one had seen before. Yost's dissertation on why his team was great has come to define the pride, image, and attitude of Michigan's football program and supporters.

And for more than 120 years, it's been the guiding light for one of the country's biggest collegiate institutions: the University of Michigan's Wolverines.

The true spark for the flame that became Michigan football came in 1898, Charles Baird's first year as athletics superintendent, when the Wolverines knocked off Amos Alonzo Stagg's Chicago club 12–11 before 12,000 in the Windy City. Hours after that game, on the train back to Ann Arbor, music student Louis Elbel wrote "The Victors." Perhaps sensing this, Baird stopped trying to ignore the country's fastest-growing sport (23 players reportedly died playing college football in 1890) and started working to become the best at it.

That quest led him to a man Michigan already knew. An accomplished West Virginia lawyer who memorized his first rulebook front to back. A man with many sides—one, as was revealed years later, that was racist. A coach who once successfully used a non-college-aged ringer with a fake name to win a rivalry game. A man whose Ohio Wesleyan team once visited Michigan Stadium before leaving under accusations of hair-pulling, choking, and cheap tackling—outrages bad enough to bar the school from future schedules.

Fielding H. Yost.

Born in the post–Civil War West Virginia mining town of Fairview in 1871, Yost grew up the son of a confederate veteran and first attended school at age 10. Unusually curious, Yost—who became town deputy at 17—went on to study law at Ohio Normal before matriculating to West Virginia Law School by the age of 25. After discovering college football in Morgantown, Yost's curiosity for the sport pushed him to Lafayette College in 1896. And after playing part in a major upset win over Penn, Yost was hooked.

Captivated by the crowds and the ability to put himself in the middle of them, Yost studied the game inside-out and determined three pillars for success—expert-level fitness, defensive block destruction, and a complete mastery of the rules. Still

PART 1: THE COACHES

working full-time as a lawyer, Yost's ideas crystalized during a coaching job at Nebraska in 1898. Dr. James Naismith worked for him as an assistant at Kansas a year later. At Stanford, in 1900, his victory over Cal drew national headlines due to tragedy when the roof of a nearby industrial building—holding spectators—collapsed, killing 23 people. He was the first person to master the concept of a football practice, showing up in full gear to physically teach each position to every player. This level of detailed instruction led to efficiency, which led to his first great innovation: the hurry-up offense.

As a player, Fielding "Hurry-Up" Yost saw how flustered defenses got when an offense altered its pace between plays. If an offense could organize itself quicker, it could control the game. His relentless training sessions were designed to simplify the in-between moments of the game, allowing his team to play twice as fast as the opposition—resulting in laughable scores, like a 76–0 win over Hastings that season. Eventually, teams began to find ways to slow Yost's offenses down—faking injuries, arguing with officials on every call, and so on. It rarely worked. And Yost—a confident, braggadocious person from birth—relished every failed effort more than the last. In his autobiography, legendary sports writer Grantland Rice recalled a conversation he'd had with Yost and Pop Warner about who invented the spiral pass. Warner looked at Yost, telling Rice it was the Michigan coach who'd invented it.

"He also invented everything else in the game," Warner added. Not getting the joke, Yost turned and sincerely thanked Warner for that admission. Yost, Rice postulated, had never met an argument—in truth or in fiction—he couldn't win. Even if he lost.

Yost's first two seasons at Michigan made him a national superstar. He came to Michigan in 1901 and, per John Behee's book *Coach Yost*, immediately promised a season-ending game with the winner of Cal-Stanford. The team "boot-camped" at Whitmore Lake that summer, practicing four hours a day. By the time Michigan opened against Albion on September 28, a 50–0 win, Yost's offense was now lightning on grass.

On October 26, Michigan hosted Buffalo, who was 4–0 and unscored upon. Yost's team led 65–0 at halftime. With 10 minutes to play in regulation, the game was called. Michigan had scored 22 touchdowns, winning by an astonishing score of 128–0. When it came time for that holiday game Yost had promised, Cal wanted no part of Yost's machine—reportedly refusing the Tournament of Roses' offer to play January 1 in Pasadena. Stanford gladly stepped up—and got destroyed. Michigan won the first Rose Bowl 49–0 via forfeit with eight minutes left and Yost's first Michigan team, dubbed national champions, outscored opponents 550–0.

By the following fall, Michigan was actually scoring *more* than a point a minute. The school received national recognition for its outstanding performance on the gridiron and all credit was heaped onto the six-foot shoulders of Fielding Yost. A budding showman with a growing ego, Yost realized exactly all of this when he stepped forward to address the crowd during that December 1902 season-ending banquet. Per Behee, every presenter that night had agreed to keep their remarks short. All but one.

"Why Michigan is Great in Football" was a 1,200-word oration from Yost's soul.

He explained how Michigan's speed was two-pronged, both physical and mental—evidenced by the fact Michigan ran more plays than any team in America, some by double. He claimed that in the previous two years, Michigan's defense had not been

PART 1: THE COACHES

scored upon "on straight football." In truth, two touchdowns were scored in that span.

Yost decided they didn't count.

"The two touchdowns made against Michigan have both been made on 40-yard runs, on plays distinctly in the nature of flukes," Yost said, per *The Michigan Daily*. "This itself is enough to show Michigan's [defensive prowess]—12 points scored against her in two years, and these on flukes."

Nobody was better and Yost had every receipt to prove it. When he got off the train in Ann Arbor to take the job in 1901, he did so with a 50-pound piece of luggage featuring nothing but personal press clippings. Writers of the age routinely noticed Yost's penchant for finding his way into newspaper photos no matter who or what the subject seemed to be.

The 1903 season was another masterclass as the Yost-led Wolverine express rolled on, starting the year with seven straight shutouts and a combined score of 437–0. The team would finish 11–0–1, the lone tie coming in what both sides would call the greatest game they'd seen: A 6–6 bout with upstart Minnesota. Yost, who actually lit a victory cigar (per the *Daily*) before Michigan's first touchdown, claimed afterward Michigan was still the better team—pointing to the fact the game was called early due to darkness.

The take in Minneapolis?

"Michigan the Mighty has fallen," *Sunday Tribune* sports writer Frank E. Force's story began the next morning. This was also the weekend Minnesota custodian Oscar Munson happened upon a Michigan-owned water jug Yost and Co. had left behind. Minnesota athletic director Louis Cooke painted the following on it:

"Michigan Jug captured by Oscar, October 31, 1903: Minnesota 6, Michigan 6."

The number 6 behind Minnesota's name was twice the size of Michigan's. Thus, "the Little Brown Jug"—one of the oldest and arguably most famous college football trophies—was born.

Michigan's Point-a-Minute era (1901–05) produced a dynasty that included an extremely sharp double-sided blade. The success created enough pressure to build a diamond mine. Yost began showing nerves late in the run, telling reporters he was "sweating blood" over a game with Stagg's Chicago team in 1904. By the close of that season, he was 43–0–1. Yost's unbeaten streak would hit 56 games until Stagg finally caught him during a 2–0 Chicago win in 1905. The first true Game of the Century.

The lone score came via safety when a Michigan returner misplayed a punt near the end zone. Denny Clark, a Detroit native and the grandson of a former U.S. Postmaster General, was reported to have been in tears over his error from the minute he was taken out of the Chicago game in '05. Fans in Ann Arbor and the surrounding area were reportedly concerned over Clark's well-being to the point he spoke to the media days later to assure them he was fine. He wasn't, though. And never really would be. The gaffe haunted Clark. He went on to serve in World War I. In 1932, at age 47, Clark shot himself in an Oregon hotel room—leaving behind a wife and three children.

"They never would let him forget it," Yost told the *Free Press* upon hearing of Clark's death. "It seemed he had lived it down, if there was anything to live down. He went out West, but he was always meeting someone who remembered the game and who remembered him as 'the fellow who lost that 2–0 game with Chicago in '05.'"

Nothing was the same after that, as rule changes led to Michigan leaving the Big Nine (formerly the Western, now known as the Big Ten) by 1908—starting a near-decade-long

PART 1: THE COACHES

period of independence before U-M returned in 1917. Michigan football's first football dynasty was also the first dynasty the sport saw outside of Princeton and Yale. Yost's Point-a-Minute teams went a combined 55–1–1 with four consecutive national titles and a total score of 2,821–42. His name is synonymous with nearly everything about the creation of Michigan football and his legacy on the playing field has been felt every day since his last as a coach in 1926. In his 1905 book *Football for Player and Spectator*, Yost—much like his memorable banquet speech—scribbled a passage Michigan coaches and players would recite for a century.

"No man can be a football player who does not love the game," Yost wrote. "Half-heartedness or lack of earnestness will eliminate any man from a football team. The love of the game must be genuine.

"It is not devotion to a fad that makes men play football; it is because they *enjoy* their struggle."

Yost's non-football side was hardly spectacular. In the book *Stagg vs. Yost,* author John Kyrk's reporting sheds light on a player loan scheme Yost oversaw well into the 1920s. His habit of pushing beyond the spirit of or discreetly breaking rules enraged peers. Yost's constant bickering with Stagg over exact rule definitions certainly played a part in turning the NCAA rulebook into the overlitigated mess it is today.

There is also the despicable matter of the fact Yost left one of his own personal requirements for a football player out of his speeches—the part where he believed they could not be Black.

Behee reported the coach often received letters from both Black and white Michigan alums recommending young Black players for Yost to recruit. Yost's answer was often subtle—but always clearly—"No."

Both Michigan and the game of football owe a great deal to Yost, the coach. The same cannot be said about Yost, the person.

Yost's postwar years were filled with equal parts success and tension. He became athletic director and football coach after the 1920 season, turning into one of the university's most powerful individuals. Fan interest exploded after the war and much of Yost's attention turned to the expansion of Ferry Field (40,000 seats) and the construction of a new indoor fieldhouse (now known as Yost Ice Arena). By year's end, Yost had a vision for an 85,000-seat football stadium on a patch of dirt between Stadium and Main Streets in Ann Arbor. We know that building today as Michigan Stadium, or the Big House.

Two days before the 1923 game against Ohio State, Yost shocked the world. Per multiple reports, the 53-year-old Yost—tears in his eyes—told the crowd at a University Press Club of Michigan event he was retiring as coach. Gasps were said to have been heard. The following day, Yost released a statement denying ever making such a comment. In those days, that's about all it took from Yost. Michigan beat Ohio State 23–0 before winning its final five games to capture Yost's sixth national championship.

Yost sort of retired in the offseason of 1924. Then again, as he reminded everyone for years, his role as AD gave him the power to delegate the head coach position however he wanted. That fall, he handed the team (and blame for two losses) to assistant George Little. By the start of 1925, with a more talented roster, Yost took the job back, booting Little off to Wisconsin. It would be his 24th season as head coach.

The "Benny to Bennie Show" of quarterback Benny Friedman and receiver/tight end Bennie Oosterbaan helped Michigan go back-to-back as Big Ten champions again, winning a share of the national title in 1925 and 1926. When Michigan toppled

PART 1: THE COACHES

Minnesota for the Little Brown Jug in a thrilling comeback victory on November 20, 1926, Yost stood with a mighty Michigan coaching record of 165–29–10—including six outright national titles and 10 conference championships. A founding father of American football.

He played the same "will-he-or-won't-he" song leading into the following season, keeping the media in suspense about his plans all the way through September. On September 16, shortly after telling his players he was done, Yost told the Associated Press he'd appointed a "board of coaches," led by assistant Tad Wieman, to run the program. A board of coaches, from someone who once wrote that "'too many cooks spoil the broth' in football as in any other realm of endeavor."

Michigan opened Yost's grand stadium on October 1, 1927, and held its dedication ceremony later that month versus Ohio State. The game, Michigan's sixth straight win over Ohio State, drew more than 85,000 people—tripling the size of Ann Arbor in one afternoon. Life looked pretty good.

Until it wasn't.

The Coaching Board collapsed in 1928. By August, Yost wanted back on the sideline. Sort of. On September 15, he announced he was un-retiring. Three weeks later, the day before the season opener, he changed his mind. Wieman, per *The Detroit News*, learned he would be head coach for 1928 when he read it in the paper the morning of Game 1 versus Ohio Wesleyan. With the staff in disarray, Michigan dropped its first opener in four decades 17–7. It was regarded nationally as the worst upset in Michigan history.

Yost was said to have been disgusted. Wieman was said to have been utterly confused. An 0–4 start would turn into a 3–4–1 season and by May 1929, Yost persuaded Harry Kipke—a former Michigan All-American who'd left the Coaching Board

11

THE PROGRAM: MICHIGAN

to run Michigan State's program—to return as head coach. His decision stunned Michigan State and offered Yost a way out of his self-created mess.

Kipke was a highly popular former player who starred in football and basketball as the first Michigan athlete in history to earn nine varsity letters and, by 1931, Michigan had won back-to-back Big Ten championships. One of the best punters Michigan had ever seen, Kipke was also credited with popularizing the cutback move as a runner. Tough as nails, he was also said to have won a fight during an intramural boxing tournament one year with a single punch. In 1932 and 1933, sparked by a thunderbolt from Detroit Northwestern by the name of Willis Ward, Kipke delivered Michigan back-to-back national titles for the first time since Yost accomplished the feat in 1904.

Ward was a Black athlete. And for some at Michigan, that was a problem. Ward was the first Black football player to wear a Michigan uniform since Yost began his association with the university. George Jewett was Michigan's first Black player in 1890, 11 years before Yost's arrival.

As a senior track star at Detroit Northwestern in 1930–31, Ward set a national high jump record while also dazzling in the hurdles. He would become known as Michigan's "One-Man Track Team" after a superstar performance at the 1933 Big Ten championship meet. As a senior in 1935, Ward began a lifelong friendship with Ohio State sprinter—and Olympic icon—Jesse Owens, besting him in two races that year.

He initially had no plans to attend Michigan, however. Ward was told Yost's Michigan athletic department would not allow a Black player on its football team. Kipke, who had saved Yost and Michigan upon returning from Michigan State, personally assured Ward that if he came to Ann Arbor, he'd get to play football. Kipke either was aware of Yost's secret racist policy and didn't care or was unaware and didn't care. Either way, Ward took Kipke at his word.

And Kipke, for his part, drew a line in the sand versus anyone standing opposite. Ward would later recall hearing stories of Kipke, on numerous occasions, going so far as to remove his coat and challenge anyone who opposed Ward's spot on the team to a fist fight. Per "Coach Yost," Kipke took his fistfight challenge straight to Yost himself. No blows were exchanged, but Yost backed down.

During a win over Princeton in 1932, Ward made a spectacular tackle that forced a fumble near the Tigers' goal line. The ball carrier, Princeton's Jack Bales, got up first and was able to retrieve the ball. However, Ward sprung up next and tore toward Bales as fast as he could—leveling him into the end zone, resulting in a safety.

"I hit him with the full impact of my 190 pounds," Ward wrote years later in the *Detroit Tribune*. "I heard his teeth rattle and the crowd roar."

After Michigan secured a 15–7 win, Ward recalled Yost—who had watched the game from the stands—planted a hug on him after the game.

"It is said," Ward wrote, "it was the first time he had ever hugged a colored player—when he hugged me." That embrace would ultimately prove hollow two years later, however, when Michigan football—and the university—encountered one of its darkest moments.

Michigan had scheduled Georgia Tech for a home game in Ann Arbor for the 1934 season. In January of that year, Georgia Tech coach W.A. Alexander wrote to Yost that "it will of course be impossible" for Georgia Tech to play in a game that included a "negro player." Alexander wrote two letters in early 1934 (January and March) to Yost asking for an assurance Ward would be benched. A.H. Armstrong, a Georgia Tech faculty rep, and Dan McGugin, Yost's brother-in-law, who helped arrange the game, wrote similar letters. There is no official record of any written communication to or from anyone at Michigan regarding the Ward matter after May 2. Behind closed doors, however, Yost had made up his mind: Ward was out.

Rumors of the decision to cave to Georgia Tech's racist demands swirled locally throughout the summer. On September 15, the *Detroit Tribune* published a massive headline that read, "U. Of M. Bows To Prejudice."

"I am greatly disappointed to learn through the newspapers that I am not to play in the game with Georgia Tech," Ward told the *Tribune* at the time. "I would give my right hand for the opportunity to play in that game."

Yost made no public comment. Ward, at the time of that publication, had not been notified by anyone at Michigan of the decision and planned to quit football until Kipke intervened. When news spread more rapidly via newspaper reports throughout September, Michigan's campus broke out in protest.

"Michigan is one of the states through which the underground railroad passed before the Civil War, by means of which many slaves secured liberation," wrote Oakley Johnson, former Michigan faculty advisor of the school's Negro-Caucasian Club, in a letter to Michigan President Alexander Ruthven on October 17. "I confess to a feeling of burning shame that the university in which I spent ten years of my life should be guilty of such crass discrimination."

Many of Ward's teammates, including his roommate—eventual U.S. President Gerald Ford—were shaken by the decision, wondering if they should play at all. A group called the "Ward United Front Committee" was formed and eventually rumors spread of a student protest planned for the game itself. Yost,

PART 1: THE COACHES

per Bentley Library, hired the Pinkerton Detective Agency's Detroit branch to investigate the committee so the school could subvert any such attempts.

On October 23, two days after Michigan's 9–2 win over Georgia Tech, Yost wrote to McGugin.

"You cannot realize the effort that was made by the colored organizations and local radical students to create trouble," Yost wrote. "The colored race must be in a bad situation judging from the number of national organizations that are organized to insure racial equality or no racial discrimination."

While Yost pretended, reality set in at Michigan. Neither the team nor Ward—who listened to the game on the radio at his fraternity house—got over the injustice and the Wolverines lost five straight to finish the year a dismal 1–7, the worst season in program history. Kipke's tenure never rebounded. Michigan went 10–22 from 1934–37. Losses to rivals Minnesota, Michigan State, and Ohio State mounted. Kipke's 1937 club improved in a 4–4 season, despite constant rumors Michigan had been subsidizing athletes under the coach's watch, and had a superstar freshman class led by Gary, Indiana, halfback Tom Harmon—a player Yost believed to be the best athlete in America. Still, on December 9, 1937, the board in control of Michigan athletics fired Kipke, a decision that stunned the former Wolverine star runner and many around the program.

The board had originally asked Kipke to resign, though the coach refused. Many things got to Kipke in the end, but Michigan's dysfunction was a theme throughout. Two days after his dismissal, the *Free Press* wrote that "it was known everywhere that Kipke and Fielding H. Yost definitely were on the outs." Many blamed Kipke's failures on the field for his dismissal. An equal number seemed to believe Yost's meddling—despite his constant denials of such—was also part of the cause.

The next two months would change the course of Michigan football history. It would also feature a power play to remove Yost. Days after Kipke's firing, alumni groups began calling for Yost's retirement into a director emeritus position and a full examination of the program. The following week, Regent David Crowley issued a public statement declaring Yost should not be allowed to pick the next coach.

The exhaustive search dragged into February, with regents shooting down numerous erroneous reports they'd already hired a coach. In truth, their sights were eventually set on Herbert "Fritz" Crisler, winner of two national titles at Princeton and a disciple of Yost rival Amos Alonzo Stagg. There was an issue, however.

The *Free Press* reported Crisler had no interest in the job unless "there was a way paved for him to assume the athletic directorship held by Yost." Ralph W. Aigler, then chairman of Michigan's athletic board and the de facto leader of the search (whether the 67-year-old Yost knew it or not), flew east to assure Crisler that was exactly what would happen. Days later, he resigned his post at Princeton and became Michigan's new head coach. Crisler was also given the title of "assistant AD" and made it clear in his introductory statement that arrangements had been made for him to eventually take over for Yost as full-time AD.

"I have no comment to make," Yost told the *Free Press* the day of Crisler's appointment.

The paper would also report that Yost, who had not been in charge of the hiring announcement, "appeared on the verge of a nervous collapse when informed that Crisler had been named assistant athletic director." One of Crisler's first moves was to bring Tad Wieman—the very same former Michigan assistant who'd been yo-yoed by Yost a decade earlier—back

PART 1: THE COACHES

as line coach. The entire move signaled the end of an era, as Yost's days in power were essentially over.

Kipke's Michigan legacy, in many ways, is the reverse of Yost's. His contributions as a human being—pushing for racial equality within Michigan football—outweighed his contributions as a coach. Yost would formally retire in 1940. Six years later, August 20, 1946, the man who created Michigan football died at 75 in Ann Arbor, surrounded by family.

2
Shifting Sands

THE PROGRAM ITSELF WOULD MOVE ON. AND CRISLER changed just about everything—including the helmet.

In those days, some teams opted to paint helmets of only downfield receivers. Crisler believed that to be as much an advantage for the defense as it was for the offense, though, and designed the wing to go on every player's helmet—hoping to give his quarterback an advantage. Thus, his first great contribution to Michigan: The winged helmet.

The other hallmark of Crisler's tenure was the talent—both what he inherited and what he would eventually assemble. All-American back Tom Harmon won the program's first Heisman in 1940, playing alongside standout QB Forest Evashevski. Quarterback Bob Chappuis, halfback Bump Elliott, and tackle Albert Wistert would come later. All would earn program legend status.

Crisler's first game as head coach in 1938 came against Michigan State in front of more than 80,000 in Ann Arbor.

PART 1: THE COACHES

From 1898 to 1933, Michigan and Michigan State played 28 times. The Spartans won twice. By the time Crisler took the field on October 1, 1938, though, mighty Michigan had lost four straight to Michigan State. It would take Crisler one game—a 14–0 season-opening win over the Spartans—to earn admiration from the Michigan faithful. Crisler's first team went 6–1–1 with a win over Ohio State and only a one-point loss to Minnesota. The program's young talent was now on display, pushing in the right direction, and fall days in Ann Arbor were happy again.

Individual talent outweighed team success for most of Crisler's run, except his final year in 1947—when everything turned magic. Crisler's Single-Wing offense—another big change—dizzied opponents and the strategic head coach pushed every right button. He was also the first major coach to take true advantage of the substitution rule, platooning for the first time that year. Michigan's 1947 club was arguably the greatest of its era, featuring five eventual Hall of Famers in Chappuis, the Elliott brothers (Bump and Pete), Wistert, and defensive end Len Ford.

The platoon system also helped Crisler build the first seriously complex college football offense. His practices were detail oriented. New formations and motions were taught. Players referred to Crisler as "the Lord." The results were dominant.

And after Crisler's "Mad Magicians" rolled through Ohio State in front of more than 85,000 on November 22, 1947, Michigan had officially punched its ticket to a Rose Bowl for the first time since Yost's boys played in the very first one. The final score was even the same. Michigan hammered USC on January 1, 49–0—just as Yost's club had done to Stanford in 1902.

Crisler resigned following the season (he'd actually made up his mind to retire from coaching before the Rose Bowl), taking over as athletic director and naming Oosterbaan—who had returned as an assistant—the new head coach. Oosterbaan's first club picked up where Crisler's left off—pitching five shutouts for another 9–0 season, giving the Wolverines back-to-back national championship runs for the third time in program history.

Michigan's program had gone through its share of drama over the first half of the century. But on the field and with a new golden boy as coach, no one could touch the Wolverines.

A four-sport icon at Muskegon High School in the 1920s, Bennie Oosterbaan was a top-flight football, baseball, and basketball player with Olympic potential as a discus thrower. He had options to play professional baseball, but instead went to Michigan to play football for Yost (and basketball and baseball for Michigan). Growing up in a religious home, part of the reason Oosterbaan opted against pro sports was the fact they were played on Sundays.

His relationship with Michigan spanned six decades. Friends teased Oosterbaan that, when it came to his alma mater, "he never left the womb"—arriving as a boy, staying through manhood and well into old age.

Crisler's decision to appoint him head coach appeared perfect. Oosterbaan, it was hoped, would combine the best of Yost and Crisler. That's not quite how it worked out, though. Crisler, like Yost, was a demanding perfectionist who could motivate through fear. Oosterbaan, a three-time All-American, truly loved sports and being part of a team. That, more than anything, was his desire for every player he ever coached—that they fall in love with football as much as he did. He taught accountability more than strategy. He was known to have said that having "backbone" was more important than learning the "wishbone."

He rarely raised his voice. Oosterbaan once told the *Free Press* it's not that he had something against yelling, he just felt it wasn't in him. Sincerity was his true stock in trade. Oosterbaan's

PART 1: THE COACHES

touch for the 1948 club, therefore, was next to perfect. The machine Crisler left behind, even without Chappuis and Bump Elliott, was finely tuned and Oosterbaan knew it better than anyone.

He also knew how cranky that machine could be if not properly fed.

Comparisons to the Mad Magicians hung over Oosterbaan's first squad every day of the year and a type of "not-impressed" vibe hung over the entire 1948 season locally, right through the final game—a 13–3 win over rival Ohio State, Michigan's fourth straight and eighth in 11 tries.

"The victory went to Michigan, the glory to Ohio State," *Free Press* columnist Tommy Devine wrote under a subhead that noted U-M's 23-game win streak and second straight national title.

Michigan had won 10 national titles in the first 50 years of the 1900s. The standard was so high, the landscape was changing. Other programs like Clarence "Biggie" Munn's Michigan State squad were catching up. No one could know it then, but Oosterbaan's first title would be the school's last for the next 50 years.

Still, by 1949, Crisler—now athletic director—began stadium expansion plans. Per Bentley Historical Library, one original plan called for a new expanded capacity of more than 125,000. They ultimately settled on 97,239 and would eclipse 100,000 seven years later.

Oosterbaan's next two seasons featured Big Ten titles, but were letdowns on the national stage—as the team went 12–5–2 with perhaps the only highlight coming by way of a 9–3 win at Ohio State in 1950's famous Snow Bowl game.

Outside of Ann Arbor, two problems brewed. In East Lansing, Munn—a former All-American at Minnesota who had worked with Oosterbaan on Crisler's Michigan staff—had Michigan State reaching unseen heights. The Spartans scored a rare win in Michigan Stadium in 1950 to spark an 8–1 season before more or less forcing their way into the Big Ten (despite plenty of pushback from Michigan) with back-to-back national titles from 1951 to '52. The '51 season included a 25–0 MSU win over Michigan in Ann Arbor.

Not only did Oosterbaan now have unprecedented competition from a legit coach at Michigan State, but the Snow Bowl in Columbus was also the final game of Ohio State football pre–Woody Hayes.

When Ohio State announced 38-year-old Wayne Woodrow Hayes as its new coach on February 18, 1951, the athletic department—and football program—was aimless. Fans wanted the legendary Paul Brown back despite the fact he hadn't been in the college game for nearly a decade. Suspense built right through the final day of a long public search, with Hayes (head coach at Miami-Ohio) coming out as the board's top choice.

"Right now," Hayes said the day he was hired, when asked about his chief rival, "I'm not worried about Michigan. I'm thinking [about our first game of next season]."

This, perhaps, would be the only time Hayes ever said such a thing aloud. It was certainly one of the last times he uttered the word *Michigan* in public.

The Toledo War gets the official credit for starting the rivalry and a win over Michigan in 1919 inspired Ohio State to build Ohio Stadium. But the Game wasn't really the Game until 1934. Coach Francis Schmidt, hired before the season after a successful run at Texas Christian, was asked about mighty Michigan in his introductory press conference. His reply created a tradition that lasts to this day.

PART 1: THE COACHES

"They put on their pants one leg at a time," Schmidt remarked. "Same as everybody else."

Schmidt's first Buckeye team hammered Michigan that year by the widest margin in program history: 34–0. Along the way, Ohio State alums formed a "Gold Pants Club," handing out small gold pins resembling football pants to anyone who beat Michigan in football. The comment, and subsequent win, created the belief that not only was Michigan beatable, but Ohio State could have everything the Wolverines had, if not more. Three straight shutouts over Michigan later, the Buckeyes had their longest win streak ever over That Team Up North and the entire state of Ohio was in love with gold pants.

The rivalry fire had been lit.

It was nearly extinguished by the time Hayes took over in '51, though. Michigan responded to the Gold Pants streak with a 10–2–2 run of its own. However, the rivalry toothpaste was out of the tube. Which is why Hayes simply wouldn't talk about it.

In Hayes' second year, there were no "beat Michigan" signs in Ohio State facilities. The *Free Press* reported that someone scribbled "79 days till Michigan" on a chalkboard in a Buckeyes locker room when fall camp opened. By Michigan week that year, the figure remained.

Hayes, who had lost his first Michigan game, downplayed the entire thing. He kept practices shorter than normal that week. The Buckeyes didn't hit on Wednesday. Thursday night featured a team dinner, complete with songs and entertainment from a magician. Per the *Akron Beacon Journal*, Ohio State officials intended to keep the word "Michigan" from being said during that year's traditional homecoming bonfire.

It all worked. On a damp day in Ohio Stadium on November 22, 1952, Michigan threw four interceptions and lost four fumbles and Hayes' Buckeyes rolled 27–7 in a game that wasn't

23

as close as the score indicated. Even the band had a bad day, messing up the "C" in their script MICHIGAN during the halftime show. The loss cost Michigan the Rose Bowl. The win crystalized Ohio State's faith in Hayes and recharged the rivalry into a new era.

Afterward, per the *Beacon Journal*, fans flooded the streets in Columbus to shout a familiar tune: "We don't give a damn for the whole state of Michigan, we're from O-H-I-O."

For Oosterbaan, things got worse in 1953. After losses at Minnesota and Illinois ruined a Big Ten title shot, Michigan traveled to rival Michigan State a wounded 5–2. It was a significant visit to East Lansing, as this was the Spartans' first season as a football member of the league (now officially the Big Ten). Michigan State, starting as an independent, had made several attempts to join dating back to 1937. Michigan officials stood in the way throughout, until December 1948, when Michigan State was unanimously voted into the new Big Ten Conference.

Now a full member, and back-to-back defending national champs thanks to Munn's leadership, Michigan State had the right to alternate home dates with Michigan as conference equals. Prior to kickoff, Michigan Governor G. Mennen Williams unveiled an award to signify the state's new annual college football showcase: the Paul Bunyan Trophy, an homage to the mythical lumberjack with Michigan ties.

The two-foot trophy, which included Michigan pine and copper, was personally selected by the governor. Neither Michigan nor Michigan State wanted anything to do with it, per reports. Neither did NBC television, which refused to air Williams' planned halftime unveiling. Per the *Free Press*, the Governor's office reached out to NBC to see if it would air an unveiling pregame. They were told "no" on that, too. The whole thing was a fiasco no one wanted to openly embrace.

PART 1: THE COACHES

The '53 game would be a celebration for Munn (who handed the program off to assistant Duffy Daugherty the next year). Munn was a captain for Fritz Crisler at Minnesota in 1931 and became his most important assistant at Michigan when he took over the program in 1938. Munn was Crisler's line coach and, per a *Free Press* report, he was Crisler's preferred successor.

So, when he left to take the Syracuse head coaching job in 1946, feathers were ruffled. And Crisler could hold a grudge like Yost. One year later, Munn was the new face of Michigan State. The two schools have loathed each other—Michigan State publicly, Michigan privately—ever since.

By 1953, Munn had built a national power. His program innovated when it recruited more players out of state. He was never afraid to recruit Black players at a time when others very much were. In his final game as head coach in the rivalry, Munn's Spartans jumped out to a two-touchdown lead early and never looked back, winning the inaugural Paul Bunyan game 14–6 and giving Michigan football its first loss ever in East Lansing.

A year later, the rivalry was officially on when Michigan drew more than 97,000 to Ann Arbor (its biggest crowd in five years) to watch talented sophomore end Ron Kramer and company dominate the Spartans in Daugherty's first season 33–7, snapping a four-game losing streak to Michigan State.

"Bennie has a great team," Daugherty said after the game. "I didn't think we were that bad. But maybe we are."

Michigan had tough losses in '54 to Army and Indiana, but Oosterbaan had rebounded by beating Daugherty's first MSU team. Entering the November 20, 1954, game in Columbus, Oosterbaan had a chance to spoil the young upstart coach's dream season. The Buckeyes were 8–0 with a Rose Bowl and national title on the horizon. Michigan, with just one league loss, had a chance to ruin it all.

For the first three quarters, the Wolverines had 82,000-plus in the Horseshoe chewing glass with the game tied at seven and the Wolverines headed for the Ohio State goal line. But as the third quarter came to a close, the Buckeyes defense stuffed Michigan four times inside the four-yard line for a goal-line stand that turned the rivalry. Hayes' now punishing offense came to life, marching 99 yards (which included a 52-yard sprint from Hopalong Cassady) from inside their own one to break the tie early in the fourth. Another touchdown late made it 21–7, giving Ohio State its second outright, unbeaten Big Ten title since 1920. Ohio State players carried a victorious Hayes off the field on their shoulders before fans tore down the goal posts.

In the Ohio State locker room, Crisler—who went 7–2–1 versus the Buckeyes before turning AD—entered to offer a congrats and a handshake to Hayes. The Ohio State coach asked a photographer to make sure the moment was documented.

"This one," Hayes, per the *Free Press,* said proudly, "I want for my scrapbook."

At his core, Bennie Oosterbaan was an elite athlete. And one of his greatest traits was the signature of any top competitor: the ability to leave a loss in the shower. Oosterbaan would never dwell on the negative, though. Not after a 17–0 loss to the Buckeyes in 1955, and again in 1957. He never hung his head and *always* moved forward.

It's why his players loved him.

It's why his rivals respected him.

"I've never coached against a finer gentleman than Oosterbaan," Hayes said, per the *Dayton Daily News,* the week of their final meeting in 1958. "If I weren't from Ohio State, I'd have to be rooting for Michigan to win this last one for Bennie."

The '58 season was a mess. Following a home loss to Illinois on November 8, only 31,000 fans showed up for the

PART 1: THE COACHES

final home game versus Indiana (a loss)—which turned out to be Oosterbaan's last in Michigan Stadium. A week later, after another loss to Ohio State, Oosterbaan formally retired from coaching. He went 66–33–4 with three Big Ten titles and one national championship.

Speaking with reporters in his office the day of his resignation, Michigan's Gentle Ben put out a cigarette and did what he'd always done. He told the truth.

"The pressure finally got me," the 52-year-old said, per Lyall Smith of the *Free Press* on Nov. 15. "Not the kind that comes from outside. Not from my bosses or the fans. I mean the pressure that builds up inside a head coach whether he wins or loses. I guess I never showed it. I'm not a very demonstrative guy—win, lose, or tie. But my heart beats just as fast as anybody else's.

"All your emotions are laid out in football. And when you share those emotions with your players, you are privileged like few men in other professions."

Oosterbaan immediately proclaimed his successor, Bump Elliott—he of Crisler's Mad Magicians, now 33 and the presumed successor for some time—more than capable. It was also revealed around this time that Michigan's athletic board, run by Crisler, had not considered anyone else for the position. Crisler was making the same hand-off move he'd made when he gave the job to Oosterbaan a decade earlier.

Only this time, the world looked much different. By the time Elliott opened his first season as head coach in 1959, Michigan had gone eight years without a Big Ten title. Elliott's first order of business, much like Crisler's had been, was to scrap Michigan's entire offense. Out with the Single Wing, in with the Wing-T, made popular at Iowa by former Michigan

THE PROGRAM: MICHIGAN

All-Big Ten QB and Crisler disciple Forest Evashevski. Unlike Crisler's seamless shift from Yost, though, Elliott's was rough. Michigan started Elliott's first season 1–3 and never recovered. A 3–1 start in 1960 was sabotaged by back-to-back losses against Wisconsin and Minnesota, and a brutal 7–0 decision at Ohio State. Year two featured an on-field low, perhaps for the entire program.

Michigan had rebounded to a 6–2 record in 1961, and while the Wolverines lost both trophy games that year to Michigan State and Minnesota, there was hope for salvation as Hayes and No. 2 Ohio State came to Michigan Stadium on November 25. The Buckeyes were once again unbeaten, but had a blemish by way of a season-opening tie vs. TCU. Their coach was also looking to prove a point.

The Buckeyes wrecked whatever hope Michigan had early and often, bolting out to a 21–6 halftime lead that only got worse. Up three scores with 34 seconds left, Hayes kept his starters on the field. Quarterback Joe Sparma hit Paul Warfield on a 70-yard throw before Sparma hit Sam Tidmore for the game's final score. Rather than kicking the extra point, Hayes kept the offense in and Sparma hit Tidmore again for a two-pointer to make it an even 50–20. Easily the most embarrassing loss for Michigan football inside Michigan Stadium.

For some reporters that day, the scene was familiar. In 1946 in Columbus, Crisler—in his penultimate season as Michigan coach—humiliated first-year Ohio State head coach Paul Bixler 58–6. Bump Elliott and Bob Chappuis, a Toledo native, wrecked the Buckeyes that day. Crisler kicked a short field goal up 55–0 late in the game. Michigan kicker James Brieske had converted seven successful PATs and the scoring record for a Michigan kicker versus Ohio State was 10. Rather than kill the clock, Crisler put Brieske in to break the record…in the Horseshoe.

PART 1: THE COACHES

Ohioans, Hayes included, clearly never forgot it.

Hayes and Elliott's postgame handshake was said to be incredibly brief, with the Michigan coach pulling away first. From there, Hayes walked over to his team and had them carry him off the Michigan Stadium field. Hayes' 1961 club—which included an assistant named Glenn Schembechler—gave him his seventh Big Ten title in 11 years and officially placed Ohio State atop the college football world.

For Elliott and Hayes, the next seven years—with the exception of Michigan's '64 Big Ten title team—featured mostly disappointing seasons as Daugherty's Michigan State club ran the league. By 1967, especially at Michigan, this was old hat.

Ohio State's once-well-oiled machine turned into a fumbling calamity, routinely outplaying teams only to lose due to self-inflicted wounds. Hayes' intensity was as relentless as it was notorious. The head coach trained mental toughness into his players daily and was never against berating a player for an error in front of the entire team, sometimes in the middle of practice. He once told a BBC documentary crew that his only rule for Ohio State's weekly Friday night team movie was that it be one "without much laughter."

"I've never seen a man make a tackle with a smile on his face," Hayes explained. "You don't laugh your way to victory."

Things were tightening in Columbus. Hayes opened 1966 hopeful that his young talent would turn fortunes, but the fumbling problems continued; worse yet, his one fierce defense had all but vanished. Washington rushed for more than 400 yards in the Horseshoe on October 1 and that season included the first three-game skid of Hayes' career.

After back-to-back home losses to open 1967, including a 41–6 drubbing versus Purdue, things boiled over at halftime of the Illinois game in week five when Hayes—beyond done with the fumbling—went after fullback Jim Otis in the locker room. Otis would later tell *The Columbus Dispatch* that Hayes screamed in his face for all to hear that the sophomore would *never* play a down for him again (he did). The Illini won 17–13.

Before the following week was out, multiple newspapers in Ohio published reports that Hayes' job—in year 17, at age 54—was in jeopardy. On the other side of the fence, Elliott followed up the great '64 season with more disappointment. Only finding a way to scratch the occasional morale-saving win against Ohio State seemed to be saving him. In the Michigan–Ohio State game of 1967, both teams entered with winning streaks—each smelling of desperation. Elliott more so.

Michigan went winless in the month of October that year, starting the season 1–5 with the low point coming during a 34–0 home loss to Michigan State, U-M's worst in the series, in front of more than 100,000. The Wolverines responded with three straight to open November, but entering the Ohio State game at just 4–5 was hardly acceptable. Some 64,000 came to see the Game in Ann Arbor on November 25, 1967.

When Michigan Stadium is full, it's a sight to behold. When it's half full, it's a seismic problem.

It was also the day Hayes' critics were silenced for good and Elliott's were empowered forever. Ohio State dominated the game, jumping up 21–0 and leading by 14 at halftime—which featured a ceremony honoring the soon-retiring Crisler—before settling for a thorough 24–14 win. Speculation about Elliott's job security immediately followed, with reports suggesting he might be the person to replace Crisler as AD.

Michigan did not fire Elliott, though. Fact was, Elliott—much like Oosterbaan—was still adored by so many in Ann Arbor. He was a World War II veteran, a Mad Magician, and one of the greatest to ever wear the winged helmet. A selfless

PART 1: THE COACHES

leader who empowered his players to shoot for the stars on and off the field.

As former Michigan lineman Dick Caldarazzo once told me, "He made you feel real."

Elliott was also the first Michigan football coach to recruit Black players consistently. In 1968, when Dr. Martin Luther King Jr. was assassinated, Elliott suspended spring drills. Per John Behee's reporting, he left it up to the team's Black members to decide when things would restart. That same year, the Wolverines elected the program's first Black captain in All-American running back Ron Johnson.

Elliott also continued to recruit elite talent, despite up-and-down performances. Ahead of the 1967 season, Elliott got in his car and made the three-hour trip from Ann Arbor to Canton, Ohio, to see a young lineman from Glenwood High School. He wasn't a heavily recruited player, but Elliott made the young man and his family feel like they were the most important people on Earth. Before Elliott's car had backed out of the driveway, young Dan Dierdorf looked at his parents and told them he would be a Michigan Wolverine, some three decades before he'd be enshrined in the Pro Football Hall of Fame, located not far from that very driveway.

Dierdorf was hardly alone. Elliott's '67 squad, the one that went 4–6, also featured underclassmen CB Tom Curtis and TE Jim Mandich—who are now in the College Football Hall of Fame. Powerful offensive guard Reggie McKenzie, another CFB Hall of Famer, was a freshman in '69. Jim Brandstatter, a burly tackle from East Lansing who would later spend five decades as a Michigan broadcaster, was also part of Elliott's rookie class.

"At 17, you don't know everything," Brandstatter would later recall. "But I knew I was going to be in good hands with Bump Elliott. I just knew it."

THE PROGRAM: MICHIGAN

That team also featured a young Mike Hankwitz, who would spend five decades in college coaching. Tom Goss, a defensive lineman from Tennessee, would become Michigan's athletic director in 1997. Henry Hill, a short tight end turned DT from Detroit, went from a walk-on to eventual team MVP in 1970. The roster was young, and no one could know it then, but it was the deepest Michigan had ever seen. And all would be on hand for Elliott's final game as Michigan head coach in 1968.

3

A New Order

FAMED MICHIGAN RADIO BROADCASTER BOB UFER OFTEN called Michigan Stadium "the hole Yost dug [and] Crisler paid for." Which was absolutely true. And by the time expense estimates for the 1967–68 fiscal year came out, Michigan's athletic department was in the red.

The Michigan Daily reported athletic expenses came in around $1.95 million—some $200,000 over budget. The cost of all that expansion (plus a new arena in 1967, now known as Crisler Center) was massive and there were a number of years under Crisler's leadership when the department spent more than it made.

That all changed March 16, 1968, when Michigan President Robben Fleming appointed 49-year-old track coach Don Canham as the new athletic director. Canham was more than a coach; he was also a businessman and a thinker. His father worked in advertising as an illustrator. He owned what was then

THE PROGRAM: MICHIGAN

known as "Don Canham Enterprises," a sporting goods business he later renamed and turned over to a trust before starting as AD. His No. 1 stated goal the night of his appointment: Filling that expensive hole with as many fans as possible.

On the field, Elliott's Wolverines surprised everyone in 1968 with eight straight wins after a season-opening loss versus Cal. They entered Ohio Stadium on November 23 at 8–1. Ohio State, however, was undefeated and on the verge of becoming a superpower.

Behind Ron Johnson, Michigan went into halftime down just 21–14—but the fourth quarter was a nightmare. Ohio State's lead exploded to 44–14 with less than two minutes to play when Hayes, after a turnover, sent in Jim Otis—his starting FB who was supposed to have never played another down—for another touchdown to give the Buckeyes an even 50.

From there, Ohio State—just like in 1961—went for two. Contrary to myth, there's no written record that Hayes actually said he tried for two because he "couldn't go for three." Instead, he said the two-point try—which failed—was an error on a botched point-after try. Elliott refused to call it cheap. Most of Michigan's roster disagreed. Johnson said as much to reporters, adding he wished he had another season of eligibility.

"The fat hog went for two," said Michigan assistant Tony Mason, speaking with the *Akron Beacon Journal* afterward.

Change was necessary. The final home game of 1968—Ron Johnson's legendary 347-yard, five-touchdown rushing performance against Wisconsin—was played on a rainy day in front of just 51,117 people. A fine crowd 40 years ago. A nightmare now.

The Michigan Daily reported Elliott had coached the '68 season under an ultimatum from the board to win or be fired—and his 8–2 season, some thought, was enough of an answer despite the Ohio State embarrassment. Canham thought otherwise, per *The Michigan Daily*. When Elliott asked for an extension after the season, Canham said no, instead offering the role of assistant AD. Which is exactly what happened, mostly in secret, throughout the month of December. It was a shrewd yet proper move, and while Elliott was taken aback at first, he quickly agreed.

With Elliott's assistance, Canham began his search with a list of 19 candidates. The Associated Press reported "rumors" that former Mad Magician/Michigan assistant Bob Hollway, Penn State head coach Joe Paterno, Georgia's Vince Dooley, and Tennessee's Doug Dickey were candidates. By Christmas Day, Canham told reporters his list was down to two names. One, per Michael Rosenberg's book *War As They Knew It,* was Paterno. The other: 39-year-old Glenn E. "Bo" Schembechler.

The man once known in Columbus as "Little Woody."

Schembechler went 40–17–3 during six seasons at Miami-Ohio by way of Hayes' staff at Ohio State. Born in Barberton, Ohio's "Magic City," Schembechler was a lifelong member of Miami's "Cradle of Coaches"—having the wild privilege of playing for two Hall of Fame coaches in college: Sid Gillman and Hayes.

The move surprised plenty, including Schembechler. For Canham, it felt perfect, even if he was an Ohioan with a name the *Daily* described as "hilarious."

During his first meeting with reporters, Schembechler explained he planned to build a program founded on toughness and discipline, but also one that fostered relationships. He told reporters he had no hobbies and the only bad habit he had time for was occasional nervous eating. He said his style could be described as militaristic, down to the last detail.

"For example," he began in his distinct cadence. "I despise long hair. It shows that someone is worried too much about himself. Football dominates a player's life during the season. He needs to think about the game and his physical condition and not about his hair."

Deep beneath all this, in Canham's head, lived a story. One of survival—and it had more to do with marketing than winning. With money in the red, facilities lagging behind their peers, and national perception falling, Canham knew a spark was needed. So he went to the oldest one Michigan had: Michigan vs. Ohio State.

The new Michigan AD went so far as to advertise the 1969 home game in various Ohio markets, not caring if a quarter of the 100,101 were wearing Scarlet—so long as they had money. He also pumped up local ticket promotion, getting advertisements in front of a reported 4.5 million in-state homes during his first three years. Crisler hated TV, Canham loved it. Tailgating was embraced. Canham noted he once spent more than $800,000 on women's restroom upgrades in Michigan Stadium to make the building more family friendly.

He spoke to the media constantly and was a promoter, reminding some of famed baseball man Bill Veeck. Or, for non-sports fans, circus legend P.T. Barnum. Canham's intense barrage of change was the boldest athletic move anybody had seen since Crisler painted the helmets.

"Nobody will ever ask me to retire from this job," Canham told the *Daily* in the spring of 1969. "If in five years things aren't going the way I want them to, I'll resign."

Many were impressed by how smoothly he handled Elliott's exit and one of his first orders of business, per the *Daily*, was to start fundraising efforts directed at alumni—another thing Crisler's old guard hated. Canham had also convinced the Big Ten not to punish Michigan over reports of an illegal loan program inside the athletic department. This, of course, they loved.

PART 1: THE COACHES

Perhaps the best description of Canham's wizardry in his new role came after he decided to install state-of-the-art Tartan Turf inside Michigan Stadium, replacing the sod (and the expensive maintenance attached to it). To offset the cost of ripping the turf out and disposing of it, Canham donated it to the nearby St. Francis of Assisi Catholic Church. Michigan didn't have to pay to get rid of its old field and Canham made sure every newspaper in America heard about how Michigan football saved a little church in need of new grass.

In the football building, the coaching switch was jarring. Elliott, like Oosterbaan, was a true gentleman and a breathing symbol of Michigan tradition. He was also beloved by his players. Schembechler was firmly not a Michigan product, a fact that refreshed some and worried others. And by the time he found footing in Ann Arbor, his players basically hated him.

This had originally been true for Schembechler with regard to Hayes, his college coach at Miami-Ohio. He was a junior at Miami when Hayes got the job in 1949, quickly installing his famed in-your-face, no-nonsense approach that was brutally honest even if it crushed a player. Schembechler did the exact same thing at Michigan, wearing the players out beyond the point of exhaustion—forcing a gaggle of them to quit before ultimately producing the famed "Those Who Stay Will Be Champions" locker room sign.

Elliott trusted his players to do the right thing until they proved otherwise. Schembechler trusted his players with nothing until they proved otherwise. And "proving it" would be no picnic. Before his first spring practice in 1969, he put buckets on the field for *when,* not if, a player would have to throw up. He used 1-on-1 wrestling as a conditioning drill.

Plenty left. Per Rosenberg in *War As They Knew It,* a player named John Prusiecki quit the team and scribbled, "And those who leave will be doctors, lawyers, engineers, architects, bishops, generals, statesmen and captains of industry," beneath Schembechler's sign as he walked out the door.

During the 1969 offseason, with Elliott still working on campus, some players went to him with complaints that they couldn't tolerate another day under Schembechler's new methods. They were used to cordial conversations. Fun was allowed. Profanity was frowned upon. Elliott stunned a few when he told them all to deal with it. In truth, Elliott—perhaps sensing what his team needed—was the person who originally pointed Canham in the direction of Schembechler.

The first defense Schembechler's staff installed at Michigan was essentially the same thing Ohio State ran. Hayes' offense was Ohio State's secret sauce and Schembechler knew it—so he copied plenty of that, too. Hayes' Buckeyes teams were famous for making the ordinary extraordinary. Ohio State's four-play Inside Belly series, for example, was hardly complex. But Hayes was the original innovator of in-game blocking adjustments—and taught every concept with punishing precision. So, Schembechler did the same at Michigan. Long gone were the days of Crisler's Single Wing, the magical spinner plays and all the downfield deception it produced. In were the days of what Hayes called "three-yarding" a team down the field with the same three concepts until the opponent broke.

On September 20, 1969—with 5,000 Vietnam War protestors marching outside—Michigan opened the Schembechler era with a 42–14 win over Vanderbilt in Ann Arbor. Michigan handed the ball to nine players (54 attempts) for 367 rushing yards and threw just 11 times.

"That's Bo's offense," junior QB Don Moorhead told reporters afterward. "It's what he calls grinding meat."

PART 1: THE COACHES

After setting a school record with 581 yards of offense in a surprising week two win over Washington, Michigan came back to Earth in week three with an embarrassing five-turnover performance in a 40–17 loss to Missouri that Schembechler called one of the worst days a team of his had ever had.

The Wolverines even had a punt blocked that day, the first of Schembechler's career. The gaffe incensed him and would for years. More than a decade later, during his very first staff meeting, assistant coach Lloyd Carr sat and listened to Schembechler begin by telling every person in the room that they were *never* to be involved in a blocked Michigan punt. Their jobs depended on it. At practice the Tuesday after the Missouri loss, Schembechler demanded his punt rush team come with everything they had—more or less threatening the offense there'd be hell to pay if another punt was blocked that season. Which is exactly what happened that afternoon. Brandstatter, who was subbing in at right tackle for an injured Dierdorf, fired off the ball and blocked his man before sprinting downfield to cover the kick. He heard no whistle. He saw no ball.

He just saw the head coach, enraged, sprinting toward him and shouting. Schembechler told Brandstatter he'd wasted a scholarship and kicked the 19-year-old off the team. Seconds later, beloved line coach Jerry Hanlon jogged over to a stunned Brandstatter and told him that not only was he not actually kicked off the team but, in reality, the missed block wasn't even his fault. The head coach, he said, would get over it. And he did, as Brandstatter would go on to become a close friend of Schembechler's for decades, right through his death in 2006.

Schembechler's temper was every bit as consistent as the one Hayes made famous. His absolute refusal to sulk was also consistent. His punishing and regimented approach to daily work kept the team's focus where it needed to be—and a week later, Michigan scored a surprising win over Purdue. The yo-yoing continued the next week at Michigan State, in Schembechler's first Paul Bunyan Trophy Game, when Daugherty welcomed him to the rivalry with 348 rushing yards in a dominant 23–12 win that put the new coach's methods right back on the hot seat—both in the media and in parts of his own locker room, but not every part.

The next week at Minnesota, Schembechler turned to younger, hungrier parts of the roster—including sophomore RB Billy Taylor, who sparked a massive 28-point second half during a comeback win.

"[This win]," he told reporters afterward, "was the making of this team."

This, more than any other moment that year, seemed to crystalize what could be. Schembechler's way was difficult, but it was working. And while those who had stayed were only 4–2, they were all starting to see what Schembechler once saw in Hayes during his playing career. The same thing Buckeye players saw in their version of the bitter old man who never stopped pushing. The true talent of a great college coach is finding a way to get an entire roster of individuals to collectively understand what it truly takes to win. Schembechler had that in spades. The next three weeks for the 1969 team were a thrash-fest: 35–7 versus Wisconsin, 57–0 at Illinois, 51–6 at Iowa.

The finale would feature Ohio State's powerhouse unbeaten "best college team ever" versus 7–2 Michigan, which could tie for the league crown by knocking off the 17-point road favorite Buckeyes. The Game of Games had finally arrived and while it wasn't perfection vs. perfection, the tension and story surrounding the new version of a classic rivalry was exactly what Canham had dreamed.

PART 1: THE COACHES

Ohio State and Michigan drew a record 103,588 on the final day of the 1969 regular season—Canham's true proof-of-concept moment.

Yost was said to have designed the famed Michigan Stadium tunnel—the only field-level entrance or exit the building's ever had—to mimic the experience of Roman gladiators entering the Coliseum. The Buckeyes played their part in the theater of the day, when two players parted from the herd and ran under Michigan's banner themselves. Standing in that same tunnel watching it all, alone in front with seniors Tom Curtis and Cecil Pryor directly behind him, was Michigan captain Jim Mandich.

One of the original renegades in this rivalry, Mandich was an Ohioan who wanted to be different. And after four years of mostly pain, he and his friends who had stayed were about to have some fun. Teammates recall Mandich, affectionately known as "Mad Dog," had tears in his eyes as he passionately rallied the Wolverines upon their entry into the arena for the biggest fight of their lives.

After surprising the Buckeyes with successful off-tackle runs on two touchdown drives to take a 14–12 lead into the second quarter, Michigan began to shock them. Barry Pierson, a 175-pound defensive back from the Upper Peninsula, fielded an Ohio State punt on his own 37 before getting outstanding blocks from Curtis, Thom Darden, and Ed Moore and sprinting toward open grass. His 60-yard return set up Michigan's game-breaking score, turning surprise into shock on the visiting sideline, where Hayes shoved a television cameraman in anger shortly after the play. It was 24–12 by halftime—and Michigan's football program would never be the same. Curtis, an All-American that year, picked off two passes in the first half and Pierson added three more after the break. In total, Michigan's defense intercepted Ohio State a whopping six times.

THE PROGRAM: MICHIGAN

Nobody scored after halftime and, in Ann Arbor, nobody cared. When the final seconds ticked off, students and fans began to storm the field. Hayes stood alone just in front of the Ohio State bench, now swarmed by jubilant Michigan fans, before taking off his hat and slowly walking away—waiting to shake Schembechler's hand in defeat. The crowd swarmed the Michigan tunnel and Mandich, the team's MVP and a consensus All-American, got stuck. He literally had to crowd surf his way to the tunnel, waving to fans on the journey.

From there, students turned their attention to the north end zone—attacking the goal post with all they had left, finally ripping it down and slowly passing it together, piece by piece, up the bleachers and onto the street. It was the greatest upset Michigan had ever pulled and one of the greatest in the history of the sport.

Rarely are eras defined by the moment that starts them, but for Bo Schembechler, this would wind up as truth. His 1969 team was, without question, the toughest he'd ever carve. A talented group, sure, but also one that had no business standing upright at season's end after all he'd put them through. Yet, there they were—Brandstatter, Dierdorf, Taylor, Curtis, Mandich, and so many more. The 1969 team's resolve and mental fortitude would become the standard for every Michigan team over the next 20 years.

"What the Wolverines did was to beat the Buckeyes at Woody Hayes' own game," *Free Press* writer Curt Sylvester wrote afterward, as Michigan clinched a stunning share of the Big Ten title and a Rose Bowl bid. "They simply overpowered him and they simply out-defensed him."

After the bus ride home, Hayes went to his campus office and started working.

The drama surrounding the victory not only established Michigan's program again, but it also exploded interest again

PART 1: THE COACHES

locally. There was more drama left for Michigan in 1969, though, as the team's Rose Bowl trip was rocked the night before. Schembechler, a man with a heart condition who had completely ignored his health, suffered a heart attack on New Year's Eve at 40 years old. Defensive coordinator Jim Young would coach the game. Michigan lost to USC 10–3 not really knowing the health status of its head coach.

A program had been established, though, and the rising star of its head coach wasn't going to tap out now. By June 1970, Schembechler had lost nearly 40 pounds and was jogging three miles a day, no longer eating pork, and monitoring his sugar. The only person seemingly unconcerned about whether or not this would ever happen again was Schembechler.

"I don't anticipate having another problem," he told the Associated Press. "I had my warning."

He also had a football war to fight. Schembechler and Hayes turned their titanic 1969 bout into a decade of rivalry masterclass that would become known as "The Ten-Year War." Hayes got revenge in 1970 after paying Michigan $80 for some film on that Wolverine off-tackle play. He then ran it all day for a 20–9 win versus 9–0 Michigan. In 1971, Michigan Stadium once again set an attendance record for the season finale, when a now heavily favored 10–0 Michigan team—veterans of '69—held off a fierce OSU charge with a 10–7 win sealed by Darden's last-minute interception. The play enraged Hayes so much he drew two personal foul flags, including one for throwing a first-down marker onto the field. He did not speak with reporters afterward—but held court in 1972, when the Buckeyes again spoiled an unbeaten Michigan season with a 14–11 win in Columbus.

The intensity turned to bitterness on the Michigan end in 1973, when No. 1 Ohio State (9–0) visited No. 4 Michigan

THE PROGRAM: MICHIGAN

(10–0) on a damp November 24. By now, everyone on both sides truly hated one another. Ohio State had messed with Michigan's banner tradition before. In '69, other than the stretch line, a few Buckeye players decided to jog under Michigan's banner by themselves. Four years later, it was a team effort—as Ohio State tore out of the tunnel first, ripping the banner down before celebrating together on the field. The Michigan Stadium outrage turned into a fever-pitched roar seconds later, though, when the Wolverines barreled onto the field—waiting for the banner to be picked up before running under it anyway.

Game on.

The Buckeyes grabbed a 10–0 lead late in the first half. Michigan roared back after a scoreless third quarter, tying the game on a Dennis Franklin quarterback keeper midway through the fourth. Disaster struck in the final minutes, though, as Franklin broke his collarbone with 2:23 to go after being hit attempting a pass. Michigan miraculously got two long field goal tries in the game's final two minutes, but All-American Mike Lantry—a 25-year-old Vietnam veteran kicker—barely missed both.

The game ended in a 10–10 tie, as did the league standings. By rule, the Big Ten athletic directors were allowed to vote on the league's representative for the Rose Bowl. Hayes told reporters after the game he figured it'd be Michigan. But some athletic directors expressed angst about Franklin's injury. The vote went to Ohio State and Schembechler erupted, accusing the Big Ten of colluding against Michigan as the Wolverines had more wins and the Buckeyes had gone the year prior and been routed. He called it the worst moment of his coaching career.

A year later, Franklin again quarterbacked a wonderful squad featuring star backs Gordie Bell and Rob Lytle, along with All-American corner Dave Brown. Once again, Michigan

PART 1: THE COACHES

started the year 10–0 before heading to Columbus. Once again, Michigan lost on the season's final day. Once again, the margin was one score. Once again, Michigan missed a field goal (with 18 seconds left) that would've changed it. After another loss to Ohio State in 1975, featuring perhaps the best defensive performance a team had ever had vs. Buckeye legend Archie Griffin, Schembechler had only four losses in his previous 70 regular season games—dating back to his debut season. All were to Woody Hayes and Ohio State.

The struggle itself had turned into must-see television. The magic of the Ten-Year War, and the Schembechler-era Michigan teams, was the relentless embrace of that struggle. Just as Yost had a half century before.

Fans responded. After drawing more than 102,000 during a win vs. Purdue in late '75, Michigan football began a non-pandemic home attendance streak (more than 100,000 for every game) that stands to this day. Best believe every result versus Ohio State mattered, but the simple fact Schembechler's Michigan kept showing up to the dance unblemished and ready for another heavyweight fight—no matter how the last one went—was all anyone ever wanted. And, thus, Ufer's full call: "The hole Yost dug, Crisler paid for, Canham carpeted and Schembechler fills."

Michigan's football program was, once again, absolutely great.

The Ten-Year War would end in Michigan's favor, when the Wolverines' undeniable growth—and the emergence of star QB Rick Leach—finally outran Ohio State with three straight wins from 1976 to '78, two at Ohio Stadium. Including Hayes' final appearance in the chapter, a 14–3 loss. Told afterward Ohio State hadn't scored a touchdown in its last three tries versus Michigan, Mt. Hayes erupted one more time.

THE PROGRAM: MICHIGAN

"I have no respect for you," Hayes screamed at *Chicago Tribune* writer Dan Israel before storming out of the press room. Ohio State fired Hayes after he punched a Clemson player on the sideline in the closing moments of the Gator Bowl that winter. Hayes died in 1987 at 74. Former President Richard Nixon delivered his eulogy.

"Little Woody" won the war 5–4–1. During that decade, Michigan went 96–15–3. In the decade prior to Schembechler's hire, Michigan had produced 10 All-Americans. During the war period with Ohio State, Michigan had 22, including consensus selections in Mandich, Curtis, Dierdorf, McKenzie, Brown, Lytle, linebacker Mike Taylor, offensive tackle Paul Seymour, defensive back Randy Logan, defensive tackle Dave Gallagher, and offensive guard Mark Donahue. Schembechler's status as a national coaching icon was cemented.

The 1978 season would also see the rebirth of another rivalry as Michigan visited Notre Dame for the first time since 1942. The original break in the series came after Yost refused to schedule the Irish—attempting to get others to do the same—after losing 11–3 in 1909 to a team coached by his former player Shorty Longman. Crisler and Notre Dame boss Frank Leahy also hated each other, with Crisler—a rule committee head—trying to ban parts of Leahy's offense.

The 1978 game would be just the third between the two schools since 1909 and it'd be a thriller. Leach, now a four-year starter from Flint, had helped Michigan turn the tide in the Ohio State series and was Schembechler's first truly great quarterback. In Notre Dame Stadium, he shook off a brutal first half with three touchdown passes after the break to topple Joe Montana and the Fighting Irish 28–14. When the '78 season ended 10–2, Leach was the greatest QB in modern school history—making the All–Big Ten team three times, setting a slew of passing records, and finishing third in the Heisman balloting as a senior.

Life without him would prove a bit awkward.

As Michigan tried to find a new offense in 1979, Schembechler took his frustrations out on a student reporter from *The Michigan Daily*. After a week four win over Cal that featured five missed field goals, putting Michigan kickers at 1 of 10 on the year, a student reporter asked the coach if he planned to put more emphasis on kicker recruiting moving forward. The reporter's account, as well as that of another nearby, is that Schembechler took offense to the question and slapped the reporter's recorder out of his hand before pushing the student's chest three times.

"If you want to make an ass out of me," the coach reportedly screamed at the reporter, "don't try to make me look bad, you understand me, son. Or I'll throw you the hell out of Michigan football." If an apology came, it wasn't published. Michigan would lose three straight to finish the year 8–4.

The 1980 season started off even worse. A narrow season-opening win vs. Northwestern was followed by back-to-back losses, putting Michigan at 1–2 and giving Schembechler a 1–5 mark over his last six games. This was, without question, the greatest in-season football challenge of the coach's tenure.

In college football, with players aged 18–22, winning can provide a cloak of invincibility to even the weakest individual. Losing, by contrast, can make the sturdiest player question whether any of it's even worth it. And by week four in 1980, Schembechler was on the verge of losing a locker room for the first time at Michigan.

"This is the test of being tested," Schembechler told the *Free Press'* Mick McCabe a day after the South Carolina loss. "And I am being tested."

The test, in reality, was change. In addition to QB changes, Michigan's staff had gone through considerable changes on both sides of the ball the previous year. The defense had been run by Bill McCartney, a former high school coach in Detroit, since 1977. The 151 points allowed in 1979 were the most by any Schembechler team at that time and by the start of 1980, he was admittedly having trouble trusting his defense—led by captain linebacker Andy Cannavino and defensive tackle Mike Trgovac.

Michigan settled on big-armed pocket passer John Wangler—from Shrine Catholic in Royal Oak—for 1980 and a legendary connection was born. Anthony Carter—a lightning bolt of a receiver from Florida who would become the greatest offensive playmaker of the Schembechler era—earned All-America honors with 14 touchdowns, and the team rattled off six straight entering a November 15, 1980, game with high-powered Purdue. There, McCartney's defense would return the favor.

Purdue All-American quarterback Mark Herrmann had thrown for 439 yards and set the NCAA's completion record a week prior. On Thursday of that week, McCartney stormed into the defensive meeting room and told his staff they were throwing out the entire game plan. McCartney's idea was to remove a defensive tackle and a linebacker from Michigan's base set, bringing in two defensive backs. The result was the advent of the nickel defense at Michigan and the Wolverines scored a third straight shutout 26–0.

The 1980 team won nine straight to close the year, securing an outright Big Ten title and giving Schembechler his first Rose Bowl victory (23–6 over Washington) in the process. The coach would go on to refer to Cannavino as the greatest captain he ever had and the 1980 squad set a new program standard for perseverance.

PART 1: THE COACHES

In January 1982, Schembechler considered leaving Michigan for an opportunity to be Texas A&M's athletic director. The A&M regents, led by future Dallas Cowboys owner Bum Bright, offered Schembechler a 10-year deal worth $2.5 million. Reports in Texas and Michigan speculated Texas A&M had offered Schembechler the job at the Shrine Game earlier in January. Others wondered if A&M officials had approached Schembechler after Michigan's appearance in the Bluebonnet Bowl on New Year's Eve. The truth, per Bright, is that Schembechler had been speaking with A&M since mid-December 1981, going so far as to visit campus with his wife, Millie. Ultimately, on January 15, it was announced Schembechler would stay at Michigan. Schembechler admitted this wasn't the first time he'd been offered a chance to leave, saying he was disappointed this one had reached the media. Though Bright told reporters it was Canham who leaked it—which in turn upped Michigan's counteroffer to Schembechler.

"We had gone as far as we were going to go and he said he had gone as far as he was going to go," Bright told the *Bryan-College Station Eagle*, saying the reported figure of $2.5 million was a bit high. "Bo Schembechler would have come [to Texas A&M] under certain conditions.... We turned him down."

With extras, Schembechler's reported Michigan salary prior to the A&M offer was $125,000. Michigan gave Schembechler a raise in the 11th hour and while Schembechler would tell reporters it wasn't what A&M's offer was, it was enough to keep him where he felt he belonged.

"I'm not in such bad shape," the 52-year-old coach told reporters on a wintry Friday night in Ann Arbor. "When I walked into this building tonight, I found a dollar bill in the snow. So don't anybody worry about me not being rich."

Michigan went 8–4 in 1982 and 9–3 in 1983 before the 1984 team went 6–6, the worst record of Schembechler's tenure.

THE PROGRAM: MICHIGAN

However, that group—not unlike Oosterbaan's 1968 club—was filled with young talent that hadn't found itself yet. Quarterback Jim Harbaugh, offensive tackle Jumbo Elliott, defensive end Mark Messner, running back Jamie Morris, defensive back Garland Rivers, wide receiver Erik Campbell, and defensive back Brad Cochran—all underclassmen on the '84 team. All soon-to-be stars.

The QB transition from Leach to Wangler earlier in the decade took a minute, but Carter was a revelation, and the offense found a way forward. The pass offense grew some under Wangler successor Steve Smith, but when Schembechler signed Harbaugh, the son of ex-assistant Jack Harbaugh, in 1983 he'd found the best pocket passer Michigan had seen to date. By 1984, the offense finally looked ready to fly, until Harbaugh broke his arm midseason, derailing the whole year and resulting in a 6–6 record.

No one picked Michigan to do anything ahead of 1985. Save for one person.

"[People] look at last year's [6–6] record, at our schedule and make predictions," Schembechler told the *Free Press* that September. "I think they've got us a little underrated. Last year was a tough year, but we might as well accept it. It hasn't had any adverse effect on this team.

"This is a better team."

He was right. The 1985 team was one of the finest Schembechler had at Michigan. Harbaugh set the single-season completion record with two games left. Against Ohio State, his beautiful 77–yard TD pass to John Kolesar served as the highlight to a 10–1–1 season that wrapped with a Fiesta Bowl win and a No. 2 overall ranking.

The '86 season started out like a house on fire, with Michigan tearing off nine straight wins to open the year. After beating

PART 1: THE COACHES

Purdue on November 8, Harbaugh had set the new program completion record (332) and Schembechler—in year 18—had officially tied Fielding Yost with 165 wins at Michigan. The following week, disaster would strike, though, as Minnesota quarterback Rickey Foggie engineered a shocking upset at Michigan Stadium 20–17, spoiling all the parties.

The Monday before the final game of that season at Ohio State, Harbaugh guaranteed a victory over the Buckeyes. His boast came on the same day his father, Jack, had been fired as head coach at Western Michigan. Jack would tell the *Free Press* he believed his son made his bold claim to take some of the negative attention away from his brutal professional setback. Either way, Jim Harbaugh would prove a man of his word—as would star tailback Morris, who erupted for 210 yards to pace a 26–24 win in Columbus.

"Jimmy was talking for all of us when he said that," Morris, who would set the school's career rushing mark in 1987, told the *Daily* afterward. The victory was No. 166 at Michigan for Schembechler, a new program record. The 1986 team would finish 11–2—his first 11-win season since 1971. Schembechler would win two more Big Ten titles in '88 and '89 before retiring and briefly transitioning into the athletic director role.

The lone on-field blemish of Schembechler's tenure was his inability to win a national championship. His 194 wins remain a Michigan record. He suffered only 48 losses in 21 seasons and won 85 percent of his conference games, with 13 Big Ten titles. In the Rose Bowl, he went 2–8 in 10 tries. Most of his players were fiercely loyal to him in ways not seen at Michigan since the days of Yost. Schembechler's program was revered in the state and many of his players became regional celebrities as a result. Michigan is a powerhouse brand today thanks in large part to Schembechler's efforts on the football field.

Schembechler's football legacy at Michigan was as undeniably successful as it was consistent.

His legacy away from football is more complicated.

A small-town Ohioan born in 1929, Schembechler came from a militaristic world and resisted his share of social change. His old-world beliefs did nothing to help the cause of female athletes during his time, as he opposed the practice of giving Michigan varsity jackets to women. Schembechler believed it would minimize the "value" of the brand. That practice wouldn't begin until 1991, after the coach's retirement and during a time he was working for the Detroit Tigers—where he'd encounter another sexist situation after criticizing a local paper for sending a female writer into a baseball locker room. One of Schembechler's former players, Warde Manuel, became AD himself in 2016 and delivered letter jackets to female Michigan athletes from 1973 to '91.

In July 2018, more than a decade after Schembechler died in 2006, a former Michigan student-athlete wrote a letter to Manuel detailing his account of sexual abuse he suffered during medical exams by a university doctor in the early 1970s. Dr. Robert Anderson began his time at Michigan in 1968, working with the football team over a span of 35 years, retiring in 2003. In the subsequent months and years that followed the original 2018 complaint, more than 1,000 people—mostly men, many athletes—came forward to accuse Anderson of sexual abuse during his time at Michigan.

A John Doe lawsuit filed in July 2020 came from a former Michigan student who claimed to have told Schembechler about the abuse in 1982. The suit also alleged Canham was told about this. Neither took any action, the suit claimed, and Anderson's abuse continued for years. Multiple Schembechler-era players from the 1970s and 1980s would come forward with similar

PART 1: THE COACHES

stories of abuse at Anderson's hand—including Chuck Christian and Jon Vaughn, both of whom would become advocates for survivors of sexual assault.

The long-running abuse was reported to have been something athletes, including Schembechler's football players, knew about. Schembechler's son, Matt, claimed to have told his father and mother that Anderson abused him in 1969. Many former Schembechler players defended their former coach, including Jim Harbaugh, stating the man they knew would have done something had he known. Others stood by their former teammates, trusting them.

Anderson (2008), Schembechler (2006), and Canham (2005) had all died prior to the initial complaint and subsequent lawsuit process, which saw Michigan pay $490 million to Anderson survivors in 2022.

In the book *Bo's Lasting Lessons*, a leadership tome authored by Schembechler and John U. Bacon (published after the coach's death), the Hall of Fame coach offered the following quote:

"When someone uncovers a scandal in their company, I don't think they can say, 'I didn't know what was going on.' They're just saying they're too dumb to do their job," he explained, before concluding, "…they know what's going on."

4

Championships and Challenges

WHEN MICHIGAN'S GREAT CANHAM-SCHEMBECHLER EXPERiment started, the university's athletic budget was $2.8 million. Some 20 years later, by 1987, that budget had swelled to $18 million and could reasonably be called a business empire—if an extremely delicate one.

With Canham set to retire in the summer of 1988, shortly after his 70th birthday—the university's mandatory retirement age—Michigan began advertising the job in the *Wall Street Journal*, *New York Times*, and *Los Angeles Times*. Canham disagreed with this, stating Michigan did not need a "businessman" but rather a fundraiser for the next stage of college athletics. Everyone knew his favorite candidate was the 59-year-old Schembechler, even after the coach underwent a seven-hour quadruple bypass on December 15, 1987, his second such procedure in a decade.

The board was hesitant, but Michigan eventually offered Schembechler the role of AD under one condition—that he retire from coaching after 1988 and assume his new job full-time in 1989. He refused. A regent told the *Free Press* the board added the condition knowing the coach would refuse, allowing the board to focus on its preferred candidate—John Swofford from North Carolina. Former players and Michigan alumni immediately voiced displeasure publicly. Asked if he was fit enough to do both jobs, Schembechler only fanned the situation by saying, "I can do anything."

After another month of this, a solution was found. Michigan offered Schembechler the job of AD and allowed him to continue coaching without restrictions—also naming U-M business operations director Jack Weidenbach as his top associate AD to handle most of the day-to-day.

The arrangement lasted about 20 months. After a Big Ten title in 1988 and another 10-win season in 1989, Schembechler found himself back in front of a microphone on December 13, 1989, announcing his retirement from coaching. Citing health and his good fortune to coach 20 years after a heart attack, Schembechler—fighting back tears—called the decision the hardest he'd ever made. The move relieved both his wife and mother.

As far as the AD job was concerned? Schembechler told reporters he didn't think it would be good for him to hang around as AD while Gary Moeller, his self-appointed successor, took over the football team.

A week later, he was out. Moving on to become the new president of the Detroit Tigers, a team then owned by Michigan grad and Schembechler friend Tom Monaghan—who had also helped up the offer to keep Schembechler at Michigan in 1982. Weidenbach would take over and become the full-time AD in 1991. Michigan's athletic department would soon enter a period of chaos, going through three ADs and off-field scandals (many rooted during the Canham era) in the 1990s.

The on-field football product Schembechler left behind, however, was still very much rolling.

On pedigree alone, Moeller was basically Schembechler Jr. He had been a captain for Woody Hayes at Ohio State before getting his first coaching gig at Miami-Ohio, working for Schembechler, in 1967. When Schembechler first reported for duty at Michigan in 1969, it was Moeller who drove his car north from Ohio through a massive January snowstorm. That is, until Schembechler got upset at how Moeller was driving, took over, and got them lost for some two hours before finding their new home. After helping establish Michigan's defense for six seasons, Moeller got his first head coaching gig at Illinois in 1976, at 36 years old. It was a mess, as Moeller went 6–24–3.

When Moeller returned to Schembechler's staff in 1980, now an offensive assistant, he was a changed coach. He'd also brought a friend with him: defensive secondary wizard Lloyd Carr. Moeller and Carr would become Schembechler's top two assistants throughout the 1980s and, along with ace strength coach Mike Gittleson, were critical in helping the coach establish a highly successful second decade.

Moeller had long been viewed as Schembechler's successor and when Carr opted to stay on as defensive coordinator, the plan was locked in. Carr considered Moeller a close friend and mentor; he also believed him to be a football genius. As a coach during an era of rapid specialization, Moeller (not unlike Yost) always maintained an ability to properly teach any position—from quarterback to defensive end to punter.

PART 1: THE COACHES

And as was the case for his old boss, Moeller's first team was stacked with talent. Michigan's 1989 squad featured young stars in defensive lineman Chris Hutchinson, defensive back/kick returner Tripp Welborne, running back Jon Vaughn, quarterback Elvis Grbac, center Steve Everitt, wide receiver Derrick Alexander, and tight end Tony McGee, to name a few. Moeller's offense had been ready for a more pass-happy transition for some time, as he and QB coach Cam Cameron worked to turn Michigan's offense into college's first pro-style vertical pass threat by the start of the decade.

There was also Desmond Howard.

A smallish former high school running back from Cleveland, Howard emerged as a sophomore in 1990 with 57 catches for 858 yards and a kickoff return touchdown. His unique blend of explosion, track speed, and body control made him a marvel with a catch radius that far exceeded his 5'10" frame.

The 1990 squad was young but incredibly gifted. The only blemishes were a four-point loss to No. 1 Notre Dame, a one-point controversial home loss to Michigan State, and another one-point loss to No. 23 Iowa. The Wolverines won six straight, including a 16–13 win in Columbus, to close the year with a Big Ten crown and much anticipation for 1991.

As the '80s turned into the '90s, college football's expansion was at an all-time high. Programs in the South began strengthening. And while Moeller's '91 squad was outstanding, it still wound up losing—by 20—at home in September to a Florida State team featuring Derrick Brooks, Terrell Buckley, Edgar Bennett, and a gaggle of other future NFL stars.

Still, Michigan suddenly had an offense recruits wanted to play in. It also had Howard. And no one in Ann Arbor had seen anything like him. A true weapon anywhere on the field, Howard was part Tom Harmon, part Anthony Carter, and part dynamite.

THE PROGRAM: MICHIGAN

In the season opener at Boston College, Howard scored on a 93-yard kickoff return and caught three touchdowns. His diving fourth-down catch in the back of the end zone to win the Notre Dame game the following week is still one of the most replayed moments in the history of Michigan football. It also firmly put Howard in the Heisman conversation. By the Minnesota win in week seven, he had scored 15 total touchdowns.

That number grew to 22 by the time Howard nestled under an Ohio State punt on his own seven-yard line on November 23, 1991, at Michigan Stadium. Howard's electrifying 93-yard punt return and subsequent Heisman Trophy pose in the south end zone put the capper on the greatest individual season in school history. And while a 10-win year would end with a sour loss to Washington in the Rose Bowl, Howard became the program's second Heisman Trophy winner that December—giving Moeller something in just his second season that Schembechler never had.

The 1992 campaign was even better, though bittersweet. Moeller continued to crank the talent and the Wolverines filled the hole left by Howard's departure with breakout star running back Tyrone Wheatley. Hutchinson, meanwhile, had exceeded all expectations in replacing Mark Messner—earning Big Ten Defensive Lineman of the Year honors. Moeller's 1992 team gave Michigan its first unbeaten season since the 1940s.

The only problem: it was 9–0–3.

From a purely talent standpoint, no coach in Michigan football history recruited better than Moeller. His first three teams put 19 players in the NFL draft—including three first-round picks. But as can often be the case with brilliant minds, communication and detailed organization had slipped under the coach. Practices began to drag. The tighter things got, the more Moeller relied on himself alone. And Michigan began to struggle closing out games.

PART 1: THE COACHES

After a tough 8–4 season in 1993 (including four losses by a combined 20 points) with mostly young talent, Moeller entered 1994 with perhaps his most talented team to date. Wheatley, a 235-pound hammer who also ran hurdles on the track team, returned after back-to-back 1,000-yard seasons. Wheatley's backup, Tshimanga Biakabutuka, a 215-pounder from Quebec by way of Zaire, was just as much of a physical phenom. Junior Ty Law—a future Pro Football Hall of Famer—was one of the most natural cornerbacks the school had ever seen.

After opening with wins against Boston College and at No. 3 Notre Dame, Michigan found itself one snap away from being firmly in the national title picture on September 24, 1994, when Colorado quarterback Kordell Stewart dropped back for a Hail Mary that would literally change lives. Stewart's "Miracle at Michigan," a 64-yard Hail Mary that went at least 70 in the air, was tipped, and landed in the arms of wide receiver Michael Westbrook for a shocking Buffalo win.

Michigan was crushed. The locker room afterward immediately struggled to process what had just happened. Finger pointing took place in the immediate aftermath, some of it ugly. The play would haunt the team the rest of the season, as Michigan fell by a touchdown less than a month later to third-ranked Penn State before a 31–19 loss to Wisconsin on October 29 and, finally, an embarrassing 22–6 loss to Ohio State. Once again, the team finished 8–4.

By the spring of 1995, Moeller's eye for talent had proven undeniable. His '95 class, in fact, might be one of the greatest of all time—as it included Charles Woodson and Tom Brady. Small mistakes, though. They usually add up. And on Friday, April 28, 1995, the 54-year-old Moeller had the worst night of his life—one his professional life wouldn't survive.

THE PROGRAM: MICHIGAN

During a night out at the Excalibur restaurant in Southfield, Michigan, Moeller drank to excess and lost himself in a public tirade most close friends were shocked to see. The head coach was arrested and charged with misdemeanor disorderly conduct and assault and battery. Moeller was released from police custody and returned to his Ann Arbor office, preparing to leave for Big Ten meetings in Florida later that day. By Sunday, news of Moeller's arrest broke—with the coach already on the road. On Monday, police described the incident publicly—including details Moeller had not shared with his bosses, resulting in Moeller's suspension by then president James Duderstadt.

Moeller left Florida and spent a day with family in Ohio before meeting with Michigan athletic director Joe Roberson. Roberson and Duderstadt allowed Moeller a chance to stay at Michigan with conditions (including alcohol counseling)—but the coach refused. A separation agreement was reached by Thursday. In reality, via reporting from Mark Snyder and myself for the book *Mountaintop: The Inside Story of Michigan's 1997 National Title Climb,* Moeller's decision to omit many damning details of his arrest to Roberson during their initial conversation—details Roberson later found out from police—led to his dismissal. Carr was named acting and, eventually, interim head coach. The following spring, during a team meeting with the players he no longer coached, Moeller told the team to learn from his mistakes. Then he said goodbye.

Carr, a former college quarterback turned high school teacher, grew up in Riverview, Michigan, alongside legendary future coaches Bill McCartney and Woody Widenhofer. His first major college job at Eastern Michigan was followed by a stint on Moeller's Illinois staff before he joined him at Michigan in 1980. The Moeller situation shocked him as much as anyone, as the coach had been best man in Carr's wedding. A defensive backfield coach by trade, Carr had great respect for both Moeller and Schembechler. He was also really nothing like either of them.

A voracious reader and lifelong learner, Carr approached football like a schoolteacher approached a classroom. He simplified everything he could control. He hated attention. He never forgot anyone's name. Moeller and Schembechler led by controlling everything the light touched. Carr led by placing trust in those he hired to do their jobs, while putting all his waking energy into controlling the small details that had cost Michigan so many times in the early 1990s.

As a recruiter, Carr's approach can best be described through the story of Todd Plate, a defensive back from Brooklyn, Michigan, who signed with the Wolverines ahead of the 1986 season. Plate had first introduced himself to Carr after a Michigan practice a season earlier, standing with his dad and eagerly pitching himself to the team's new defensive coordinator as a prospective walk-on.

"He's a player," Plate's father said to Carr, who tried his best not to roll his eyes before pointing the pair in the right direction and rushing home for dinner with his kids.

Some four years later, Carr looked onto the Michigan Stadium turf and saw Plate standing opposite Ohio State leading receiver Jeff Graham on a third-and-goal from the four-yard line. The Buckeyes ran a fade right at Plate, who had not only been a star scout team player but had also proved his father right by earning a scholarship. The former walk-on played press coverage perfectly in the end zone, finishing through the ball and breaking up a touchdown in the biggest game of the year with the Big Ten title on the line. The Buckeyes settled for a field goal and Carr made a mental note.

THE PROGRAM: MICHIGAN

He'd tell the story of Todd Plate to coaches throughout his career, insisting that *every* kid who touches the program matters—and could be the difference between a championship or second place.

He coached through an ultimatum from Michigan administration to get the interim tag removed in 1995. Carr was able to keep Michigan's program out of the ditch in '95 and '96, but by the start of 1997—with Michigan now having suffered four straight four-loss seasons—Carr, once again, believed his job was on the line. His team, led by fifth-year senior QB Brian Griese, Woodson, a titanic offensive line, and the most talented defense in modern school history, felt it, too. And rallied around him as a result. For the first time in a generation, Michigan players were freer to speak their mind within the program. Freer to dress the way they wanted, to be who they wanted and play the way they wanted.

The result—for the first time in a decade, Michigan played free, loose, and for nothing but each other. The team elected a walk-on captain in linebacker Eric Mayes. Younger players started to feel more comfortable around older players. Old frustrations were aired out as, in reality, Carr sensed what nobody else had: Michigan's football family needed to heal so it could move forward together. Which is exactly what happened.

Carr and first-year DC Jim Herrmann—a former Michigan linebacker—installed an exciting new fire-zone defense that revolved around Woodson's presence as the nation's best defensive player. By the middle of that '97 campaign, after several appearances on offense while also anchoring the country's top-ranked defense, Woodson announced himself as the country's best player, period, when he made a ridiculous one-handed sideline interception at Michigan State that has since made its way onto more posters than the Ohioan can count. Michigan

PART 1: THE COACHES

survived a scare versus Iowa and crushed unbeaten Penn State in Happy Valley 34–8 in arguably the most impressive regular season win in modern program history.

And, like Howard six years prior, Woodson's punt return touchdown against Ohio State in the finale—capping an 11–0 perfect regular season—sealed his Heisman victory. Woodson would become Michigan's third Heisman winner that December and the Wolverines, now led by a thoughtful coach no one really wanted in the first place, were on the verge of a national title.

Everything came together at the Rose Bowl on January 1, 1998, in ways it never had for Schembechler or Moeller. Carr's unbeaten Michigan squad found a way to topple big-armed Washington State QB Ryan Leaf in the season's final game and while the national title wound up split with Nebraska, it was Michigan's first since 1948.

Three years prior to that national title, the program was on its knees and without direction. Michigan administration nearly cut the Schembechler line, and many did not want Carr as head coach. He proved them all wrong. In 1997, Michigan went from a powerful Midwestern program known throughout most of the country to a national powerhouse with a global brand.

It was impossible to know then, but Carr's ability to rejuvenate the program—and his 1997 team's ability to come together as one—saved Michigan football.

The unlikeliest of leaders with the steadiest of hands, Carr went 32–5 from 1997 to '99 and by 2004 his Michigan program had produced a national title, five Big Ten crowns, a Heisman winner and more than 40 NFL draft picks. Three of his players (Woodson, Steve Hutchinson, and Brady) would enjoy Hall of Fame pro careers. When players entered his office to talk, he had them read a word from the dictionary upon entry. Carr's contributions to the Ann Arbor community, specifically his work with C.S. Mott Children's Hospital and the ChadTough Defeat DIPG Foundation (named for his late grandson), last to this day. He spoke in a signature tone that was both direct and whimsical at the same time, with the ability to pivot from deadly serious to dryly hilarious multiple times in one sentence.

His 2006 club would start the year 11–0, losing a No. 1 vs. No. 2 game at Ohio State by three points—the day after Schembechler's death—at Ohio Stadium. After a tough 2007 campaign, featuring a stunning upset loss to Appalachian State, Carr retired from coaching.

In just 13 years as head coach, Carr managed 122 wins—placing him behind only Schembechler and Yost at Michigan. His players revered him as a combination of a second father and favorite teacher. They came to him for advice on everything—from marriage to business—for the rest of their lives and he returned every call. In 2011, Carr would become perhaps the unlikeliest of inductees into the College Football Hall of Fame. During a 25-year reunion for the 1997 team in 2022, Michigan dedicated the stadium tunnel in Carr's honor.

"My name is up there," Carr, still with that signature tone, told a slew of his former players the afternoon of the dedication, "because my guys put it there."

Carr's retirement was the end of the Schembechler coaching line. The 28-day search for his replacement, led by AD Bill Martin, was all over the place. There were flirtations with LSU coach Les Miles, a former Schembechler assistant loved by some and loathed by others in the Michigan family. Rutgers coach Greg Schiano actually turned the job down. By mid-December, with erroneous media reports and fan angst growing, Martin landed on West Virginia coach Rich Rodriguez—the opposite of a "Michigan Man" in just about every way.

PART 1: THE COACHES

Rodriguez brought change, fast and furious, to a Michigan program that was in need of more speed and a fresh look on offense. The problem? Carr's offense was more or less the exact opposite. Rather than slowly integrate his spread system, Rodriguez believed it best to establish a new identity immediately—even if growing pains happened. They did. The defensive changes weren't any better. Plenty of attrition happened before Rodriguez's first season, with several players—including big-armed pocket passer Ryan Mallett—transferring due to the fact the new coach's system no longer fit their talents. Traditions were changed. Rodriguez fired all of Carr's assistants, save for one, including legendary strength coach Mike Gittleson—a move that did him no favors with the legion of legendary former players who now barely recognized the place.

The result was a disaster.

Rodriguez's first season in 2008 was the worst in modern program history. Michigan went 3–9 and missed a bowl for the first time since 1974. He never recovered. The aftermath set Michigan back at least a decade. His second year began under the cloud of an NCAA investigation into improper practice methods and ended with another losing season 5–7. By year three, once-mighty Michigan was officially staggered, and Rodriguez's new era was already on the hot seat. The pot boiled over with a humiliating 52–14 loss to Mississippi State in the Gator Bowl on January 1, 2011. After three years, Rodriguez—at 15–22 with just six Big Ten wins (zero vs. Michigan State or Ohio State)—was fired by new Michigan AD David Brandon.

Brandon, a former Michigan regent and Domino's Pizza CEO who played under Schembechler, tried to put tradition back into the program when he hired former Carr assistant Brady Hoke, who had gone 49–50 in eight years at Ball State and San Diego State. Hoke was a beloved defensive line coach

THE PROGRAM: MICHIGAN

on the '97 national title squad and a wildly popular pick among former players. He would not, however, be the answer to anyone's prayers.

Hoke reestablished several Michigan traditions—including general defensive football, which had vanished under Rodriguez—and shocked everyone with an 11-win Sugar Bowl season in 2011. Led by a dedicated group of fifth-year seniors, many recruited to the program by Carr, the group, at times, felt abandoned by the Michigan family during that period and expressed as much even after their successful final campaign.

It would be the best Hoke had. A defensive line coach who had never coordinated either side of the ball, Hoke was an outstanding recruiter who was beloved by his players and their families—but on the field, his program was disorganized and without an offensive identity. Not unlike the blunder Rodriguez had made three years prior, Hoke opted against keeping the spread offense dynamic QB Denard Robinson thrived in—resulting in an awkward attack that eventually lost steam and fell apart by year four.

Moreover, Hoke's staff was never strong enough, and his program's general discipline was never sound enough. Recruiting was generally terrific; the results, however, were middling. In four years, Hoke went 31–20, with a 2–6 record vs. Michigan State and Ohio State.

By the end of the 2014 season, after a 5–7 campaign lowlighted by off-field drama resulting in the firings of both Hoke and Brandon, Michigan football was back to a modern low point and in need of new life.

Then, after a month of speculation, new life appeared.

Jim Harbaugh, just two years removed from a Super Bowl appearance with the San Francisco 49ers and now football's hottest coaching free agent, returned home to Ann Arbor on

PART 1: THE COACHES

December 30, 2014—hired by interim athletic director Jim Hackett during a month-long search that captivated the NFL and college football worlds. Most media speculation throughout early December leaned toward Harbaugh, who had been fired by the 49ers after a falling out with management, finding another job in the NFL, with Michigan being a dark horse option at best. As the month wore on, though, Michigan slowly turned into the favorite to land the coach's services.

In reality, Harbaugh had held interest in coaching at Michigan since his professional playing days ended in the early 2000s. Late during his playing career, Harbaugh worked as a volunteer assistant coach for his father, Jack, helping him build a I-AA national champion at Western Kentucky. During Harbaugh's down periods in the offseason, he joined his father on the road and learned how to recruit—driving all over the Southeast, especially Florida, scouting and collecting talent. In the 1990s, while playing in the NFL, Harbaugh personally recruited Willie Taggart for his father out of Bradenton, Florida—showing up in the Manatee High School cafeteria one day out of the blue to have lunch with a bunch of shocked kids. Taggart would become a star at Western Kentucky before embarking on his own coaching career, which has included head coaching stops at Oregon and Florida State.

Always his own person, Harbaugh bucked advice from many he trusted—including Raiders owner Al Davis—when he opted against working his way up the assistant coaching ladder in favor of a head coaching job at the University of San Diego, a non-scholarship program in 2004.

There, in his early forties, Harbaugh worked relentlessly to build a winner. He never stopped thinking like a player, even as a coach. At San Diego, he joined his players for push-ups at practice. He ran gassers up a hill with them until, like them, he puked. Harbaugh went 29–6 in three years and persuaded a completely down-on-its-luck Stanford program to give him a chance in 2007. In his debut season, Harbaugh improved the team win total by three and engineered the largest upset the sport had seen—beating No. 2 USC as a 41-point underdog. His presence was indefatigable. He pitted players against one another in everything they did, every second of every day, and never let off the gas—willing people (some talented, some not) to achieve above their believed level.

"He takes losers," a former Harbaugh player at San Diego once told me, "and turns them into winners."

A year later, when Michigan's job came open, Harbaugh expressed interest. Michigan officials, however, did not believe he was ready.

By December 2014, Harbaugh had the football world in his palm. After resurrecting Stanford, Harbaugh's first run as coaching's hottest free agent happened in 2011—once again when Michigan's job was open. Brandon, however, had other plans—and Harbaugh joined the San Francisco 49ers, where his tour de force would continue with a 44–19–1 run over four years that included a Super Bowl appearance and three trips to the conference title game. Michigan was, at this point, beyond desperate and Harbaugh—finally—was more than wanted by the place he'd long desired. On December 30, Michigan introduced Harbaugh in front of hundreds of reporters in Ann Arbor—the largest non-game media gathering Michigan had since Schembechler's retirement. Fans stood outside Michigan's Junge Family Champions Center, faces pressed against the glass on a cold winter morning, hoping to get a look at what many teary-eyed supporters deemed their savior.

Harbaugh's Michigan homecoming was national news for more than a calendar year, as his 2015 team shocked the country

PART 1: THE COACHES

with a 10-win season in year one. Hoke's teams had always been talented, but Harbaugh's punishing discipline—reminiscent of his college coach—had immediate results. His methods were chaotic by design. On the eve of his first training camp, players still hadn't been told what time practice started the next day. Once Harbaugh's players learned how to adapt to that chaos, football became easy.

The 2015 season would be, perhaps, the greatest coaching job of Jim Harbaugh's life. The 2014 squad had won five games and Michigan's incoming recruiting class for Harbaugh's debut season was ranked in the 30s nationally. The 2015 team would be the least talented group Harbaugh coached at Michigan.

It might've also been his favorite—at least for a while.

Led by Iowa transfer quarterback Jake Rudock; former walk-on center Graham Glasgow; tight end Jake Butt; and a young, talented defense, Harbaugh's first Michigan group stunned the Big Ten with a 9–3 regular season that was capped with a dominant win over Florida in the Citrus Bowl—doubling the previous year's win total and, in many ways, creating false expectations locally and nationally.

The 2016 team, led mostly by the veteran players Harbaugh had turned around a year earlier, started the season 9–0 for the first time in a decade and set the table for the most anticipated Michigan–Ohio State tilt since the No. 1 vs. No. 2 game in 2006. The second Harbaugh–Urban Meyer game was easily the most memorable—with league and national title implications—and most controversial.

Just two years removed from a losing season, Harbaugh had No. 3 Michigan in double overtime against No. 2 Ohio State in front of more than 100,000 terrified observers at Ohio Stadium. A titanic battle, and one of the most-watched regular season college football games ever, came down to a fourth-and-1 rush

69

attempt by quarterback J.T. Barrett with Ohio State driving for a win in the second OT. Barrett was tackled right at the line, forcing the officials to review the actual spot. Michigan's sideline erupted as it saw the replay live in the stadium, believing it had stopped Barrett short and won the game. Everything changed seconds later, though, when the official returned to the field and signaled a first down for the Buckeyes. One play later, Curtis Samuel broke a touchdown run to give Ohio State the Big Ten East title and a clear path to the College Football Playoff. Michigan's reward? Second place.

"I'm bitter," an enraged Harbaugh would bark afterward, saying he believed the officials cost Michigan a victory. "Bitterly disappointed in the officiating."

The loss was crushing. Not just because Michigan had been so close to getting out of the chokehold Ohio State had it in, but also because the Wolverines knew they were about to restart. Harbaugh's first two teams, led by hungry veterans who'd been embarrassed during the Hoke era, went 20–6. His 2017 team was one of the youngest he'd ever coached, highlighted by a flashy top-five recruiting class and almost no collective winning experience. Expectations continued to soar, but for the first time in his coaching life, Harbaugh was unable to meet them.

After losing starting QB Wilton Speight to a spine injury in September, Michigan cratered with embarrassing losses against Michigan State and Penn State before finishing the year on a three-game skid. By the close of 2017, Harbaugh was 0–3 vs. Ohio State and 1–2 vs. Michigan State, had zero Big Ten titles, and was without momentum for the first time as a coach.

Three of Harbaugh's first four Michigan teams (including the 2018 group) would win 10 games. Still, problems rose. Despite his reputation as a quarterback guru, Harbaugh's

PART 1: THE COACHES

inability to fix Michigan's most important position haunted his teams. The offense stagnated. Coaching turnover—both due to the talent Harbaugh attracted and the demand he put on it—was constant. By 2020, Harbaugh was 47–18. But he was 0–5 against Ohio State and Michigan's Big Ten title drought was still alive.

Other problems persisted as well, specifically Harbaugh's awkward approach to dealing with his contract. Or, rather, not dealing with it. Harbaugh originally signed a seven-year deal with Hackett, Michigan's interim athletic director, ahead of 2015. By 2016, though, former Harbaugh teammate Warde Manuel was appointed full-time AD. Harbaugh, now working without an agent, more or less postponed extension negotiations through the first half of his deal and by the end of 2019, there was still no resolution.

The 2020 season would be the penultimate year in Harbaugh's initial contract. For recruiting purposes, allowing a coach to enter the final two years of his deal without an extension is highly unfavorable. Yet, Harbaugh's refusal to discuss an extension—and Michigan's refusal to push him—put everyone in a corner. Once the COVID-19 pandemic hit, everything fell apart. Harbaugh's militaristic style was no longer preferred by players or fans. The team bottomed out with a nightmarish 2–4 season—outraging the fan base. Many fans and media members called for Michigan to fire Harbaugh.

Michigan did not fire Harbaugh. Instead, Manuel offered him a new five-year deal at a reduced salary. A pay cut. Bonuses and escalators (as well as a deferred compensation package) made Harbaugh one of the highest-paid coaches in college football for the first six years of his tenure. Now he was toward the bottom of the Big Ten. Publicly, Harbaugh shrugged it off.

"I'd do this job for free," he'd later claim.

Privately, though, per multiple sources around the coach—the pay cut was the beginning of the end of Harbaugh's time at Michigan.

It was also the spark that reignited his career.

Because when Jim Harbaugh has an enemy, his record's pretty damn good.

"Captain Comeback" completely retooled his staff heading into the 2021 campaign, bringing back former Michigan players Mike Hart and Ron Bellamy as assistants while injecting much more youth into the program elsewhere. He hired young defensive wizard Mike Macdonald from his brother, John, and the Baltimore Ravens to lead a new, fun, player-led defense. Michigan went from a military-style program to a player-run operation where athletes were free to share their thoughts and feelings almost overnight.

Harbaugh's greatest attribute—his ability to adapt and survive—showed up again.

"We're going to do it," Harbaugh told the world that summer of Michigan's goal to beat Ohio State and win the Big Ten, doubters be damned. "Or die trying."

Michigan's 2021 season was something out of a storybook. Unranked and counted out when the year started (including by some inside its own university)—and counted out again after a four-point OT loss to rival Michigan State in October—Harbaugh finally found his stride as Michigan's head coach.

It was also the year his offensive line finally clicked. The QB problems were one thing, but Harbaugh's incredibly complex—and effective—run game was a bear to install. It took him the better part of five full seasons and recruiting cycles to build proper OL depth. By 2021, he'd finally found it. Behind a dominant fivesome of Andrew Vastardis, Andrew Stueber,

PART 1: THE COACHES

Ryan Hayes, Zak Zinter, and Trevor Keegan, Michigan's run game exploded. The Wolverines led the Big Ten in rushing for the first time in Harbaugh's tenure (earning the offensive line its first Joe Moore Award) and became a football-playing picture of their head coach.

Tough, relentless, and never out of a fight.

And on November 27, 2021, inside Michigan Stadium, the pain finally ended. After eight straight losses to Ohio State (four straight in its own building) and just one win over the Buckeyes since 2003, Michigan finally got off the mat. Hassan Haskins rumbled for a rivalry-record five rushing touchdowns, Aidan Hutchinson was unblockable, and the Wolverines outrushed Ohio State 297–64 in a 42–27 thrashing that was one of the most emotional wins the program had ever seen. New Buckeyes head coach Ryan Day had boasted about what he and his program planned to do to Harbaugh, as the Game did not happen in 2020 due to COVID. After a two-year wait, the tables turned.

"Sometimes," Harbaugh said afterward, "people that are standing on third base think they hit a triple."

The 2021 team gave Michigan its first Big Ten title since 2004 a week later by blasting Iowa in the Big Ten championship game before bowing out to national champion Georgia in the College Football Playoff semifinals. The loss stung, but Michigan's fan base was all the way back in love with Harbaugh. Both the coach and the administration knew as much.

The first seven years of Jim Harbaugh's run at Michigan featured rumor and speculation about his return to the NFL. Multiple NFL teams expressed interest in Harbaugh during those seven years. However, per multiple sources, the coach never reciprocated interest.

Then Michigan cut his pay and he responded by winning a Big Ten title. Harbaugh, who swears in another life he'd have been a judge or lawyer, now had his leverage back. When he flew to Minneapolis to interview with the Minnesota Vikings in early February 2022—the week of National Signing Day—multiple people inside Michigan's administration believed the Wolverines would have a new coach come fall.

That's not what happened, though. Harbaugh, to the surprise of some in his circle, was not offered the job during his trip to Minnesota. Instead, the Vikings were interested in further conversation at another date. Harbaugh was not. He phoned Manuel that night and told him he'd be back at Michigan for 2022. He signed a restructured deal with the school later that winter. But the drama was hardly over.

Michigan had lost the greatest player of the Harbaugh era in Hutchinson, who went No. 2 overall to the Detroit Lions in the NFL draft, but the returning core would be the best of Harbaugh's career. With pandemic-era players receiving a sixth year of eligibility and transfer movement easier than it had ever been, Michigan retooled a seasoned squad with more veteran talent at critical spots ahead of 2022 and, more importantly, had finally found its next great quarterback.

Not unlike two decades earlier with two kids named Tom Brady and Drew Henson, Michigan found itself with a veteran captain at QB (Cade McNamara) and a prodigious sophomore (J.J. McCarthy) behind him. In 2021, McNamara had held off McCarthy, the most talented passer Harbaugh had signed since Andrew Luck. That wouldn't be the case in '22. The two split time early, but by conference play Michigan went with McCarthy—an uber-athletic five-star passer from Illinois who'd never lost a start as a prep quarterback.

The move was exactly what Michigan was missing. Its offense had transformed into a spread version of Harbaugh's smash-mouth run game and McCarthy's arm—and legs—was

PART 1: THE COACHES

the ingredient to put it over the top. The other factor in 2022 was the best kicking battery in program history: placekicker Jake Moody and punter Brad Robbins. Moody initially came to Michigan as a walk-on before quickly earning a scholarship and the starting job—setting a record with six field goals against Indiana as a true freshman in 2018. Robbins arrived the same year as the son of former Harbaugh teammate and Michigan punter Monte Robbins. By 2022, Moody was the defending Lou Groza winner and Robbins had been one of the top punters in the league for three years. Moody broke Garrett Rivas' all-time field goals made record that season and the following spring, both Moody and Robbins were selected in the NFL draft.

Paced by another top-end offensive line and the dynamic rushing duo of Blake Corum and Donovan Edwards, the defending Big Ten champs blasted through their first 11 opponents, nine of them by double digits. Day's Buckeyes, meanwhile, shell-shocked after what had happened a year prior in Ann Arbor, spent the 2022 season trying to project an image of improved toughness.

It was a mirage.

Michigan's offense again dropped the hammer on Ohio State, this time in Columbus, rushing for 252 yards and throwing for 278 in a thorough 45–23 thrashing that formally announced the Wolverines as true national title contenders for the first time since 1997.

It wasn't to be, though, as Michigan's freight train of a year met the same result as the previous seven Harbaugh teams in the postseason—a loss. The heavily favored Wolverines struggled defensively versus fast-paced TCU after a month-long layoff, resulting in a shocking 51–45 setback at the Fiesta Bowl in Arizona.

The offseason would again feature a brief NFL flirtation by Harbaugh, this time with Denver—despite saying a year prior he was done with such things. He wasn't, though. He also wasn't over the pay cut. Or what some around him would deem as a "lack of support" from an administration that included some who wanted him gone just two years prior. And while Manuel wasn't one of those people, he had delivered the pay cut. And that was enough.

Harbaugh had seemingly found motivation through his perceived enemies for the title pushes in 2021 and 2022. In 2023, the enemy list grew.

He returned to Michigan in 2023 with Corum, Edwards, McCarthy, and the bulk of his offensive line and defense still intact. However, that August, Michigan announced it was suspending Harbaugh three games for recruiting violations the NCAA claimed took place during a COVID-19 dead period. No. 2 Michigan outscored East Carolina, UNLV, and Bowling Green 96–16 in Harbaugh's absence. He returned to the sideline for a win over Rutgers on September 23, Michigan's 14th straight Big Ten win, but more trouble was ahead.

In October, Yahoo! Sports reported an NCAA investigation into violations over alleged sign stealing. Reports would eventually uncover a scheme concocted by staffer Connor Stalions, who was accused of filming the sideline of future Michigan opponents from the stands during advance-scouting trips. He resigned in early November. The Big Ten began its own investigation into the matter in October and on November 10, it suspended Harbaugh for the team's remaining three games.

Michigan, 9–0 and ranked No. 3, found out about the suspension during the team's flight to its November 11 game at No. 10 Penn State.

PART 1: THE COACHES

Motivated on behalf of their coach and now led by interim boss Sherrone Moore, Michigan's offensive coordinator and offensive line coach, the Wolverines ran the ball 32 straight times and didn't throw a pass in the second half during a 24–15 win.

A week later, Moore was head coach for Michigan's 1,000th victory as a program, a 31–24 win at Maryland. And on Nov. 25, it would once again be No. 2 Ohio State vs. No. 3 Michigan—just like 2016. This time, though, in Ann Arbor. With Moore on the sideline and Harbaugh watching from home, Corum set a program record with his 22nd rushing touchdown of the year in a 30–24 win that gave the Wolverines three straight over the Buckeyes for the first time since 1997.

With their "one-track mind," the 2023 Michigan Wolverines welcomed Jim Harbaugh back a week later for another Big Ten championship game win over Iowa—Michigan's third straight crown. The victory set up a matchup with Nick Saban and Alabama in the Rose Bowl on January 1, Michigan's first trip since (you guessed it) the 1997 season.

Wearing '97 Rose Bowl throwback uniforms, McCarthy and the Wolverines put on a show for the ages. Roman Wilson's touchdown catch with less than two minutes to play pushed the game to overtime, where Corum would end it with a 17-yard touchdown run—the 56th of his career, a new school record.

The day Harbaugh took the Michigan job, he likened his career to that of a carpenter. One who built "great cathedrals" that could be celebrated forever. The process of building those cathedrals is what drove him. And on January 8, 2024, at NRG Stadium in Houston, Texas, Harbaugh finally got to deliver one to his alma mater.

"It went exactly how we wanted it to go," Harbaugh said afterward. "None of us are up here taking a deep, long bow—because, we know, this was about good old-fashioned teamwork."

No. 1 Michigan finished off the first 15–0 season in school history with a dominant 34–13 win over No. 2 Washington for the program's first national title since 1997, its first outright since 1947. Less than a month later, Harbaugh was in Los Angeles wearing a different shade of blue as the new head coach of the Chargers.

Michigan went 89–25 with three Big Ten championships and a national title during Harbaugh's run. His wins were fourth on the school's all-time list, behind Schembechler (194), Yost (165), and Carr (122). In the end, he did it his way. And as strangely as he had arrived, Jim Harbaugh—one of the top-performing individuals in Michigan football history—was gone.

"Someday when they throw dirt over top of me, someone who's eulogizing me—someone on this team or a teammate of mine—if they would simply say, 'He was a Michigan man,' that would mean everything to me," Harbaugh said after the national title game, his last as head coach. "We slip and we fail sometimes. But a Michigan man makes it right.

"I'm not the definition-maker of what a Michigan man is or isn't, but that's what's inside me."

PART 2: THE HEISMANS

5
Tom Harmon

NOT LONG BEFORE HIS FIRST DAY OF FOOTBALL PRACTICE AS a freshman at Horace Mann High School in Gary, Indiana, a 14-year-old Tom Harmon won a pair of roller skates at a local theater in a gum-chewing contest.

Either thinking about a new career as a roller skater or not thinking at all, Harmon found himself at practice with a wad of gum in his mouth. And when coach Doug Kerr heard it snap, he booted Harmon on the spot. The youngest of six, with two older brothers already playing college football, being thrown off the team on day one wasn't an option. So, Harmon spit out the gum and flatly refused to leave.

Per a recounting in the *New York Daily News*, Kerr spotted Harmon jogging around the practice field in a varsity uniform and told Harmon to change into an older, more worn-out freshman shirt. Minutes later, a now ragged Harmon fielded a punt on his own 10-yard line and ran it back 90 yards for a touchdown. Doug Kerr never cared about bubble gum again. Harmon made varsity and was offered that first jersey back. The freshman, now full of surprises, declined.

He'd stick with No. 98.

For Harmon, the number became part of his life's fabric. He explained in his book, *Pilots Also Pray*, he felt it brought him luck and insisted it follow him through high school and into college. It'd eventually be painted on the side of his World War II patrol plane.

Modern readers may see the awkward number and think it's why he stood out. But it's not. Harmon's electric ability to bring adults out of their seats just by checking into a football game became legendary. Even in places his team was hated. Often misunderstood as a showboat, Harmon's most famous moniker—Old 98—was actually rooted in humility. It wasn't actually his first nickname, either.

Born in tiny Rensselaer, Indiana, Harmon grew up in a big, close family. Harmon wrote in his book that before he was born, his siblings had agreed each child would help pay for college for the next. The oldest, Sally, took on the sacrifice of skipping college to get things started for the other five. They gave one another pet names. In fact, Sally was the one who picked Tom's middle name, Dudley, based on the name of a boy she'd been dating at the time.

As a kid, Harmon attended school at the Cathedral of the Holy Angels. So, in reality, Kerr wasn't his first football coach—a nun was. In his free time, Harmon bothered his older brothers, Harold and Gene, tagging along anywhere they went. He played football, baseball, and handball with the older boys. Now and again, someone would give him a buck to buzz off. Harmon always took the money to see Saturday-afternoon movies at the theater. He loved Western films and Tom Mix was his favorite cowboy. After carrying on to his brothers one day about watching *Ace of Cactus Range,* his first nickname, "Ace," was born.

Playing at Horace Mann in what sportswriters then referred to as one of the country's toughest leagues, the Northern Indiana High School Conference, Harmon led the nation in scoring with 123 points in nine games during his senior season of 1936.

A halfback, passer, return man, punter, and kicker, Tom "Ace" Harmon turned from a sensation to a Midwestern schoolboy legend that year. During a game against Oak Park, per the *Times* of Hammond, Indiana, Harmon had a 51-yard kickoff return, two 22-yard scrambles to set up scores, three completions for 71 yards, and every punt of the ball game. Some 8,000 fans came to see Harmon and Horace Mann beat division rival Emerson on November 12, 1936, and sportswriters declared him the greatest halfback the region had ever seen. In his final high school football game, Ace notched runs of 85 and 70 yards, scoring four touchdowns, to help Horace Mann win its first NIHSC title. Later in his senior year, after wrapping up a terrific basketball career, Harmon broke the state record in the 200-yard low hurdles at 22.6 seconds.

Harmon picked Michigan for a few reasons. Kerr was an alum, it was close to home, and two of his friends, Bill Dwyer and Doug Geisert, were also going. He also made a visit to campus with Kerr once during his time at Horace Mann and fell in love.

"Even today, I believe that Ann Arbor in the fall is the most beautiful town in the world. And I have seen a few other beautiful towns since that day," Harmon wrote in his book. "I don't know how to say it, but the fact is that Ann Arbor in autumn is *it.*"

Published rumors that Michigan paid Harmon to commit persisted throughout the summer and into the fall of his freshman year (first-year players were ineligible then). He made several denials and, per *The Michigan Daily*, actually asked Harry Kipke if he could get a job—claiming he barely had enough cash to eat. His other problem was school itself. Harmon admitted to struggling with grades his freshman year, writing in his book they were poor enough to have made him ineligible had he been on varsity. One of his campus jobs was as a clerk at Slater's Bookstore in Ann Arbor—a hangout for players back then. Harmon credited Florence Slater, owner of the bookstore, for helping him improve his schoolwork ahead of his first varsity season.

On the field? Harmon's freshman crew, including quarterback Forest Evashevski, beat Kipke's final varsity team both times they scrimmaged that fall. It would be the best Kipke would ever see of Harmon as Michigan's head coach, though, as he was dismissed following the '37 season.

Harmon entered 1938 excited to play for incoming coach Fritz Crisler and to become the feature playmaker in the new coach's Single Wing attack. Crisler, however, had other ideas.

When training camp ended, Crisler listed Harmon as a starter—but not at the position he wanted. The coach, in what would become the first of many savvy moves at Michigan, stunned the speedy sophomore when he named him the team's starting right halfback—known as the offense's chief blocking back. Harmon wrote the decision left him "bitterly disappointed" in the moment and once he entered the season opener against Michigan State for his first carry, late in the second quarter, he tripped over his own feet and stumbled for a minimal gain.

Something happened that day, though.

The Michigan State game to open 1938 was one of the most anticipated in recent memory. The previous fall, coach Charlie Bachman's Spartans had made history with their fourth straight win in the series—all of them in Ann Arbor. After the 19–14 win, per the *Lansing State Journal*, MSU fans rushed the field and attempted to tear down Michigan's goal posts—only to be thwarted by the home fans. By the eve of the 1938 game, the *State Journal* reported that Ann Arbor police used tear gas to disperse rowdy fans from city streets. More than 80,000 people showed up and despite the fact he barely touched the ball, Harmon *did* help Michigan snap its losing skid to Michigan State and, for the first time, saw what true college football jubilation looks like. Years later, Harmon appreciated what Crisler had done for him in that moment.

"I had come to Michigan to set the world on fire, according to what the newspapers had to say about me," Harmon explained in his book. "The bench is a great leveler."

His role increased in a win over Chicago and the aforementioned Minnesota loss, and was peaking heading into October 22, 1938, at the Yale Bowl in New Haven, Connecticut. After Michigan fell behind 13–2 at halftime, Harmon opened the quarter with a 54-yard pass that set up Michigan's first score. Trailing by five in the fourth, Harmon struck again with a 40-yard rope to Norm Purucker before dazzling the crowd with a zig-zagging run that broke three tackles. Later, on a fourth-and-goal from the three, Harmon hit John Nicholson for a touchdown and left an upset-minded 45,000 at the Yale Bowl stunned.

By this point, Harmon had shown some of what made him a schoolboy legend in Chicago. He had a dazzling 54-yard run in the score-fest versus Chicago. Michigan knew he could punt and kick. But after the third quarter of the Yale game, the Wolverines found out the Ace could also throw. Harmon hit Purucker on a 54-yard strike on the opening drive of the second half. Two plays later, Michigan had its first touchdown of the day. There were no more nasty articles about an overhyped

THE PROGRAM: MICHIGAN

prospect. Harmon had arrived. Michigan went without a loss the rest of 1938, finishing Crisler's first season 6–1–1 with Harmon earning All–Big Ten honors.

The magic of the Ace, however, was just beginning.

Just weeks after the football season ended, Harmon made Bennie Oosterbaan's travel squad for the basketball team. Two weeks later, Harmon stepped in for injured center Jim Rae and dropped a game-high 14 points against Wisconsin in a narrow loss. By the end of the month, Harmon made history as the first person to wear No. 98 as a full-time member of the Michigan starting five.

Football was the main event, though, and by 1939 everyone expected greatness. Though Harmon played what was known as "right halfback" in Crisler's system, a more modern comparison to what his primary position was would be something to that of a very fast option quarterback with a great arm—who also kicked, punted, and returned everything. By 1939, Harmon's mesmerizing athleticism helped him master literally every action a player could make on a football field.

In the 1939 season opener, once again against Michigan State, Harmon put it all on display. On the final play of the first quarter, Harmon caught a short pass on the MSU 47 before immediately juking a defender to head for open grass. He set up his next cut five yards ahead of the defender, breezing by two more tacklers and running away from a fourth. At the 14, he stopped on a dime to change direction and break a fifth tackle before a gaggle of exhausted Spartans hauled him down inside the five.

Michigan State's defensive 11 spent the ensuing timeout between quarters sitting in the Michigan end zone exhausted, trying to catch their breath. Michigan led 26–0 at the half, besting the Spartans for a second straight year.

PART 2: THE HEISMANS

Harmon's junior year was off to a hot start and, while his week two matchup with Iowa star halfback Nile Kinnick was a big deal, news of war in Europe had become impossible to ignore. Nazi Germany invaded Poland on September 1—roughly five weeks before the season started. Harmon wrote in his book that while the situation in Europe was certainly talked about inside Michigan's locker room, most still believed the conflict to be something they'd never deal with in person.

"What had we gained out of World War I but a lot of bad debts?" Harmon wrote of his thoughts at the time. "Hadn't it been the war to stop wars? It hadn't succeeded, and why should we get into another one?"

Neither Harmon nor Kinnick could know it when they shared a field at Michigan Stadium on October 7, 1939, but the war would become a massive part of both their lives. Kinnick entered the game as the senior star, Harmon the junior. Kinnick was a 5'8", 170-pound whirlwind who—like Harmon—did everything from throwing to kicking to making would-be tacklers look foolish in space. The "Cornbelt Comet" played an average of 57 minutes per game in 1939 as a three-way star.

On Iowa's second possession, Kinnick dropped to pass. After evading a tackler, he uncorked a bomb to Floyd Dean that cleared the defense and went 70 yards for a touchdown. The rest of the day would belong to Harmon.

After he opened Michigan's scoring with a two-yard plunge to tie the game, Harmon got the better of Kinnick near the Iowa goal line when he sailed over an intended receiver to intercept a pass in the end zone. He'd break the tie later in the first half, cutting back a sweep—Harmon's signature—for a two-yard touchdown. His own 30-yard scamper after a blocked punt would set up Harmon's second score of the half, which made it 20–7 Wolverines at the break.

THE PROGRAM: MICHIGAN

In the third quarter, with Kinnick leading another promising drive, Harmon stepped in front of another pass—this time at full speed—and sprinted untouched down the visiting sideline for a 90-yard interception return touchdown. The pick-six would be the final score of a 27–7 Michigan win. Including point-after attempts, Harmon scored all 27 points. It would be the only blemish of Kinnick's spectacular 1939 season, which ended with a Heisman Trophy that December. Two Decembers later, three days after the attack on Pearl Harbor, Kinnick reported for service duty in the Navy. In June 1943, at 24, Nile Kinnick died off the coast of Venezuela during a training flight emergency landing.

Harmon's 1939 season continued a week after the Iowa game with a four-touchdown performance during an 85–0 thrashing of a Chicago program that was about to be discontinued. On October 28, Michigan welcomed Yale and Harmon dazzled one more time with three touchdowns (and the extra points). After a 27–7 win, Michigan was 4–0 and Harmon led the country with 73 points. Shortly after the game, per the *Free Press*, Harmon even got to meet Miss America 1939, Patricia Donnelly, who was in town to visit campus.

Harmon's All-America status was all but cinched in the season's first month. As a junior with growing national celebrity, he was on the cover of *TIME* magazine by November. But as would be the case during his time in Ann Arbor, the season would be crippled by a handful of brutal moments. Eight turnovers at Illinois and a flat start vs. Minnesota resulted in back-to-back losses, as Harmon and Co. settled for a 6–2 season. Harmon finished the year a consensus All-American and finished second to Kinnick in the Heisman voting.

Every summer during college, Harmon returned home to Gary to work a job as a lifeguard. The summer before his senior year of 1940, Harmon recalled running in the sand with friends more than he'd ever done in his life. By the time he reported to Michigan for training camp, he'd never been in better shape.

Before the start of the semester, Harmon took two weeks to drive his aging mother to South Dakota to see relatives. He recalled it was the first time in his life he'd paid for one of his parents to do anything. After returning home, he became more determined than ever to use his football stardom to buy his parents the best life he could. In 1940, Harmon and his teammates signed a pledge (without the staff's knowledge) not to drink, smoke, or break training during the season. Harmon wrote in his book that he never broke from his training regimen a single day during his Michigan career—and 1940 would be no different.

"It wasn't hard to hold to," Harmon wrote, "when football was a matter of life and death to you."

On September 28, 1940, Tom Harmon—the gum-chewing skater boy from Indiana—turned 21. This was also the date of Michigan's season opener at Cal's Memorial Stadium. Among the more than 35,000 fans in the Berkeley bleachers that day was a 23-year-old John Fitzgerald Kennedy—a recent Harvard graduate who was spending the fall auditing business classes at Stanford. It would be the first time anyone west of Illinois got to see Tom Harmon play football.

He settled under the game's opening kickoff on his own six-yard line before veering left and simply running away from 11 defenders—sending the kicker flopping to the ground with just a wiggle of his shoulders. One play, one Harmon 94-yard kickoff return for a touchdown. On the second play, he kicked the extra point. Harmon added a 75-yard punt return touchdown and an 82-yard touchdown run…before halftime. On the long touchdown run, an angry Cal fan stormed the field and attempted to tackle Harmon inside the five. The Ace, appearing a bit surprised at first, merely sidestepped the fan, breaking a tackle from a 12th Bear on the way to the end zone.

Harmon finished Michigan's 41–0 win with 131 yards on 16 carries, five completions for 39 yards, three punt returns for 90 yards, a kickoff return for 94 yards, four total touchdowns, and four extra points. Thirteen years later, then Senator John F. Kennedy told a group of Boston College supporters the best football player he ever saw was former Yale star Clint Frank. The second best?

"I saw [Tom] Harmon score 21 points on his 21st birthday in the first half of the game against California," Kennedy said.

The following week against Michigan State, the Harmon train rolled on with 170 yards of offense, 50 return yards, and three touchdowns in a narrow 21–14 win. On October 12 at Harvard, Harmon put up 181 yards of total offense with three total touchdowns—and an interception on defense—in a dominant 26–0 win. After a quiet one-touchdown, one-field-goal showing in a 28–0 win over Illinois, Harmon went bonkers again on October 26 in Ann Arbor against Penn, rushing 28 times for 142 yards to go along with three completions for 51 yards and a touchdown in a hard-fought 14–0 win. He also punted 12 times for 442 yards in that game, helping the Wolverines maintain field position throughout.

On November 9, 1940, it was No. 3 Michigan at No. 2 Minnesota with everything on the line. The biggest game of Harmon's career. On a rain-soaked, muddy afternoon in Minneapolis, Harmon was limited to 59 yards on 29 carries—but still managed to go 10 of 14 through the air, including a first-quarter touchdown pass to Evashevski to give Michigan a 6–0 lead. Kicking in the rain, Harmon barely missed the PAT. Michigan's defense controlled most of the first half, until one play with four minutes to go in the second quarter—when Bruce

Smith broke through the line for an 80-yard touchdown run that was followed by a successful kick to make it 7–6 before the half. Playing on a wrecked field in the second half, Harmon and the offense made it inside the five once—but stalled out. Michigan finished the game with 15 first downs to Minnesota's five. But the Gophers won on the scoreboard 7–6, spoiling the Wolverines' perfect season.

After the final horn, Harmon quietly made his way into the locker room, where he promptly sat down and sobbed.

"I don't think that I have ever experienced a greater disappointment in my life," he wrote.

Michigan followed its heartbreaking loss to Minnesota with a seven-point win over Northwestern before Harmon decided to go out in style. In his final game as a college player, at Ohio Stadium, Harmon rushed 25 times for 136 yards, went 11 of 22 through the air for 151 yards, had 81 return yards, picked off a pass on defense, scored three touchdowns, and kicked four extra points. As the final seconds of a dominant 40–0 Michigan win over Ohio State ticked down, reporters swarmed Harmon on the visitors' sideline. Now clearly the Heisman front-runner, the boy from Indiana wiggled free with flash bulbs popping before jogging solo down the sideline toward the Michigan locker room.

The greatest player in the country had completely controlled the sport's greatest rivalry like never before seen. Along that final run, Tom Harmon of Michigan—inside Ohio State's beloved Horseshoe—received a standing ovation.

For Harmon, football was a means to an end—helping his parents. Harmon had no intention of playing professional football, saying he only saw a good amount of money for a short time. He studied speech at Michigan and immediately used his stardom to go on a speaking tour that December. With the money earned, Harmon had enough to give his parents a better life and created more opportunities for himself—including a Hollywood film: *Harmon of Michigan*.

Harmon won the Heisman that November, topping Texas A&M running back John Kimbrough, finishing a remarkable run that featured national scoring titles in 1939 and 1940. He still hated the attention, writing in his book he wished his entire team could have shared the honor with him and that the trophy had always felt "empty" to him due to the Minnesota loss.

By the fall of 1941, Harmon had started a radio career at WJR in Detroit when he received his draft letter. On November 5, he enlisted in the U.S. Army Air Corps and would serve in World War II—earning both a Purple Heart and a Silver Star. Harmon married actress Elyse Knox, whom he met filming *Harmon of Michigan*, in 1944 and after a brief career in pro football, transitioned back into broadcasting (and eventually publishing). He and Elyse had three children—Kristin (who married singer Ricky Nelson), Kelly, and Mark. All three of his children went into acting, with Mark (an All-American at UCLA) earning multiple Emmy nominations as of 2023.

In March 1990 at 70 years old, Harmon suffered a fatal heart attack after a round of golf in Los Angeles. He loved the sport of football until the very end. During an interview with the *Nevada State Journal* in 1977, he explained his frustration with the modern game in that it had "too many takers."

"I remember football so well," he said. "You played football because you loved it. You would rather play football than eat."

In life, and in football, Tom Harmon never took more than he gave.

6

Desmond Howard

ONE SUMMER DAY BETWEEN YEARS AT ST. JOSEPH'S, A private Catholic school on the shore of Lake Erie in northeast Cleveland, Desmond Howard went to work with his father.

J.D. Howard was a tool and die maker who repaired machines at Osborn Manufacturing in Cleveland in order to pay tuition at St. Joe's. His message was singular and unrelenting: Education equals a better life. If Desmond wondered why his father harped on this so much, that doubt faded hour by hour inside that hot, thick factory air.

"I couldn't see how he did it," Howard said, shaking his head almost at a loss for words, during an interview with Charlie Rose in 1997. "I still can't."

Though they divorced in his youth, his parents, J.D. Howard and Hattie Dawkins, both remained firm influences in their children's lives. In his book, *I Wore 21*, co-authored by Bill Roose, Desmond recalled walks he and his father took around

Cleveland. If they passed a corner with a drug dealer, J.D. told him to take a look and remember that in 20 years—when he and his brothers had finished school—those boys would still be standing on that corner.

Always the smallest and the fastest on any field, Howard was 5'8" and weighed 155 pounds by 1986, his junior year at St. Joe's. His diminutive frame concerned every coach he ever played for. It also fueled his furnace.

One of those coaches, for a time, was Ohio prep legend Bill Gutbrod. Gutbrod began his run at St. Joe's when it opened in 1950. By Howard's junior year, his program had churned out a handful of NFL players, including the Golic brothers, Bob and Mike. St. Joseph's entered the '86 season with a massive offensive line, a college quarterback named Elvis Grbac, a handful of senior backs, and one tiny junior. Three players ran for touchdowns in a by-committee approach during a season-opening win over Shaw. By Week 2, though, injuries forced Gutbrod to go with the little guy nobody could ever catch. The result: Howard scored five touchdowns, including a 72-yard kickoff return, and made a diving first-half interception to spark a win over rival Euclid.

"This is the greatest moment of my football career," he told the *Plain Dealer* afterward, flashing the ear-to-ear smile and signature Woody Woodpecker–like laugh that would become his signature.

The moment was, once again, proof his parents' approach to hard work was correct. St. Joe's was on the north end of Cleveland. Howard lived on the south end. He woke up at 5:30 every morning and took a two-hour bus ride to campus while many of his childhood friends slept in before going to school in the neighborhood.

During his senior season, Howard exploded. His stretch from October to mid-November was especially dynamic. In week seven vs. fellow power St. Ignatius, Howard scored the game's only touchdown—a 50-yarder in the second quarter—and then made two interceptions in the final three minutes of regulation to secure a 7–0 win. A week later in the mud vs. another rival, Massillon, Howard again scored the game's only touchdown and had another pick in an 8–0 win. Then, against North Canton on Halloween, Howard rushed for 248 yards and two scores before adding the game-sealing interception (his 10th of the year, a school record) in a 21–14 overtime win.

While never blessed with size, Howard was doubly blessed with athletic twitch and explosion—making his cuts in space absolutely lethal and giving him an uncanny ability to adjust his body in midair for off-target throws. Howard didn't jump or run at the NFL combine, but had he done so, his vertical and long jump numbers at 5'9" would've been more impressive than his 40 time. In a dozen ways, he was a football talent at least a decade ahead of his time.

Howard rushed for 1,499 yards and scored 17 touchdowns for St. Joe's, adding 10 interceptions as a first-team All-Ohio performer. Despite his size, Howard was now a national recruit. He was not, however, a priority in his own state. Ohio State fired coach Earle Bruce the week of the Michigan game during Howard's senior season. A program in turmoil, the Buckeyes' staff only made one in-school visit with Howard, his father told ESPN years later. Ohio State's chaotic mess would be Michigan's gain when Howard picked the Wolverines—joining Grbac—just before signing day in early 1988.

On signing day, he was clear: Michigan had recruited him as a running back. Then he got to campus, where he discovered how recruiting actually works. Howard may have been led to believe, or even told, he was being recruited as a running back.

In reality, he was recruited by Schembechler's staff as an athlete without a position.

Within his first week of practice, Schembechler and offensive coordinator Gary Moeller asked Howard to move to wide receiver. As a prep running back, Howard estimated he'd caught one pass in his career. He caught more balls on defense as a safety. He'd blocked a bit, but not like Michigan receivers blocked.

There was also the matter of fact that Michigan's offense under Schembechler rarely threw the ball. Anthony Carter had rewritten Michigan's record book as a wide receiver before graduating in 1982, but the former All-American had to max out every chance he got—never making more than 51 catches in a season. In the years since Carter had graduated, not a single Michigan WR had come close to matching his yardage production.

Howard took a redshirt his freshman year and, like most prep superstars in that situation, he struggled. Howard has long been vocal about his relationship with Michigan athletics counselor Greg Harden, a longtime university staffer who helped Howard (and many other young athletes) sort through mental challenges.

The bench, as Tom Harmon wrote, was still a great leveler.

Another monumental thing that happened during Howard's freshman year was an opportunity to hear Dr. Harry Edwards speak. Howard came to Michigan to study communications, hoping for an eventual career in media, and wasted no time diving in. He believed in dressing for the future he saw for himself. On his first day of class at Michigan in the fall of 1988, Howard showed up in a suit and tie, carrying a briefcase.

If an important speaker gave a talk somewhere on campus, Howard found it. Which is how he ended up in front of Edwards, the famed sociologist and civil rights activist who started the Olympic Project for Human Rights. Two members

PART 2: THE HEISMANS

of the OPHR, Tommie Smith and John Carlos, became famous for their Black Power salute on the medal podium at the 1968 Olympics. A large part of the professor's talk also reminded Howard of what his father had preached—there is so much more to life beyond athletics.

The following spring, Howard took a trip to California to see his brother, Jonathan, who was stationed there in the Air Force. Upon arrival, Howard forced one of Jonathan's friends to drive him to Cal's campus in Berkeley, where he'd wander unannounced to the sociology building before plopping in front of Edwards' office. After about 45 minutes of waiting, Edwards rounded the corner—and a lifelong bond was established. Howard left with a signed copy of *The Struggle That Must Be* and a new perspective on life.

By the time Michigan's 1989 season opened, Howard was a different person. He was still mainly a blocker—but thanks to new perspectives shown by Harden and Edwards, Howard was becoming a *tenacious* blocker. Former wide receivers coach Cam Cameron recalled in *I Wore 21* that Howard was the only wide receiver he had at Michigan to record a "triple knockdown" block—meaning he knocked the same defender over three times in one play.

"That's the kind of blocker Desmond was," Cameron said.

Howard earned playing time right away as a redshirt freshman, seeing reps on the opening series against Notre Dame. He even hauled in the first catch of his career, a 17-yard post, midway through the first quarter. In time, Moeller and Cameron would revolutionize the pass game at Michigan. But this was 1989 and still very much a Schembechler operation. Howard also found himself behind talented veterans Greg McMurtry and Chris Calloway—two future draft picks. Howard flashed his return skills against the Irish, exploding down the home sideline for a 38-yard runback in the first half. But he had competition there, too, in Tripp Welborne—arguably the most talented defensive back Schembechler ever signed. Once again, Howard was dealing with the bench.

By 1990, though, change was on the way. Schembechler retired, Moeller took over as head coach, and the time to throw the ball was here. Starting with the season opener at Notre Dame.

Trailing 14–3 with four minutes left in the first half, Howard exploded toward the middle of the field on a post route and ran away from the entire Irish defense, right into a beautiful throw from Grbac in the back of the end zone—a 44-yarder, the first touchdown of the Moeller era at Michigan. Midway through the third quarter, lightning struck again when Howard caught a three-step stop route, juked a tackler, and ran away from two more for a 25-yard touchdown. Howard often simplified his adjustment to wide receiver by explaining that after he caught a pass, he simply turned "back into a running back." No. 4 Michigan fell to No. 1 Notre Dame that night 28–24 but Howard had made his mark with six catches for 133 yards and two touchdowns—just the 14th time in program history a player not named Anthony Carter finished a game with at least 130 receiving yards.

Michigan followed the Notre Dame loss with wins over UCLA, Maryland, and Wisconsin. By the time the Wolverines hosted Michigan State on October 13, the Wolverines were ranked No. 1 and Howard was already at 19 receptions for 330 yards and five touchdowns.

The 1990 Michigan–Michigan State battle became known as the "No. One vs. No One" game—dubiously in Ann Arbor, fondly in East Lansing. The underdog Spartans were physical up front and Michigan was sloppy. The underdog Spartans moved in front 21–14 after a Hyland Hickson touchdown run midway through the third quarter.

The MSU lead lasted 13 seconds.

Howard caught the ensuing kickoff at the six-yard line, then began a slight veer to his left before turning on his signature second-level afterburners near his own 30-yard line. The kid neighborhood pals used to call "Magic" exploded down the home sideline before, as if having eyes in the back of his head, veering back toward the middle of the field to run away from one more tackler during a 95-yard kickoff return touchdown to tie the game.

But, as had been the case all day, MSU quarterback Dan Enos and the Spartans' ground game continued to have Michigan's number—marching 70 yards in nine plays to take another seven-point edge 28–21 with less than two minutes to play. Howard, once again, put on his "Magic" cape and put the team on his back—making a fourth-down catch to keep the last-ditch drive alive before hauling in a 25-yarder to put the Wolverines inside the Spartans 10 with 10 seconds left. Howard had made eight catches for 140 yards and had the kickoff return. On the next snap, MSU coach George Perles sent three defenders toward Howard's side of the field—which included two corners right over top of him. This left Derrick Alexander 1-on-1 toward the wide side of the field, and his easy catch in front of an MSU defender made it 28–27 with six seconds to play.

With college football still six years away from overtime rules, Moeller opted to go for the win—something his players completely backed him on. The two-point try saw Howard get a 1-on-1 matchup with MSU corner Eddie Brown. The Michigan star beat Brown clean off the line on a slant route, bad enough to be a full yard in front of him as Grbac threw the ball to open space. Just then, Brown reached out and tripped Howard just before the ball arrived, causing an incompletion. No pass interference was called, and Michigan left Howard's breakout game of 1990 heartbroken.

Another bitter one-point loss to Iowa the following week officially wrecked Michigan's year, as a very talented young squad finished 9–3 with a Gator Bowl victory versus Ole Miss—featuring 10 Howard touches for 226 all-purpose yards and two touchdowns. When the season ended, the sensational redshirt sophomore had posted 63 catches for 1,025 yards and 11 touchdowns. He became just the second player in school history to top 1,000 yards, joining Jack Clancy in 1966. His 24.3 yards per return was a Michigan record.

Howard's breakout season as a redshirt sophomore, despite almost zero production his first two years, was enough to put him on NFL draft radar entering the winter of 1991. In the locker room after the Gator Bowl, though, Howard told reporters he'd already made up his mind—he, and the rest of Michigan's talented junior class, was coming back.

Grbac, Howard, Alexander, and an offensive line anchored by stars Steve Everitt and Greg Skrepenak pushed Michigan to No. 2 in the AP's initial Top 25. Howard had some preseason All-America honors, but was hardly at the top of anyone's list. *The Sporting News* published a list of 10 favorites for the Heisman in its summer preview magazine. The top three were Houston quarterback David Klingler, BYU quarterback Ty Detmer, and Georgia Tech quarterback Shawn Jones. One Michigan player made the list. At No. 10: running back Ricky Powers. No receivers were listed.

It would take one week for Howard to show the world that was an error.

On the first play of the second quarter, Howard took over. With Michigan trailing 10–0 facing a third-and-4 on the BC

19, Grbac took a five-step drop versus pressure and lofted a ball high into the middle of the end zone toward Howard, who was running a route toward the corner. However, in the blink of an eye, the All-American contorted his body and floated behind a defensive back for an acrobatic touchdown grab, Michigan's first of the year.

Penalties and missed opportunities kept the score at 10–7 going into the break. However, on the first play of the third quarter, Boston College decided to kick the football to Howard. No. 21 fielded the ball on his own seven and began to veer toward his right before slamming his right foot into the turf and exploding into a tiny crease that turned into a 93-yard sprint. Howard ran away from the entire BC kickoff team, motoring by the kicker without breaking stride before cruising the final 20 yards with one arm in the air. Howard's electric display continued in the fourth quarter when he won a slant near the goal line by at least five full steps on an eight-yard touchdown to give Michigan a 21–13 lead. Then, with less than two minutes to go, Michigan's magic man put the first game of the year on ice. Grbac, pressured again, lofted another high throw down a seam into the end zone toward Howard—who beat his man inside before leaping into the air for his *fourth* touchdown of the game.

When the game started, Howard was considered good. By the time it ended?

"Heisman Trophy candidate written all over that one," CBS announcer Brent Musburger howled as Howard celebrated a day that featured seven catches, 183 total yards, and a career-best four scores.

The beauty of playing at a place like Michigan in those days was the opportunity to play on national television early and often. By the end of college football's first weekend in 1991, Desmond Howard was becoming a big name.

A week later inside Michigan Stadium against seventh-ranked Notre Dame, it got even bigger.

It was another top tilt between the Wolverines and Fighting Irish, a nationally televised bout that'd be one of the most watched of the year. For Howard, it was the biggest single showcase opportunity of his young life.

And with one touch early in the second quarter, he began taking advantage. Howard took a reverse handoff from Powers and exploded into open field before juking one DB off his feet and sprinting untouched for a dazzling 29-yard touchdown run. Through six quarters, Howard had scored on a catch, a kickoff return, and a run.

He was just getting started.

Getting an education was Desmond Howard's No. 1 reason for returning to Michigan in 1991. Putting every ounce of his being into football was No. 2. With Michigan clinging to a three-point lead facing a fourth-and-1 midway through the fourth quarter, two decisions were made that would change the rest of Howard's life. First, Moeller elected to go for it. Michigan would line up in a heavy formation and bluff run, only to have Grbac throw a quick hitch to Howard for an easy first down—provided the coverage was right. The second decision was Grbac's. On the sideline before the play, Howard's ex-prep teammate told the head coach that if the corner sat on the hitch, he was going to give Michigan's All-American a fade into the end zone.

Nobody blinked.

"You know what we're going to do right now?" Moeller asked no one and everyone in his headset with roughly nine minutes to play in the game. "He's going to throw it to Desmond and Desmond's going to score a touchdown."

Grbac took the snap and rose up as if to throw a quick hitch. Howard got the look he wanted and immediately went

PART 2: THE HEISMANS

to the fade route. Grbac pulled back the hitch and lofted a ball high toward the back corner of the same end zone where Howard had been tripped into a drop versus Michigan State a year earlier. Shortly after the ball left the QB's hands, he thought it was too far and would fall incomplete. But Howard, showing off his trademark second-level speed, turned on extra gas around the 5-yard line and exploded by two Irish defenders before leaving his feet—extending to a full horizontal—and hauling in a miraculous diving catch for a 25-yard touchdown.

"Oh my god," Moeller exclaimed on the headset before taking a long pause. "That kid is unbelievable."

It was Howard's sixth touchdown in two weeks. More important, it was *another* spectacular play—this time on a national stage. "The Catch" would be clipped and shown over and over on highlight shows in the immediate aftermath. Notre Dame coach Lou Holtz compared Howard to former Notre Dame star Rocket Ismail after the game.

In those days, and really throughout the history of the program, Michigan football has been against public Heisman Trophy campaigns. Other schools would use billboards, mouse pads, T-shirts, coffee mugs, and anything else they could think of to advertise preseason favorites throughout the '90s. Michigan never did any of this, for a few reasons.

One, the "team" at Michigan was always the thing—figuratively and literally. Two, when your program is hot enough to put more than 100,000 people in uncomfortable bleachers every fall Saturday, you don't need to advertise. The Michigan–Notre Dame game was the season's first big national showcase and Howard—who had some sizzle entering the season—stole the show.

A week later, Howard was featured on the cover of *Sports Illustrated*—the first time a Michigan football player had gotten the coveted magazine spotlight since Rick Leach in 1976. The

Wolverines' schedule that season would feature three top-10 opponents in the first month. The Notre Dame win was followed by a home loss to No. 1 Florida State, but Howard's momentum hardly slowed as he still scored twice. And after two more touchdowns in a 43–24 win at No. 9 Iowa on October 5, Howard's touchdown total was up to 10 after four games—and Michigan's 51-year Heisman Trophy drought looked to be drawing its last breath.

The Michigan State game on October 12 was more of the same. A year after the infamous two-point-conversion no-call, Howard brought an entire case of revenge for the Spartans in East Lansing—making four catches on the Wolverines' opening possession, including an easy seven-yard touchdown on the exact route (in pretty much the same spot of the end zone) on which he'd been interfered with a year prior.

As had been the case all year, Michigan State's early strategy was to crowd the line of scrimmage and leave Howard alone in single coverage outside. The offense threw several quick hitches wide and let Howard run by whichever Spartan was across from him. Or, sent him deep and let him win that way. When defenses adjusted, Michigan's run game ate people alive. Howard finished the MSU game with eight catches for 101 yards and two scores and the Wolverines' 45 points in a three-score win were the most they had scored in the rivalry since 1947.

No. 21's Heisman campaign was also starting to gain traction in opposing locker rooms.

"In my estimation, Howard's a better football player than [ex–Notre Dame star] Rocket Ismail," MSU cornerback Alan Haller, who'd become the school's athletic director roughly 30 years later, told reporters afterward. "I played against both players and he can do more on the field than Rocket. He can catch and he's a heckuva blocker."

The magic continued a week later with three more touchdowns against Indiana, including another diving catch in the corner of the end zone on a fade route, and a dazzling 71-yard fourth-quarter kickoff return to set up the game-sealing score in a 24–16 win.

Most teams tried all they could to avoid kicking the ball to Howard, knowing what he was capable of. Moeller did his best to give opponents no choice, often surrounding Howard on the kickoff team with other terrific athletes like Tyrone Wheatley. The choices were to kick it out of bounds and take a penalty, kick it short and give up field position, or take your chances deep. Indiana's first kickoff of the game was short and gave Michigan the ball near midfield. This one went deep, and turned into a bigger disaster.

"I don't think you can give the Heisman Trophy to anybody but Desmond Howard this year," broadcaster Gary Danielson remarked after the play. "He's the most electrifying football player I've seen.... He absolutely changes the game."

The season hadn't reached Halloween and Howard was now pretty clearly without an equal in the Heisman race. Through six games, Howard had scored 15 touchdowns. As an offense, Michigan had scored 24. What's more is that he did all this on just 34 receptions. The Wolverines were still absolutely a run-first offense, but for the first time in program history, the team's offensive game plan revolved around a wide receiver.

When defenses crowded the line of scrimmage, Moeller threw the football. When they adjusted to Howard, he ran it. In a hundred ways, Desmond Howard was a decade ahead of his time as a football player, maybe more. He used his size to his advantage in ways people never thought possible and his explosion, no matter his height, was out-of-this-world great. He'd eventually win a Super Bowl MVP as a kick returner, but the only coach who truly understood the full value of Howard's athleticism was Moeller—who was squeezing every drop out of it in 1991.

The marriage was nearly perfect. Howard was a team-first player and had been since high school. Moeller understood Howard was the most gifted athlete he'd ever coached and knew it was his responsibility to maximize those gifts while they were together. However, he also knew he had to do this without sacrificing the team. Michigan did not morph its offense to bend around Howard, despite the fact Grbac was a future NFL quarterback himself. Howard's opportunities came organically throughout the course of Moeller's game plans. And what made Howard extra special was the fact that nearly every time his number was called in 1991, he delivered.

In a 59–14 win over Northwestern on November 9, Howard only touched the ball five times offensively. He used those five touches to gain 120 yards and score a touchdown. Michigan was 8–1 and Howard had recorded a touchdown catch in nine straight games to start a season, a new NCAA record. In total, he'd caught a touchdown pass in Michigan's previous 11 games. Howard's touchdown against the Wildcats, a 64-yard screen pass, gave him 120 points—breaking Harmon's record of 117 with three games left. The touchdown was also his 20th of the season, which broke Ron Johnson's program record of 19—all rushing—back in 1968.

After two more touchdown catches in a win over Illinois, Howard entered the Ohio State game with 58 catches for 854 yards, more than 500 return yards and 21 total touchdowns. During the *first* game of the year at Boston College, Michigan defensive back Lance Dottin boldly told Howard he was about to be a Heisman Trophy candidate and if he scored that day, he should do something special in the end zone. Howard, who

PART 2: THE HEISMANS

scored four times that day, laughed it off as far too premature but definitely stored the thought in the back of his mind. Saving it for a special opponent.

Desmond Howard's final game in Michigan Stadium came on an overcast, windy afternoon on November 23, 1991, versus Ohio State—the school he'd grown up watching in Cleveland. His trepidation about where the Buckeyes were headed after the firing of Earle Bruce proved correct, as now fourth-year coach John Cooper entered 1991's version of the Game with a 27–17–2 mark and an 0–3 record vs. Michigan. For Cooper, things would get worse before they got better. Specifically that afternoon at the hands of a Cleveland kid who was about to win the Heisman Trophy playing for Ohio State's biggest rival.

With Michigan in control of the game, up 17–3 with less than five minutes to play in the first half, Howard fielded a high punt at his own 7-yard line before shaking his shoulders, planting his right foot in the ground, and juking the pants nearly off Ohio State's 30 as he began to roar upfield. At his own 18-yard line, Howard simply ran through another tackle attempt before veering toward the OSU sideline with the jet boosters fully engaged.

"One man," legendary ABC broadcaster Keith Jackson shouted, pointing to just one would-be tackler standing between Howard and immortality. "Goodbye," he continued, after Howard scorched by punter 23.

"Hello, Heisman."

In what would become one of college football's most iconic moments of the 20th century, Howard—who covered the 93 yards virtually untouched—motored toward the middle of the Michigan Stadium south end zone and flashed the pose John W. Heisman turned into the sport's greatest individual trophy.

There are not five more famous plays in college football. Howard's magical moment in the season's biggest game was as poetic as it was spectacular. A perfect snapshot of his marvelous two-year run and the ideal capper to a truly historic season. Howard's 22nd touchdown made him the first wide receiver in the Big Ten's century of football to lead the conference in scoring.

Three weeks later on December 14 at New York's Downtown Athletic Club in Lower Manhattan, Howard won the Heisman Trophy with more first-place votes than any player in the award's history. The final tally saw Howard receive 640 first-place tallies. The next-closest was Washington defensive lineman Steve Emtman, who recorded 29. His final margin of victory over runner-up Casey Weldon (Florida State QB) was the second largest in history, only trailing O.J. Simpson's win in 1968.

Hattie and J.D. proudly watched the ceremony together in Cleveland. J.D.'s shirt read HEISMAN HOWARD'S DAD. Hattie wore one that read MAGIC'S MOM. It was a moment they shared as a family, as all the years of sacrifice proved worth it. It was also a moment that would change all their lives.

It's been nearly four decades since Howard's magical 1991 season, and while he's enjoyed both an NFL career and a fruitful run as a broadcaster, he's *still* most remembered for his Heisman win at Michigan.

He entered Michigan as a short kid without a position. And thanks to a personal drive and inherited work ethic, Desmond Howard left as the program's single greatest offensive player.

7
Charles Woodson

IT WAS DECEMBER 1994, AND THE MICHIGAN RUNNING BACK room was shook.

A prep All-American from Ohio who'd rushed for nearly 6,000 yards was going to be a Wolverine. Already one of the deepest position rooms in the country the previous fall, Michigan had just welcomed two new prep stars to the backfield a year earlier in Chris Howard and Chris Floyd.

"Howard!" shouted a jubilant Jim Herrman, then a defensive assistant under Lloyd Carr, as he approached the young running back in the hall. "We got this kid coming in…he's better than Ty Law."

Around the corner, Floyd heard the same thing. He also got a name—Charles Woodson. The name meant nothing to Howard, a native Louisianan. But Floyd was from Detroit and knew exactly who Woodson was. He immediately informed his young cohort of Woodson's prep stats, including how he'd just won Ohio's Mr. Football after rushing for more than 2,000 yards and 30 touchdowns. Panic washed over the two. They had spent one year stuck behind Tyrone Wheatley. They would spend 1995 behind Tim Biakabutuka. And however much longer after that behind this new sensation.

"Who is this guy playing against?" Howard shouted to himself. "Blind people!?"

Indeed, Charles Woodson's reputation had preceded him.

It wasn't always that way, though. Born in northern Ohio on October 7, 1976, to Solomon and Georgia Woodson, Charles had clubfoot as a baby and had to wear braces on his legs before his second birthday. He earned the nickname "Poochie" as a boy over his affinity for the 1980s television jingle written about a pink toy dog marketed for young girls.

"Poooooo-chie! Poochie for Girls!"

Around this same time, Woodson's older brother, Terry Carter, was working on his own nickname—Local Legend. A track sprinter, wrestler, pitcher, and, of course, running back—Terry dominated every sport he touched. Playing for the Fremont Ross varsity football squad as a sophomore in 1987, Terry went in to replace an injured starter in game one and never left the lineup. He finished his career with three straight 1,000-yard seasons—passing former Michigan star Rob Lytle on the school's all-time rushing list before heading to Miami University (Ohio).

Woodson would later refer to Terry as his "rabbit," the person he'd found himself chasing since as far back as he could remember. Sibling inspiration saw Charles essentially grow up the same as his brother. In Little League baseball, he hit for power. He, too, was a running back on the gridiron. He won medal after medal in the long jump and 100-meter in youth track meets. Perhaps the only difference was that Terry wrestled in the winter. Charles preferred to play point guard on the basketball court. Until he got home—and had to wrestle Terry for "fun."

Woodson's sophomore year at Ross coincided with the senior season of star running back Tyrone Price, who'd rushed for more than 1,000 yards the year prior—pushing Charles to wide receiver and defensive back. There'd be no clear early path to the field as there had been for Terry. It wouldn't matter.

In his second game on the Ross varsity squad in 1992, per the *Fremont News-Messenger*, the 6'1", 175-pound Woodson scored on the team's first offensive snap—a 24-yard pass from Brian Wilson. He later returned a fumble 50 yards for a touchdown and picked off a pass in the opponent's red zone. The following week, he was in the end zone again with an 85-yard interception return for a touchdown on a play where he batted the ball to himself and brought it back to the house. By the fifth week of the season, Woodson had scored a touchdown via rush, reception, interception return, fumble return, and kickoff return.

"Poochie" was now a bulldog—with a rocket strapped to his back. Despite starting the year as a skinny nobody behind a Division I player, Woodson was voted Ross' most valuable player as a sophomore—finishing with 44 tackles, six picks, multiple defensive touchdowns, and a kickoff return score as the team's leading receiver and second-leading rusher. By the middle of basketball season the following winter, his head coach declared Woodson—now his starting point guard and leading scorer as a sophomore—the best player in the conference.

He was just getting started.

Through his first seven games of 1993, Woodson rushed for nearly 900 yards and 16 touchdowns—despite being out sick for a game. In week nine against Napoleon, Woodson scored six touchdowns in a game...for the second time in a month.

THE PROGRAM: MICHIGAN

He finished his junior year with more than 1,500 yards and 27 touchdowns, earning first-team All-State honors.

As an athlete with good size, Woodson's only holes were in the eye of the beholder. He was so good at so many things, his consistency often lulled scouts and evaluators into thinking he appeared slower or less explosive than he actually was. In reality, Woodson's superior athleticism just made everybody else look slower. Woodson had 4.3 speed in the 40-yard dash, and he could dunk and do all the things a supremely talented athlete could.

Chris Howard wondered if Woodson had been running against blind people in high school. In reality, it was Woodson who had eyes in the back of his head. As a runner in the open field, he used his blend of speed and burst to run away from people after setting them up with his field vision. Opponents stopped kicking the ball to him at some point during his sophomore year. He still managed to find it and break off long returns. His favorite run play was an inside trap because he loved how well his offensive line blocked it. On defense, he'd line up as a single-high free safety and just roam the field—picking off passes and stopping the run from anywhere.

He was the best athlete on every playing surface he touched, and everybody knew it, which often led to challenges. During a basketball playoff game his junior year, Woodson got ejected after punching an opponent who'd thrown him to the ground after a layup. His teammates responded by erasing a halftime deficit to secure an upset win.

Woodson became a national football recruit during his junior season, though most believed his childhood affinity for winged helmets would push him north. Fact was, Fremont, Ohio, is actually closer to the University of Michigan than it is to Ohio State. Woodson played high school at Ross, where Lytle—onetime owner of Michigan's all-time rushing record—had starred. Michigan was

PART 2: THE HEISMANS

on TV as much as, if not more than, Ohio State. Speculation grew in the summer of 1994 when Woodson attended Michigan's summer camp and left with the defensive back MVP award.

His senior season on the Ross gridiron was more or less a coronation for the greatest player the area had ever seen. Every week it was something new. Despite teams trying not to kick to him anymore, Woodson still returned a punt 84 yards for a touchdown versus St. John's in week two. He also ran for 205 yards that night—parents' night. Against Findlay, per the *News-Messenger*, 211 of his 256 rushing yards came on three carries. Two weeks later, after missing a game with a knee injury, he ran for 250 yards again. Then, on October 22, 1994, Charles Woodson officially became an Ohio schoolboy legend.

Playing against Clay High School in Oregon, Ohio, Woodson ran for a school-record 335 yards and seven touchdowns during a 72–0 romp. A week later, Woodson set Ross' single-season rushing record and passed his brother, Terry, on the school's all-time rushing list. He'd finish his career as Ross' all-time rushing leader with 3,861 yards—posting 2,028 rushing yards and 38 touchdowns in just 10 games.

Woodson's recruitment was hardly a wild affair. Growing up, Terry had been a Michigan fan. So when the annual Michigan–Ohio State showdown came on TV every November, Charles did what his brother did: He rooted for the Wolverines. There was also something about those helmets he couldn't shake, and he loved watching Michigan games on TV. Lytle had not only starred at his high school, but he was also an assistant coach on the Ross staff during Woodson's historic run. Ohio State, in reality, never had a chance with Charles Woodson. Notre Dame and Miami (Fla.) were the only other teams to get visits, and per a former teammate, Woodson spent most of his time in South Bend telling everyone he'd be playing in Ann Arbor.

The only mystery was *what position* he'd be playing.

Lloyd Carr would eventually take over as head coach in 1995. But Woodson committed to Michigan in December 1994, when Gary Moeller was still head coach. Carr, defensive coordinator at the time, was with Moeller and Woodson at a downtown Ann Arbor steakhouse the weekend of his visit and figured he'd simply sit back and watch the head coach reel in the program's next great running back. Carr's roots in Detroit made him an ace recruiter for Moeller in the midwest, which included Ohio.

Carr had driven by Fremont more times than he could count during the early part of the '90s, including a gaggle of trips to Sandusky to persuade a young tackle named Orlando Pace *not* to sign with Ohio State. Years later, when both men were part of the same 2013 Rose Bowl Hall of Fame class, Carr whispered in Pace's ear that he *still* believes the Buckeye legend and Pro Football Hall of Famer would've looked better in blue.

He knew all about Woodson. Or so he thought.

The words "I think I'd like to play defense" hit Carr's ears like a record scratch. In those days, if Michigan was recruiting an athlete of Woodson's caliber, the kid almost *always* wanted to run the football. Woodson was different. He told Carr and Moeller he believed the secondary would give him a longer career and offer a cleaner path to the NFL. Recruits did not talk like this back then. Veterans didn't talk like this.

No one argued.

For most 18-year-olds entering Michigan's football program—no matter the era—the process of "proving it" takes a while. Tom Harmon and Desmond Howard spent their first year on the bench. It took Tom Brady three and a half years to prove it. Brian Griese needed four.

It took Charles Woodson one day.

PART 2: THE HEISMANS

Like any big-time program, Michigan football is filled with internal moments of folklore. People remember every syllable of Bo Schembechler's "the Team" speech. Players can recall how the air smelled in the stadium the morning of the 1969 Ohio State game. They remember how they felt when John Wangler hit Anthony Carter against Indiana in 1979. And they remember every second of that time Charles Woodson stepped to Amani Toomer and lived to tell about it.

Scot Loeffler remembers the actual play—Brown Indiana 17 Pivot. It was fall camp of 1995 and Woodson, a true freshman corner, had drawn Toomer in a live team drill. Toomer's reputation at the time was that of the best athlete on the roster. And, more importantly, one of the toughest people—player or coach—in the program. Freshmen didn't try Toomer. Most veterans didn't.

But when Loeffler ripped a near-perfect throw toward the sideline—exactly where Toomer liked it on this particular route—he saw something different. Woodson read the play perfectly, almost as if he was in the huddle, exploding through Toomer for a pass-breakup that nearly stopped practice it was so shocking. Nobody beat Toomer like that, least of all a kid most people (outside of the running back room) had never heard of.

Things got more intense from there when an infuriated Toomer got up and drilled Woodson with a right hand directly to the head. A full-blown fistfight broke out between the baddest senior on the team and the freshman from Ohio. When the scrap was over, nobody questioned Charles Woodson ever again.

Freshmen at Michigan didn't excel. The program was built to prohibit it. High schoolers, no matter how talented, showed up every fall believing they were ready to skip the line only to discover exactly how hard a Mike Gittleson strength program was. Most workouts were designed to mentally break freshmen of poor habits, to help them learn how to play at the next level. Charles Woodson didn't need any of that.

If it took most freshmen 15 seconds to finish a drill, Woodson could do it in 10. Classmates would find themselves in search of the nearest puke bucket on a practice field or weight room only to see Woodson, doing the same amount of work, barely sweating.

"I never played with anybody else like Charles," said former All-American Michigan offensive tackle Jon Jansen, who also played a decade in the NFL. "[Some, like Champ Bailey or Sean Taylor,] were close. They were really good. Special. But not Charles special."

Jansen entered the program a year ahead of Woodson as a big, skinny tight end who was quickly pushed to the offensive line room. He remembered *exactly* how hard every drill Michigan threw at incoming freshmen could be in comparison to high school. Gigantic, world-class athletes nearly being brought to tears over an inability to put one foot in front of the other in a state of total exhaustion.

A particular drill that tore everyone up was a high-knee agility drill where players had to run through a maze of tight elastic bands without getting their feet caught. Everybody messed it up the first time. Some never got it right.

"Then Charles comes in and, like, dances through it at full speed," Jansen recalled in the book *Mountaintop: The Inside Story of Michigan's 1997 National Title Climb*. "He made everything we thought was hard look so easy."

As a kid, Woodson had spent so much time chasing Terry, trying to be everything he was as a runner. But once he told the Michigan coaching staff his plans to transition to defense full-time, Charles started to chase something else—true greatness.

Woodson was a natural at every sport he touched. One of those kids who could've been a professional basketball player had he chosen to pursue it. But he chose football. He also chose cornerback. At Ross, Woodson also played deep safety—running down interceptions other kids couldn't sniff. He was a power hitter in Little League who played basketball and track through high school. The summer of 1995 was the first time Woodson was allowed to specialize in one thing. And it's when he began to soar.

Woodson won Michigan's nickel corner job ahead of the '95 season opener against Virginia on August 26. He made a tackle that helped force a punt on his first series. Early in the fourth quarter, with Michigan trailing 14–0, Woodson undercut a slant route from standout WR Germane Crowell and nearly had his first college interception as the ball bounced off his hands. The play forced Virginia to settle for a field goal to make it 17–0. Michigan would, of course, go on to win that one—the first Lloyd Carr ever coached—by a score of 18–17.

He was in the starting lineup the following week. He'd never go back to the bench.

Against Memphis on September 9, Woodson got his hands on another throw—this time perfectly reading a screen pass before cutting in front of a stationary receiver—and didn't drop it. Woodson's first career interception set up the first Michigan touchdown of the game in a 24–7 win.

"That there," remarked TV color analyst George Perles, the recently retired longtime Michigan State head coach, "is a Sunday play."

By the time Michigan went to Michigan State, the Wolverines were a surprising 7–1, ranked No. 7, and Woodson had become a fixture in the defensive backfield. The freshman who'd stopped looking like a freshman on day one of practice had two interceptions and a fumble recovery and was among the team leaders in tackles. His transition from offense to defense was so smooth many had already forgotten how dominant his days as a running back were.

And entering Spartan Stadium on November 4, Woodson had yet to face a situation on a football field he couldn't master or dominate. Then he met Derrick Mason and Muhsin Muhammad. The dynamic Spartan receiver duo, both future pros, went bonkers against a now-overconfident Michigan secondary—combining to catch 13 Tony Banks passes for 187 yards (Banks threw for 318). On Michigan State's final possession, with Michigan up four, Mason badly beat Woodson on a fourth-down corner route to keep the game alive. Four plays later, Woodson saw an interception bounce off his hands directly into Mason's for another big chunk. One snap later, Mason scored the game-winner—shocking Woodson and the Wolverines.

The final touchdown hadn't come against Woodson, but the freshman left East Lansing devastated. He'd felt solely responsible for a loss and didn't understand how to process it. He worked hard like everybody else, but to this point in his career—it had all been so easy. This was not easy.

"That was one of those things that happened in life. Where, like, what can I change?" Woodson recalled in *Mountaintop*. "What can I change?"

When Woodson got off the team bus in Ann Arbor, he went into his dorm room, grabbed a pair of clippers, and shaved his dreadlocks. The following week, in horrific weather at home against Purdue, Woodson made his third pick of the season in a defense-dominated 5–0 Michigan win that sealed Carr's status as permanent head coach. He followed that up with two picks against Ohio State, silencing Biletnikoff winner Terry Glenn, to finish 1995 as the Big Ten freshman of the year.

Michigan's season, however? A mixed bag. The Ohio State win quenched the rage from those who never wanted Carr, but not for long as a bowl defeat saddled Michigan with four losses for the third straight year. Little changed in 1996. The offense struggled, the defense dominated, and Woodson looked like a superstar.

This was even clearer in the '96 season opener versus Illinois.

After struggling early on offense again, Michigan mounted a drive into the Illini red zone toward the end of the first quarter. On a second-and-10 from the Michigan 13, Woodson split wide left in a three-receiver set and ran a streak into the end zone as a decoy—allowing running back Clarence Williams to break wide open over the middle for what should've been an easy touchdown. Scott Dreisbach's throw, pressured as it was released, fell to the ground two feet short of the target.

Three possessions later, up 7–5, Carr stopped with the decoy stuff. Woodson took a reverse handoff from Williams and stormed into open grass for the first time since his high school days. In the broadcast booth that day working alongside ABC's Bob Griese—whose son Brian had told him all about No. 2 ahead of the game—offered a prophetic warning:

"Look out."

Everything an elite player does is different. They stand differently. Walk differently. And when they touch a football, they'll make your neck hairs stand at attention.

Woodson floored through the Illini defense along the home sideline just as those running backs feared he might once upon a time. His first offensive touch in college went 57 yards and was Michigan's most electric offensive moment in a year.

"You have to utilize special players," Carr said afterward, "who have special abilities."

However, as was usual at the time, the offense managed just a field goal out of Woodson's spark before settling for a 20–8 win. That, more or less, is how the 1996 season went. Against Indiana,

Woodson was a major part of the offense with four catches for 55 yards (along with a full load on defense). Woodson also ripped off a magnificent 57-yard touchdown run on a reverse where he ran through and away from six tacklers before gliding the final 30 untouched. Michigan needed every inch of that run as it held off the Hoosiers 27–20.

Individually, Woodson was thriving. As a team, Michigan was barely surviving. Woodson was a big part of the offense again at Purdue on November 9, catching three passes for 43 yards—but the rest of the offense bottomed out. Michigan lost three fumbles—including one on the goal line, by defensive tackle-turned-fullback Will Carr—in a brutal 9–3 loss that shook the program to its core. Two weeks later, after another loss to Penn State that saw no offensive touches for Woodson, a bubbling pot boiled over.

The Monday of Ohio State week, with Michigan sitting at an unacceptable 7–3, Woodson and Carr got into a disagreement on the practice field and the sophomore star walked off, fully intent on transferring. Woodson's back hurt, literally (he was rehabbing an injury) and figuratively (he'd been carrying Carr's team). The threat was bad enough for Carr and his assistant coaches to spend the rest of the day trying to figure out how to change their best player's mind—but when the final staff meeting began that night, Carr told the room they'd be without Woodson against Ohio State.

Carr's last-ditch effort was a phone call to Woodson's mother, Georgia, whom he'd gotten to know well during the recruiting process. Both he and defensive backs coach Vance Bedford pleaded with her to talk with Charles. She did exactly that, telling her son to remember he'd picked Michigan for a reason—for what it could do for his future on and off the field—and he'd be staying there for that same reason.

PART 2: THE HEISMANS

The turning point in Charles Woodson's football career came from that phone call, because he listened to his mom. On Tuesday he was at practice. By Saturday, November 23, in Columbus, Ohio, Woodson was a different person.

He broke up three passes, made nine tackles, and dazzled on punt returns as Michigan stunned No. 2 and previously unbeaten Ohio State in a 13–9 win at the Horseshoe. As a sophomore, Woodson set a new school record for pass breakups (15) and earned first-team All-America honors. He also caught 10 passes for 139 yards and a touchdown and rushed six times for 152 yards and a score.

Michigan finished 1996 with its fourth straight four-loss season. But in the win against Ohio State, Carr had made the critical decision of pivoting from Dreisbach to Brian Griese at quarterback—and had found his voice as the leader of the program in the process.

Entering 1997, the sky would be the limit for Woodson. In his journal leading up to the season, Carr dreamed about starting the season in a four-receiver set with Woodson split wide. The Wolverines now believed they had the best individual player in the country and Carr was hell-bent on wringing out every drop of talent Woodson had to give in what would be his final year on campus.

The change in Woodson after his near exit before the Ohio State game was obvious to anyone watching. Like every great player who'd ever come before him at Michigan, the better Charles Woodson got, the harder he worked.

During one particularly difficult summer workout ahead of the 1997 season, strength coach Mike Gittleson couldn't help but take note that the team's best player was suddenly working harder—and faster—than everyone else on the roster. His quest was simple. His mother told him he was going to stay at Michigan for a reason. That reason: to prove he was the best amateur football player in America. When Gittleson had the Wolverines run stadium steps that summer, Woodson attacked every one of them as if they were opposing ball carriers. His maturity as a leader was exploding. His seriousness as a competitor was through the roof.

When it came time to fill out individual goal sheets later that summer, Woodson's index card listed one thing: He wanted to win. Every game. Every award. Everything.

Which is exactly what happened.

With first-year defensive coordinator Jim Herrmann running Michigan's new fire zone defense, Woodson was free to put everything he had on full display. In a stunning thrashing of No. 8 Colorado in the season opener, Woodson made a leaping sideline interception the first time the Buffalos tried him and was an active blitz participant the entire game. By the fifth game of the season, Michigan had given up only two touchdowns and teams had more or less stopped trying Woodson. And, since Michigan played a lot of quarter-quarter-half deep coverage, with Woodson taking half the field, opponents didn't have many places to throw the ball. Or run it.

After a thrilling comeback victory over Iowa on October 18 put Michigan at 6–0 for the first time in more than a decade, the Wolverines traveled to 5–1 Michigan State, where Woodson—no longer in need of dreadlocks—got his payback at Spartan Stadium. Michigan's now ferocious defense swallowed the confident Spartans early and often, intercepting MSU quarterbacks six times in total—tying a school record. Woodson had two of them, including a spectacular one-handed sideline interception late in the third quarter that would become a signature highlight for both the program and Woodson.

The pick came against a throw from QB Todd Schultz that was intended for the bench area. Woodson, who jumped higher

PART 2: THE HEISMANS

than anyone thought possible that day, soared into the air for a spectacular one-handed catch that left the stadium breathless. Even more so when, upon his descent, he gracefully placed one foot in bounds.

For Michigan football, the 1997 season was a dream. The year that washed away the sadness of the Moeller exit and more than five decades of national title frustration. It was the year Lloyd Carr stamped himself as a Hall of Famer, the year Michigan football reintroduced itself to the national stage, and the year Charles Woodson became a household name. The pick against Michigan State was his Heisman moment.

When the game ended, a still-shocked Carr raced to the locker room to watch the replay of a catch he still couldn't believe he'd just watched.

The buzz continued two weeks later when unbeaten Michigan destroyed No. 2 Penn State in Happy Valley—using Woodson's talents on offense as a wide receiver during a nationally televised broadcast—to push the Wolverines to a No. 1 ranking at 9–0. After besting Wisconsin in week 10, Michigan was set for Ohio State. The shoe was on the other foot now, as Ohio State had the chance to play national title spoiler.

Woodson, the greatest individual player in school history, did not let that happen. In Michigan's monumental 20–14 win, clinching an 11–0 mark and a Big Ten crown, Woodson intercepted a pass in the end zone, caught a pass on a touchdown drive, and scored on a 78-yard punt return down the Buckeyes' sideline that stands as one of the most memorable moments in Michigan Stadium history.

Decades later, Carr would simply refer to this play as "a work of art."

When the year started, Woodson was silently sweating on the stadium steps while Tennessee's Peyton Manning received

123

THE PROGRAM: MICHIGAN

every ounce of Heisman Trophy buzz. After Woodson crossed the goal line against the Buckeyes, though, things looked different. On December 13, 1997—with fellow Hall of Famers Manning and Randy Moss sharing the stage—Woodson became the first primarily defensive player in the history of college football to win the Heisman Trophy. Michigan's third player to win the honor.

After Michigan won the Rose Bowl on January 1, securing the school's first national title in 50 years, Michigan staffer Scott Draper stood outside the team hotel performing a head count for those heading back to Ann Arbor. There was one player he couldn't find, though. Until, that is, he saw a stretch limo parked near the team busses. Out of curiosity, he peeked inside to see who'd ordered the cush ride.

It was Charles Woodson. Sitting with a smile stretched across his face in the morning California sun, legendary status already cemented in Michigan, the 21-year-old soon-to-be superstar put on a pair of shades and started the cruise toward his happily ever after.

As of this book's writing, it'd been more than 25 years since Woodson captivated one of the largest football fan bases in the country. His Pro Football Hall of Fame career, and subsequent run as a broadcaster, has made Woodson a legend in other parts of the world. He's a Raider. A Green Bay Packer. Georgia's son. Terry's younger brother. The kid from Fremont who looked like he was running against blind people.

At Michigan, he more or less keeps a key to the city. Woodson's been a highly present supporter of Michigan athletics every day since he left. Though, in some ways, he never really has. Because in Ann Arbor, Michigan, Charles Woodson is simply known as the best to ever do it.

The greatest individual football player in the history of Michigan's football program.

PART 3

THE FAMILY

8

The Quarterback Standard

It was September 17, 1977, and Michigan was hosting Duke for the second game of quarterback Rick Leach's junior season. Already a two-year starter on his way to becoming the greatest in program history, Leach broke the huddle and swaggered to the line of scrimmage the way he always did.

Leach didn't have a walk. He had a stride. He played the quarterback position with rhythm, like a drummer keeping time in a rock band. It was fourth-and-1 from the Duke seven and on the 22nd play of one of the most mesmerizing drives he'd ever led, Leach strode toward the line of scrimmage before planting both feet on either side of center Walt Downing—shimmying himself into a crouch as he surveyed the defense one final time. On the sideline, kneeling just outside the end

THE PROGRAM: MICHIGAN

zone (nearly *on* the field) was a 13-year-old Michigan ball boy capable of mimicking Leach's every move. That stride. The way Leach would adjust his chest plate with his right hand before licking his left and settling into that famed crouch. The kid—son of a Michigan assistant—played catch with Leach before practices and alternated between a source of entertainment and annoyance for everyone in the program.

Leach barked his cadence under center so hard his body rocked backward. Just enough to pull the entire defensive line offside as he called for the ball. Leach took a wide step to his right as he began down the line, putting a fake into the belly of fullback Russell Davis before exploding off tackle and into the end zone. It was the 34th touchdown of Leach's already historic Michigan career and it capped the longest scoring drive in the history of college football's winningest program—22 plays, 89 yards, and more than 12 minutes of clock consumed. It's a Michigan record that stands today. The first person to greet him in the end zone was not a teammate, but that 13-year-old ball boy.

This was not the first time Jim Harbaugh lost himself in football at Michigan Stadium.

It was hardly the last.

The modern quarterback lineage at Michigan is incredibly unique and one of the greatest in the history of the sport. After Leach, who pursued pro baseball after college and was drafted by the Denver Broncos in 1979, Michigan had a 30-year stretch that saw 10 of its quarterbacks drafted into the NFL. Nine of them started in the league. Four (Jim Harbaugh, Elvis Grbac, Brian Griese, Tom Brady) were Pro Bowlers. Four (Grbac, Griese, Brady, Chad Henne) won Super Bowls. One (Brady) is known as the greatest to ever play.

However, among that group of passers, there is only one 3,000-yard passing season in college (John Navarre's 3,331 yards in 2003 is still a Michigan record). These quarterbacks would lead the longest run of success in modern Michigan history. None of them was built alike, though a commonality existed. From the first to the last.

They *lived* to compete.

The story of Tom Brady going from seventh stringer at Michigan to global icon has been told more times than anyone can count. What's rarely discussed, though, is the fact Michigan had *seven quarterbacks* capable of winning a football game against pretty much anyone. At all times. That was very real. The competitive cauldron in Michigan's quarterback room—especially throughout the '80s and '90s—is the furnace that forged the program's post–World War identity.

Leach, of course, was the original standard.

A three-sport schoolboy legend at Flint Southwestern, Leach—who was actually born in Ann Arbor—came to Michigan as an 18-year-old freshman in 1975. Multi-year starter Dennis Franklin had just departed, and the only junior backup, Mark Elzinga, had varsity experience. The timing was right. But that's not why Rick Leach made history at Michigan.

Leach's prep stardom made him a legitimate college prospect in three sports. His father, Richard, caught for Michigan's 1953 national championship baseball squad. Rick, who was also a standout guard on the basketball court, picked football *and* baseball when he followed his dad's path to Ann Arbor. A natural athlete who carried himself with the confidence reserved only for those who make the hard look easy, Leach's ability to inhale information without making mistakes blew Schembechler away in the summer of '75.

The coach who'd become famous for his advice to *never* start a freshman anywhere so long as he could help it, told reporters he'd already contradicted himself on that one long ago—adding no other coach in America was crazy enough to start a true freshman quarterback.

"No one else has Rick Leach either," he added.

The 1975 season was a resurgence of sorts for Schembechler's Michigan. Leach's first start against the Buckeyes was a 21–14 loss, as Ohio State stretched its unbeaten streak vs. Michigan to four years. The game was a battle, though, as Michigan snapped two-time Heisman winner Archie Griffin's record streak of 31 straight 100-yard rushing games. Leach partly proved the old Schembechler right by throwing 12 interceptions in just 100 attempts. But he was a terrific leader, as the coach had already proclaimed, of Michigan's option-based ground game, mixing in the occasional bomb from his live left arm. Michigan went 7–1 in the Big Ten that year, ending the season ranked No. 8 nationally to the surprise of many and delight of everyone in Maize and Blue.

Leach never left the field again. The 1976 team reached No. 1 before a late loss at Purdue spoiled a terrific 10–2 Big Ten title season featuring a win over Ohio State. Leach added two more wins over Ohio State and two more Big Ten titles with 10-win seasons in 1977 and 1978. His only problem was the Rose Bowl. His Michigan teams went 0–3 in Pasadena, including a 17–10 loss as a senior—a year when Leach finished third in Heisman voting. By the time Leach left Michigan, he was decidedly the program's most successful quarterback and his fame throughout the state rivaled that of any pro sports star in Detroit. He started 47 games at Michigan and rewrote the record book, setting new marks in passing, total offense, and touchdowns. His 82 career touchdowns were an NCAA record and his 6,640 yards of total offense set a Big Ten mark. In every way, Leach became an on-field extension of Schembechler. Incredibly tough, lightning quick, and capable of exploding (in

PART 3: THE FAMILY

a good way) at any moment. His presence became legendary. And his absence became difficult to overcome.

Michigan's offense went through a difficult transition in 1979. After years of being spoiled by Leach's special combination of option prowess and arm talent, Michigan was forced back to Earth—and, with that, forced to pick a lane.

But not before trying to drive in two at the same time.

Veteran B.J. Dickey, a good option QB, had served as Leach's backup. John Wangler, a pocket passer with a cannon, represented the stylistic shift many fans felt was long overdue. Dickey was the team's starter for the first half of '79, though he rotated some with Wangler. When Wangler was in the game, Michigan was more apt to lean on a newer vertical pass game. When Dickey was in the game, it was more of a familiar and traditional Michigan attack. On paper, this always makes sense. In real life, it almost never does. Without a clear leader at QB, Michigan's offense was all over the place that season.

Though 1979 did produce one of the single greatest moments in college football history.

On October 27, homecoming, with six seconds left and Michigan–Indiana tied at 21, Wangler dropped back and fired a beautiful strike between the numbers and into the arms of a streaking Anthony Carter—who famously did the rest. Wangler's famed "54 Pass Post" to Carter for a game-winning touchdown, including Bob Ufer's euphoric call, is one of the most replayed plays in the history of the sport. And it came in a game Wangler didn't start.

Wangler earned four starts to Dickey's seven that year and, with Michigan 8–2 entering the Ohio State game, Schembechler made it a three-man situation when he surprised the Buckeyes by starting freshman option QB Rich Hewlett over Wangler. It didn't work. The Buckeyes weren't caught off-guard and after a scoreless 26 minutes, Schembechler went back to Wangler. Wangler's arm kept Michigan in the game, but this—a balanced pass offense as opposed to an option-heavy attack—was once again a backup plan. During Leach's freshman year in 1975, San Diego State's Craig Penrose had led the country with 2,660 passing yards. By 1979, not only had four quarterbacks hit 2,600 yards—two of them eclipsed 3,000, including 3,720 from BYU's Marc Wilson. While Michigan was dominant running the ball in the early '70s, high school pass offenses were blossoming. By the end of the decade, that trend reached college. The '79 season and the 1–2 start to 1980 was the final straw for Schembechler, who went all-in on Wangler and changed the program as a result. Wangler and Carter helped spark a nine-game win streak to close the '80 season, resulting in a surprise Big Ten title and a new outlook on life.

Then, on January 1, 1981, led by a pure passer in John Wangler, Michigan's balanced offense was too much for Washington as Michigan rolled 23–6, snapping Schembechler's Rose Bowl skid and giving the coach his *first* bowl victory at Michigan.

"I love the forward pass," Schembechler quipped afterward.

Wangler's performance in 1980, and subsequent Rose Bowl win, was revolutionary. Nationally, he's known for the famous throw to Carter. In Ann Arbor, he's known as a legend despite really only starting one season. Even with limited attempts, Wangler's 2,646 career yards ranked No. 2 on the program's all-time list when he was done.

In 1981, Wangler passed the torch to highly athletic passer Steve Smith, who helped Michigan continue its offense growth. The following winter, Schembechler picked up the phone and called a kid who would eventually catapult Michigan all the way out of the option era.

PART 3: THE FAMILY

The kid, now a young man, who'd run into the end zone to greet Rick Leach against Duke.

After moving to California midway through his high school career following his father Jack's departure for Stanford, Jim Harbaugh entered the winter of 1982 with a heavy decision. An underdog even when he's favored, Harbaugh would later claim he was lightly recruited. Which isn't true. Harbaugh, per the *Crestline* (Ohio) *Advocate* (Jack's hometown newspaper), had interest from 30 colleges across the country. His eventual finalist group featured Arizona, Wisconsin, Stanford, Cal, Western Michigan (his father's new school), and Michigan.

Harbaugh nearly became a Badger, as Wisconsin head coach Dave McClain had been a college teammate of Jack's at Bowling Green State. Moreover, his mother, Jackie (also a BGSU alum), was highly fond of McClain. Which mattered. A lot. When Jim and John Harbaugh first asked to play tackle football as kids, it was their mother—not their football-coaching father—who went to Tom Minick's pee wee practices (alone) to audit the coach's overall competency and safety protocol. The Harbaugh boys did not put on a helmet until Jackie, who knew more about the game than the rest of the neighborhood had forgotten, determined their coach knew what he was doing.

Jim also nearly became a Western Michigan Bronco. Jack took the Western Michigan job just as Jim was finishing high school. Jim would later tell *Sport Magazine* he'd have gone to Western Michigan had his dad actually asked. Jack—fully aware of the national opportunities his son had—didn't push his agenda. He never formally offered or asked Jim to attend WMU as part of his first class, supporting him to make his own choice. Schembechler called late in the process. He claimed to be late on purpose in an attempt to avoid claims of nepotism. None of it mattered. It was the only call Jim Harbaugh ever wanted.

THE PROGRAM: MICHIGAN

The son of a coach, he'd never spent more than a handful of years anywhere growing up. The years he spent in Ann Arbor, though, were his formative ones. Where he'd stored most of his core memories.

Born two days before Christmas 1963 in Toledo, Ohio, Jim Harbaugh first moved to Ann Arbor in the winter of 1973. That fall, Jackie made her visit to Tom Minick and Jim played tackle football for the first time. His first team—the Ann Arbor Junior Packers—practiced on a large patch of grass near an elementary school on the city's south end, about three miles away from the family home. When nine-year-old Harbaugh first got in the tackling line and saw the opposing runner was more than twice his size, he nearly quit. Only he didn't. He bit his lip, walked to the line, and got steamrolled. In the process of being steamrolled, though, he grabbed a limb—and never let go, making his "first career tackle." It was both the first and last time Jim Harbaugh was intimidated on a football field. Decades later, he'd use the story of "tackling Ralph" to inspire his 41-point underdog Stanford squad prior to its historic upset over USC in 2007.

Harbaugh spent much of his formative years riding his bike around Ann Arbor, playing football in the street or church parking lots with friends. Basketball in Michigan's intramural building and running through entire baseball games in his mind (alone) by throwing a ball off the house (or a local storefront) to himself until someone told him to stop. By 1974, Jack and some of the other coaches had persuaded Schembechler to allow staff kids at practice. At Iowa, coaches became so annoyed with Jim running onto the field during drills they threw him out. Jack never forgot it. Jim annoyed Schembechler, too, but nobody ever banned him from the field. Jack never forgot that either. Instead, if Jim became too much of a hassle, the coach merely had a few players tape him to a locker until he calmed down. Eventually, he became a ball boy—and became obsessed with every aspect of Michigan's program.

He could recite his batting average to a stranger at a moment's notice. Same with his football stats, assist-turnover ratio, and win-loss record against John in checkers. If something had a score, Jim Harbaugh was obsessed with winning that thing. And when he was let inside Michigan's walls for the first time, he became obsessed with the Wolverines—memorizing stats, plays, opponents, mannerisms, whatever. He'd scour the locker room for wristbands with friends after home games. On Monday, he'd sell them at school for a dollar. He got ejected from a Little League baseball game. Got into fights on the wrestling team. At Stanford, he became famous for bloody-nosed pick-up games with other coaches. He never forgot the names of the two quarterbacks Schembechler offered before him in 1982 (Dave Yarema and John Congemi). He played laser tag during his bachelor party and won by scoring all his points against one 10-year-old.

A lot of people say they're competitive.

Few have walked it, every day of their life, quite like Jim Harbaugh.

Fire burns two ways, though. On the day of his first team meeting at Michigan in 1982, Harbaugh hitched a ride to campus with childhood friend Jim Minick. On the way, the muffler fell off. Harbaugh and Minick used coat hangers to temporarily fix it, but Harbaugh still showed up 10 minutes late.

"Sometimes," he'd fondly recall years later to longtime college coach Gerry DiNardo, "the car really does break down."

Schembechler didn't care. Incredulous the son of a coach would be late for *his first meeting of college football,* he famously barked at his new pupil, "You will never play a single down at the University of Michigan your *entire* career."

Harbaugh began 1982 behind Smith and junior backup David Hall as the Wolverines' third stringer. Michigan's offense, meantime? It missed Wangler. The passing game was inconsistent, turnovers followed, and Michigan got off to another nightmarish 1–2 start. At home against Indiana in week four and up 10–0 late in the first half (without an injured Carter), Schembechler ran out the clock near midfield before the break and received an ovation of boos from Michigan Stadium. Michigan ran the ball 62 times that day in a 24–10 win. Indiana used two quarterbacks to throw the ball 49 times. One of them was named Cam Cameron, a North Carolina native who also played basketball at IU for Bob Knight—a close friend of Schembechler's.

A year after that game, Cameron was a GA on Michigan's coaching staff. An hour after that game? Schembechler told reporters anyone who booed could "go to hell."

Smith, and Michigan, found a way more than they didn't throughout 1982 and 1983. The Wolverines went 8–1 in Big Ten play in '82, winning the league. In '83, Michigan's offensive line and defense continued to churn as the record improved to 9–3—including a spectacular day from Smith in a November win over Ohio State. Ahead of the '84 season, optimism for the next chapter of Michigan football was high. Largely because the player Schembechler said would never play a down at Michigan was finally ready to be its starting quarterback.

A process that took a while.

Tall and rangy with the quickness of a point guard and decent speed, Harbaugh was the rare prospect capable of leading any offense. His whole life was football, a family business. As a kid, he prayed nightly to become 6'2" because he'd read that was the preferred height for a pro quarterback. He talked about playing in the NFL to teammates in high school. There's never been a backup plan. His mantra became simple: "I'm going to play as long as I can, then coach as long as I can, then I'll die." There is no in-between. There is nothing else.

One of Harbaugh's closest friends at Michigan was linebacker Andy Moeller, son of then assistant Gary Moeller. The two went to Pioneer High School together. They were roommates and about as close as one could get to a best friend. Jamie Morris, on the other hand, was a pint-sized running back from the Northeast who was *never* afraid of standing up to anyone over anything. Including Harbaugh. Once during practice, Moeller and Morris got tangled up after a tackle and started to scrap. Harbaugh, out of nowhere, torpedoed his way in between the two, not to get in Morris' face but to begin legitimately fighting Moeller. To a point where *that* had to be broken up.

"*Do not go at my running back like that!*" Harbaugh bellowed.

Andy may have been his best friend, but Morris was in his huddle. That, to Harbaugh, was always more important. That's not to say he always treated those inside his huddle as family. The younger version of Harbaugh was not opposed to calling out offensive linemen for missing blocks, or receivers for not making enough of an effort on a throw. Schembechler once told *Free Press* columnist Mitch Albom a story from Harbaugh's freshman year. One day in practice, after taking a late hit from a defender during a play, Harbaugh got up and threw the ball directly into the guy's face mask. He ran hot and often struggled to bring himself back to neutral in time for the next play.

Albom also wrote how Schembechler was more hands-on in practice with Harbaugh at a young age than he'd been with any QB since Leach. He was intensely hard on him. At one point early in his career, dorm officials cited a handful of players for drunk and disorderly conduct and damaging school property—Harbaugh being one of them. Schembechler responded by throwing him off the team. Harbaugh told him he wasn't involved (he wasn't), and Schembechler told him to prove it (he did). Later in his career, Harbaugh and QB coach Jerry Hanlon famously stopped speaking to each other over an argument that more or less boiled down to Harbaugh trying to coach his teammates rather than simply worrying about his own job. The spat didn't last, of course, as Harbaugh long considered Hanlon one of his favorite coaches. But it was indicative of who he was. Stubborn. Intense. Never wrong—except when he was.

Harbaugh could be an adventure.

But he was an undeniably talented one.

By the end of spring practice in 1984, Harbaugh was now clearly Michigan's best quarterback and looked ready to help launch the Wolverines' offense into the stratosphere. His first start came on September 8, 1984, at Michigan Stadium against Jimmy Johnson, Bernie Kosar, and No. 1–ranked Miami, which was already 2–0 with wins over ranked foes in Florida and Auburn.

If he was nervous early, he didn't show it. Harbaugh's first throw as Michigan's starting quarterback was a beautiful 15-yard out for a first down. Moments later, he lofted a perfect ball right from the right hash to the left sideline that went 16 yards and hit Steve Johnson in stride for a first down inside the Hurricanes' 12. Two runs later and Michigan had the game's first lead. Three hours later, Jim Harbaugh scored his first win as a starter 22–14 against the No. 1 team in the country.

Inconsistencies followed in a humbling home loss to Washington and wins over Wisconsin and Indiana. Michigan's young roster was still 3–1 and feeling good entering Spartan Stadium on October 6. The offense struggled early during Harbaugh's first rivalry appearance, as Michigan trailed 13–7 early in the third quarter when Harbaugh handed the ball to running back Jamie Morris on an off-tackle play. Morris was drilled by two players, causing a fumble. Harbaugh—standing some 10 yards away—started to sprint toward the ball, colliding head-first with two defenders. Michigan State recovered the fumble and Harbaugh's season was over just five games in. He'd broken his left arm. Schembechler visited Harbaugh in the hospital after his surgery. Before the coach left, Harbaugh asked him for one favor.

"Don't forget about me."

During Harbaugh's decade as Michigan's head coach from 2015 to 2023, he routinely visited injured players in the hospital. When star lineman Zak Zinter went down with a severe leg injury midway through the 2023 Ohio State game, Harbaugh—suspended by the Big Ten and watching outside the stadium—met Zinter at the emergency room rather than stay to celebrate with the rest of the team.

The fact Michigan's offense became inept without Harbaugh—resulting in a 6–6 record, the worst of the Schembechler era—made it impossible to forget Harbaugh. The 6–6 record shook Michigan's program and support base. The core of returners in '85 felt responsible and, like their quarterback, worked as if their careers were on the line. The result was one of the most memorable seasons in modern Michigan history.

Unranked in September, by October Michigan was surging and Harbaugh was one of the country's top passers. In five games, Michigan went from unranked to No. 2 nationally and was 5–0 for the first time in eight seasons. A brutally hard-fought two-point road loss to Heisman candidate Chuck Long and No. 1 Iowa on October 19 and a bitter tie at Illinois two weeks later were setbacks. But by November, at 6–1–1, Michigan's offensive confidence was through the roof and its defense was decidedly the best in America once again.

THE PROGRAM: MICHIGAN

On November 9, Michigan hosted Purdue and star QB Jim Everett, one of the top passers in America and a Heisman candidate. A week prior versus Northwestern, Everett had gone 23 of 31 for 292 yards and two scores...in the first half. Sportswriters entered the game raving about Everett. They left raving about Harbaugh and his defense. The Michigan QB went 12 of 13 for 233 yards and three touchdown passes (in about one half) while the Wolverine defense harassed Everett into a miserable 12-of-22, 96-yard, one-interception performance in a 47–0 romp.

Michigan entered the finale with Ohio State at 8–1–1. With the game tied 3–3 early in the second quarter, linebacker Chris Spielman forced a fumble on a screen pass to give the Buckeyes the ball deep in Michigan territory. Six plays later, Keith Byars scored from two yards out—just the fourth touchdown allowed by Michigan's defense that season—to make it 10–3 Buckeyes.

By now, though, Harbaugh was on his way to mastering the art of the comeback. Especially immediately after a bad play. Following the turnover and Ohio State score, Harbaugh settled the Wolverines with a 25-yard bullet to tight end Eric Kattus down the middle to reignite the crowd. Seven plays later, after Harbaugh converted a fourth-and-1 sneak, the QB hit Gerald White (after bobbling the snap) over the middle on a third-and-goal play to tie the game just before the half. Entering the fourth quarter, with Michigan now leading 20–10, Harbaugh was 8 of 8 for 76 yards on third down. And after Ohio State cut Michigan's lead to three with 10 minutes left, Harbaugh capped his trademark performance with a signature play that said everything about him. On second-and-7 from his own 23, Harbaugh faked a hand-off on a seven-step drop and turned around in time to see a blitzing safety steaming toward him unblocked. In that microsecond, Harbaugh had

PART 3: THE FAMILY

three choices: dump it off, run away, or take the hit and let it rip. He chose option three. Leveled as he threw, Harbaugh's ball traveled about 40 yards in the air and right into the arms of John Kolesar, who took it the rest of the way for a 77-yard touchdown. When Kolesar crossed the goal line, Harbaugh was still on the ground being checked by an official. He took a beat, rolled over, picked himself up, and power-jogged off the field with the look of a football superhero. It was the second-longest pass in Michigan history and Harbaugh's 18th touchdown of the year, breaking Smith's school record of 17.

The 1985 team would finish the year 10–1–1, successfully erasing the embarrassment of 6–6. Thirty years later, at the team banquet following Harbaugh's first season as Michigan head coach, more than 30 members of that team were in attendance to celebrate the 2015 team for winning 10 games and erasing the pain of a five-win season a year prior.

"This was the greatest day of my life," Harbaugh said after the Ohio State win in '85. "I don't know what else to say."

Michigan entered 1986, Harbaugh's fifth and final year with the program, with more than a dozen returning starters and was viewed as a legit national title contender. The Wolverines opened the year ranked No. 3, surviving a test at Notre Dame in week one and another against sophomore Deion Sanders and Florida State in Ann Arbor before rolling to a 6–0 start in Big Ten play. When 9–0 Michigan went to Minnesota on November 15, it was ranked No. 2 with history waiting the following week in Columbus. Harbaugh was a legit Heisman contender and on the verge of potentially giving Schembechler his first national title.

Instead, disaster struck. Michigan turned the ball over three times and watched QB Rickey Foggie lead a balanced Gophers offense down the field on the final drive of the game just before

Chip Lohmiller ruined Michigan's perfect season with a 30-yard field goal as time expired, handing the Wolverines a 20–17 loss.

Harbaugh was devastated.

"I feel sick," he told reporters after the game. "My heart bleeds."

Two days later, it got worse. On November 17, Western Michigan fired Jack Harbaugh after five years with the program. He had gone 25–27–3 at a woefully underfunded program, telling the *Free Press* after his firing that WMU noted a lack of fundraising growth as a reason for his termination. Later that day, 22-year-old Jim Harbaugh—Jack's middle child—sat in front of TV cameras some 100 miles east of his heartbroken father and proceeded to make another headline for every newspaper in America.

"We're going to play in the Rose Bowl this year," Harbaugh said emphatically. "I guarantee it. We'll beat Ohio State and we'll be in Pasadena on January 1."

The comments shocked the college football world, though they merely surprised teammates and coaches at Michigan, who shrugged them off as Jim being Jim and began to work even harder to make sure their QB didn't wind up looking like a fool. Was Harbaugh *that* confident in a win over the Buckeyes? Maybe.

He also might've been trying to make sure his father's firing wasn't front-page news in Detroit the following morning, something Jack told *Free Press* writer Mick McCabe. Mission accomplished. The local papers led with Jim's Ohio State promise while news of Jack's dismissal—one Schembechler roasted—was beneath the fold.

In Jim Harbaugh's world, two things exist. One is football. The other is his family. Everything else is noise. He put himself, and by proxy his football team, ahead of his father's pain when the week started. By the time it ended, the team showed Harbaugh how much it had his back.

PART 3: THE FAMILY

On game day, Harbaugh threw two first-half interceptions, the second inside the Ohio State 10. He'd been able to pull Michigan out of the fire so many times. Now, it was someone else's turn. Morris rumbled for 210 yards and two touchdowns, Moeller made 13 tackles and Ivan Hicks batted a pass away from Carter in the end zone on the final drive as the Wolverines forced Ohio State into a missed 45-yard field goal with 1:06 and no timeouts remaining.

Earlier in the game, the crowd had been so loud with rage toward Harbaugh that his offensive line couldn't hear audibles at the line, forcing him to start cupping his hands as he shouted. A huge part of Michigan's success that day came at the line of scrimmage as Harbaugh, now a master of how the run game worked, was simply walking to the line of scrimmage and counting bodies. If Michigan had more blockers on one half of the line, that's where Harbaugh checked the ball. Over and over. The hand-cupping was necessary. But Harbaugh being Harbaugh, he started cupping his hands and shouting at the line even when Michigan *wasn't* changing plays, just to throw the Buckeyes off. Now, with Ohio State out of chances, that same crowd was silent.

Harbaugh, a week after guaranteeing victory over Michigan's most hated rival, took three knees inside Ohio Stadium. After the third, Harbaugh got off the ground just as Michigan's sideline stormed the field. After getting the game ball from the official, Harbaugh turned around and saw his dad. Jack stood jubilant opposite his son, arms extended wide. Jim, the game ball secured in one arm, raised the other high in the air before bear-hugging his father on the *new* greatest day of his young life.

"I knew what I was doing," he told reporters after the game. "I had no second thoughts about it. It was exactly what I needed personally."

Ohio State, meantime, was devastated. Spielman finished the '86 game with 29 tackles in one of the most iconic defensive efforts in college football history. He and Morris would become friends later in life, with the Michigan running back often joking that every one of those 29 tackles came a little closer to the goal line. Carter caught two touchdowns. None of it mattered. Also on the Ohio State sideline that day was a 22-year-old first-year graduate assistant from Ashtabula, Ohio, named Urban Meyer. Someone else who never forgot Harbaugh's guarantee.

Michigan's 1986 season would end with a loss in the Rose Bowl, but it changed the program forever. Harbaugh rewrote the school's passing record book, ending the year as the all-time leading passer with 5,449 yards and a career completion rate above 62 percent.

Jim Harbaugh, the ball boy who couldn't stay off the field, had officially revolutionized the quarterback position at Michigan.

9
Passing through Pressure

Brian Griese grew up with the words of a legend ringing in his ear.

"Don't plan on doing what I did."

The son of the one and only NFL quarterback to lead his team to a perfect season, Griese's father, Bob, never pushed his boys to play football. While the Hall of Fame former Miami Dolphin never banned the sport from his sons Scott, Jeff, and Brian, he was sure to warn all of them that the life he built by playing professionally was not a realistic goal.

The message resonated. But all three of his boys wound up playing college football just the same. Brian, the youngest, was a bit different, though.

Football was *not* going to be Brian Griese's life. He played because he loved it. But his college choice would be about academics, which is why Michigan—one of the schools that did *not* offer Griese a scholarship—became his pick. He arrived as a walk-on in 1993, firmly No. 5 on the depth chart inside a QB room now dripping with pressure. The pressure to compete. The pressure to perform. The pressure to innovate. The pressure to win.

And, again, the pressure to replace a legend.

Elvis Grbac's parents, Ivan and Cecilija, left Croatia and migrated to Cleveland, Ohio, in the '60s before Elvis was born. He wasn't named after the famous singer. Elvis was actually a pretty common name in Croatia. He went to St. Joseph's in Cleveland, the same high school as Desmond Howard. Playing in that run-heavy offense, Grbac barely threw the ball. However, Michigan's staff knew of the massive 6'5", 240-pound prospect's arm as he'd developed a reputation in the area as a baseball pitcher. Moeller and Cameron saw a cannon with a terrific frame and a whole lot to work with.

Grbac arrived on campus in 1989, Moeller's third season as Michigan's offensive coordinator and 10th back with the program since returning to Schembechler's staff in 1980. Cam Cameron, who'd joined the program as a graduate assistant during Jim Harbaugh's run as a starter, was now in his eighth season as a Michigan assistant and his influence over the offense was immeasurable. Not only had Cameron helped Harbaugh find new heights as a passer, but he helped Moeller modernize the pass game completely during the latter half of the 1980s. A process that began with Harbaugh, but reached warp speed under Grbac. The '89 season was Schembechler's last and Moeller's fingerprints were all over it.

The offense Schembechler had installed to change Michigan's program 20 years prior was now but a memory. The new offense was no longer rooted in the option. In fact, it wasn't rooted in

PART 3: THE FAMILY

anything. Moeller and Cameron built one of college football's first truly balanced, pro-style offenses at Michigan, and it began to attract talent in areas the program hadn't seen before. There were no gimmicks or dozens of variations on a single theme. Moeller's offense, in theory, could execute any concept an NFL team ran—run or pass. Receivers Chris Calloway and Greg McMurtry were legit NFL prospects. The program had signed Howard and Detroit native Derrick Alexander that year. All four of those players would enjoy lengthy NFL careers thanks in part to the exposure they received in Michigan's new system. That, almost by itself, created a reputation that developed into a WR talent pipeline the likes of which Michigan had never seen. One that stretched well into the 2000s.

The quarterback, of course, was the centerpiece to it all. Not only as a passer, but also a coach on the field. Moeller's offense was complex for its time and included constant checks based on defensive looks—meaning the quarterback wasn't just responsible for executing after the snap, but also responsible for making sure the offense was in the right play *after* he called it in the huddle.

Senior Michael Taylor had the top spot to begin 1989 after coming off the bench a year prior to spark a 9–2–1 Big Ten- and Rose Bowl–winning season.

"Michael may be one of the smartest kids I've ever had," Moeller told the *Free Press* in 1989 after Taylor finished '88 as the Big Ten's most efficient passer. "He's like a point guard. Michael understands the game so well."

Physically, though, Taylor was struggling. The 1989 season opener was a titanic matchup between No. 1 Notre Dame, the defending national champions, and No. 2 Michigan at Michigan Stadium. Taylor, who broke his collarbone late in 1988, battled shoulder issues throughout training camp leading into the season. Schembechler and Moeller's problem was obvious: Start a very limited, albeit extremely savvy Taylor against the No. 1 team in the country or start a healthy true freshman named Elvis who'd barely thrown the ball in high school.

Taylor's week of practice leading into the Notre Dame game featured almost zero passing. His arm couldn't handle it. Then, early in the third quarter against the Irish, trailing 14–6 and having only attempted six passes, Taylor took off to scramble on a third-down play and was leveled by multiple defenders, resulting in a back injury.

Ready or not, Elvis Grbac was on the dance floor.

Grbac had impressed coaches with how quickly he was able to grasp Moeller's complicated system. To a point where he entered the first game week of the season as the team's backup, having taken several first-team reps in practice in case Taylor couldn't go. He projected confidence when he entered the huddle for the first time, with teammates telling reporters afterward that Grbac gave a mini speech in an effort to calm nerves just before taking his first snap.

If it worked, those nerves likely came flying back on Grbac's second snap when he turfed a wide-open throw in the flat. His third snap was worse, as he launched a third-down throw recklessly over the middle toward no one in particular. The ball had enough heat on it to break a board, but it whistled a good 10 yards ahead and in front of the intended target. His first series was a disaster. But the great thing about freshmen—especially ones who were raised by European parents who knew almost nothing about the pressures of major college football—is how short their memories can be.

On the second snap of Grbac's next possession, Moeller called a play action concept that sent McMurtry on a 20-yard post. Grbac's massive frame covered a good 12 yards just on his drop before he rifled a laser into the arms of a striding McMurtry for 30 yards and a first down. Grbac hopped in the air like a kid on Christmas as the ball landed safely in McMurty's hands before striding to the next huddle with the confidence of a man who'd forgotten he'd never done this before.

Three plays later, this time on third-and-20, Grbac ignored his safety valve underneath and launched a perfect ball to McMurtry on a deep corner route that covered 30 yards and reignited Michigan Stadium. Grbac finished the drive with a blistering fastball through two defenders and into the hands of tight end Derrick Walker for a touchdown to get Michigan back within one score. Grbac finished his debut 17 of 21 for 134 yards and two touchdowns as Michigan's offense exploded in the fourth quarter. Rocket Ismail's two second-half kickoff return touchdowns and Notre Dame's subsequent 24–19 win overshadowed Grbac's debut, but close observers saw the future in the form of the giant right-hander with the famous first name.

Grbac got his first start the following week at UCLA and the game went about the same. A poor first half followed by inexplicable late life from the Michigan quarterback almost no one had ever heard of three weeks ago. Grbac led two late scoring drives, including the game-winning field goal march, in a thrilling 24–23 win out west. Taylor returned later that year to finish off another Big Ten championship season—but the youngster had made his mark.

The 1990 season, Moeller's first as head coach, was all Grbac. And Michigan's offense exploded. The sophomore set a program record with 21 touchdown passes, including four in a Gator Bowl win over Mississippi State. Michigan's offense averaged a school-record 432.5 yards per game and Grbac led the Big Ten in passing efficiency as the Wolverines lost three games by six points, sharing the Big Ten title with Michigan State, Illinois, and Iowa at 9–3.

By the start of 1991, Grbac began to outgrow even Moeller and Cameron's expectations. As Grbac's confidence soared, so did Moeller's. With Howard on his Heisman run and Grbac playing the best ball of his life, Moeller's offense set a Michigan record for pass attempts in 1991 and Grbac broke his own single-season touchdown record with 25—a mark that still stands today. Grbac also became the first quarterback in modern Michigan history to lead the country in passer efficiency, as Grbac's 1991 season was the best the school had ever seen: 152 of 228 (66.7 percent) for 2,085 yards, 25 touchdowns, and just six interceptions.

The regular season was brilliant. The postseason would be anything but.

Michigan entered the Rose Bowl on January 1 with national championship hopes still alive. The fourth-ranked Wolverines had a chance to beat No. 2 Washington (11–0) and if Nebraska could upset Miami in the Orange Bowl, Moeller would have something in just his second season that Schembechler never delivered—a national title.

The Huskies had other plans. Beno Bryant rushed for 158 yards, star receiver Mario Bailey was terrific, and Billy Joe Hobert tossed three touchdown passes. Michigan's offense, playing without star center Steve Everitt—who sprained his ankle late in bowl prep—did not cross midfield in the first half. Grbac's inability to escape and the absence of Everitt—coupled with Washington star DT Steve Emtman—was disastrous for the Wolverines, who couldn't get the ball to Howard in his final game. For the first time under Moeller, the quarterback's inability to run had come back to haunt him. A day that began with national title hopes ended with bitter disappointment.

PART 3: THE FAMILY

Michigan's 1992 season produced one of the best and most frustrating years in program history. Grbac's performance was no exception. Already arguably the most accomplished passer in Michigan history, Grbac entered the year with Heisman Trophy expectations. And parts of his season-opening performance against No. 3 Notre Dame lived up to it—as he threw for 242 yards and two touchdowns. He also threw three interceptions, including a rushed pick on the final play of the game that preserved a 17–17 tie.

The pressure on Grbac that season was unlike anything a Michigan quarterback had ever seen. The same could be said for the team in general. The 1991 season—Howard's success and the national title contention—had vaulted Michigan into the national championship discussion in ways not really seen during the Schembechler era. The old coach never won a national championship at Michigan. He also never talked about winning one, purposely putting all the program's focus on the Big Ten and the Rose Bowl. College football, and the expansion of cable television, exploded in the 1990s. The game became a more nationally consumed product, which led to more interest in the national title picture.

All that pressure came to a head on November 14, 1992, when Michigan fumbled a staggering 10 times—losing four of them—during a cold and windy Ann Arbor day against unranked Illinois. The day was a microcosm of where the program was at the time—10 fumbles, two interceptions, and a ridiculous 523 yards of total offense to keep Michigan in the game. Trailing by three on the final possession, Grbac hit his first six passes to push Michigan to the Illinois 17 with 1:07 left. A touchdown kept Michigan's national title hopes alive. A tie kept only a shot at the Rose Bowl. Grbac's hand was hot, but Michigan opted for conservatism. Moeller called a run on first down—against a blitz Grbac didn't see pre-snap—and lost six yards. After an incomplete pass on second down, Moeller—now clearly playing for the tie—ran the ball on third down before winding the clock all the way down to 19 seconds before kicker Peter Elezovic hit a 39-yarder to tie the game at 22–22. The home crowd booed Moeller's decision *during* Elezovic's successful kick. Michigan, as Moeller had hoped, ended Grbac's final season in the Rose Bowl—finishing an awkward 9–0–3 after another tie with Ohio State in the regular season finale.

Grbac's final game at Michigan featured a bit of everything, including a revenge comeback victory over Washington in the Rose Bowl. It also represented the potential of what might have been if a few breaks had gone an inch the other way. Tyrone Wheatley exploded for 235 rushing yards and Grbac was effortlessly good in a 175-yard, two-touchdown day as Michigan won 38–31. Grbac left Michigan as the most accomplished passer in school history, the first to throw for 6,000 yards. He helped push the offense to unseen heights and put Michigan in the national conversation, creating a new standard for the position in Ann Arbor.

For Michigan at the time, the recruiting pitch for quarterbacks was simple—come to Michigan and see if you can run an NFL offense better than the best of your peers. They took as many talented arms as they could find. No one's spot was held over seniority—they had to earn it. Every day. A year after taking Grbac, Michigan brought in his clone in the form of Todd Collins—another gigantic passer at 6'4", 225, with a big arm, a top-10 prospect at his position. Next came in-state schoolboy legend Jay Riemersma, a three-sport standout who was also nationally ranked. In 1992, Grbac's senior year, Michigan signed its highest-rated passer to date in the form of Eric Boykin—the No. 5–ranked QB in the class from Dayton Meadowdale who

PART 3: THE FAMILY

turned down Ohio State to play in Moeller's offense. They one-upped themselves in 1993, taking No. 4–ranked Scot Loeffler—from Bo Schembechler's hometown of Barberton, Ohio. There was also, of course, Brian Griese.

Griese entered the program telling himself he would have fun and focus on his schoolwork in order to set himself up for a business career. He would not get lost in the fishbowl of competition inside that quarterback room.

The things we tell ourselves.

Griese, just like his dad, *loved* football. More specifically, he loved playing quarterback. Also, like his father, he couldn't really run. He was a pocket passer all the way and while he was agile enough to move his way out of trouble, Griese's biggest on-field asset was his brain.

Even in the early 1990s, *many* college offenses were still entrenched in the option. Playing at Miami's Christopher Columbus High School, Griese had the green light to call audibles at the line of scrimmage, something he did (correctly) often. This happens now and then today, but it almost never happened back then. The summer before his senior year, Griese went to Bill Walsh's quarterback camp at Stanford and left with the MVP award.

Still, his situation was complex. Griese was still processing the loss of his mother, who lost her battle with breast cancer when he was 12. He wanted to go to school somewhere away from home in south Florida and had the offers to do just that. Purdue, his father's alma mater. Indiana, Purdue's hated rival. Bill Walsh and Stanford. Griese was the 15th-ranked pocket passer on recruiting guru Tom Lemming's list for 1993. But as he navigated the scene, Bob's words rang more clearly. He picked Michigan largely because of its academic reputation. However, not long after arriving on campus, he realized the other reason for his choice.

153

He also loved to compete.

Loeffler and Griese eventually became lifelong friends, but as freshmen quarterbacks in the same class—they didn't like each other. No one really did. The room was very tense. After spending the first half of his career backing up Grbac, Collins entered 1993 confident and ready. He looked like Grbac, he moved like Grbac, and even threw like him. He had some of the same issues, too. Specifically, he was a huge player who wasn't very mobile. Moeller's offense was all about timing at every level; there wasn't room for improvisation. If anyone made a mistake, the whole thing fell apart. The pressure to keep that up was immense and nobody felt it more than the quarterback. Collins also had a high release, meaning throws could sail on him—occasionally leading to interceptions. Additionally, if someone took Michigan's run game away, it was difficult for Collins, who relied heavily on play action throws, to maintain efficiency.

Collins' two years as Michigan's starter, the final two of Moeller's tenure, was a war of two extremes. When it was right, it was elite. He threw for 274 yards in the 1993 season opener and led the Wolverines to a 28–0 win over Ohio State in the regular season finale. He also threw three interceptions against Notre Dame, struggled to move the ball at Michigan State, and had turnover issues in all four of Michigan's losses in a disappointing 8–4 campaign. The 1994 season was similar. Collins was great against Colorado and had Michigan on the fringe of 3–0 and two top-10 wins. But Kordell Stewart's Hail Mary was a bit better. Collins had his struggles as a starter, but he was also snakebitten by tough luck and growing frustration within the program over close losses under Moeller.

By the fall of 1995, a once-promising QB succession plan now looked markedly different. Moeller had been fired. Cameron

PART 3: THE FAMILY

was coaching in the NFL. Riemersma moved to tight end. Boykin transferred to West Virginia and Loeffler, the most touted of them all, had suffered a career-ending shoulder injury. When Lloyd Carr took over as an interim in 1995, his top options were Griese—who had yet to start a game—and sophomore Scott Dreisbach, an athletic, 6'4" passer from Indiana who was supposed to be Moeller's next Grbac.

Dreisbach had also been overlooked because he played in a run-heavy prep offense. Moeller had been fired *after* spring ball, which gave Carr little time to sort out his quarterback plan. He'd remembered how highly Moeller thought of Dreisbach's potential, and his arm talent was undeniable. The decision to start Dreisbach frustrated Griese, but it proved correct in the opener when Dreisbach hit Mercury Hayes in the corner of the end zone at the buzzer for a thrilling one-point win over Virginia. Dreisbach's future at Michigan—and his entire football career—changed over the next month, though, when he suffered a serious thumb injury in practice ahead of a week five game vs. Miami-Ohio.

Now, suddenly and almost out of nowhere, Griese—onetime fifth-stringer and still a walk-on—was Michigan's starter. His debut against the Redhawks was smooth. His second start, against Northwestern, was a nightmare. Against an upstart Wildcats defense, led by future head coach Pat Fitzgerald, Griese had three completions and two picks after halftime, finishing 14 of 34 for 96 yards in a shocking 19–13 home loss. It was Michigan's first loss to Northwestern since 1965 and the first in Ann Arbor since 1959. Griese played the rest of the season, but nerves from that loss never left as Michigan finished the year 9–4.

Stuck between trying to do what he felt Moeller would've done and trying to find his own voice, Carr went back to

THE PROGRAM: MICHIGAN

Dreisbach in 1996 but *very* similar results followed. The offense stalled against Northwestern, again, and lost to the Wildcats for a second straight year. Michigan beat Michigan State, but fell apart a week later during a 9–3 loss at Purdue. Michigan entered its date with No. 2 Ohio State at 7–3 with zero momentum. Dreisbach's thumb never fully recovered and his ability to handle a snap specifically suffered greatly. At halftime in Columbus, trailing 9–0, Carr benched Dreisbach and went back to Griese. The fourth-year walk-on shook off the whiplash and proceeded to deliver a program-changing play when he hit Tai Streets on a slant against Shawn Springs for a 68-yard score that silenced Ohio Stadium and sparked a dramatic 13–9 Michigan comeback victory.

For Griese, the victory was the close of a two-year whirlwind that left him exhausted and nearly done with football. In the spring of 1996, Griese had been through a humiliating public ordeal when he was arrested outside an Ann Arbor bar. Still grieving the loss of his mother and frustrated over not playing, Griese felt like the win over Ohio State that year—the second of his career—was a feather in his cap and a reminder of his father's original words: Football was not going to be his life. Griese's immediate plans post-1996 were to leave Michigan and begin a postgraduate scholarship program at George Washington before beginning his life outside the game. He was done with college football and Michigan.

For at *least* a few days.

Back home in Florida during the first week of January, Griese had dinner with his brother, Jeff—who could tell what was going on. His message to Brian was easy: He had the rest of his life to be a businessman. He only had *one* more year of football with his friends. Even if it meant sitting the bench and cheering on Scott Dreisbach or Tom Brady. A few days later, he showed up in Lloyd Carr's office to tell him he was all-in no matter what.

So sure he was leaving campus, Griese finished the 1996 season and didn't bother to secure a lease for the following year. When he showed back up in Carr's office in the winter of '97 to tell him he'd be all-in, no matter what, he did so while living in the closet of friend and basketball player Travis Conlan's apartment.

Suddenly unburdened with the pressures of living up to his family name or surviving the intense fishbowl that was Michigan's quarterback room, Griese rededicated himself to the game in ways he'd never done before. Carr told him to drop weight, so he did. Immediately. Decades later, Carr recalled how every time he'd stand up from his desk that spring he would see Griese outside his window doing wind sprints.

The bond between Carr and Griese is unlike any other quarterback–head coach duo in the history of Michigan football. Carr absolutely entered 1997 with his job on the line. He was 17–8 and the few who did believe in him were running out of ways to calm the irate. Griese, and many of the older players on the team, knew exactly that—and felt responsible for it.

Carr had always been a player's coach. He'd also been an old high school teacher. He was stern but loyal and caring. Like his predecessors Moeller and Schembechler, Carr gave himself to the team and game completely—but more than that, he worked to develop each player's mind beyond the field. He put some of his favorite literature excerpts in playbooks. Inspirational quotes and speeches became part of the program. He gave out popsicles after hot practices in August. He knew players' extended families, their friends, their girlfriends, their hopes, their fears.

Griese knew how much Carr cared. Others did, too. In 1995, team captain Jarrett Irons told then athletic director Joe Roberson on a team plane that if Carr wasn't given the full-time job in 1996, then the team needed to find a new captain. Many of the issues that had led to Carr's eight losses over the previous two years were small errors derived from the head coach—and, as a result, the team—trying to be someone else. Specifically a combination of Moeller and Schembechler. By September 1997, Carr and Griese were done being anyone but themselves. For better or worse.

And the results were historic.

In the decade since Carr had taken over Michigan's defense, the Wolverines had finished at least second in the Big Ten in points-against seven times. The 1997 season would be Carr's masterpiece, with Charles Woodson leading a historic unit. It was Griese's poise, though, that proved the difference between another pretty good year and a truly elite one.

Many of Griese's predecessors at Michigan had solved their problems with aggression. Leach ran people over. Harbaugh refused to throw an incomplete pass. Grbac could throw the ball through a wall. Griese chose a calmer approach. His total command of what Michigan was trying to do on every snap gave Carr an extra coach on the field and hardened the quarterback's confidence. He took safe throws when they were open, he was outstanding off play action, and his mastery of when to check to a run was critical.

With a national TV audience watching, and Bob Griese nervously calling the game in the press box, Brian Griese showed the world the new version of himself—the one that slept in Travis Conlan's closet and watched film until 2:00 AM—on September

13, 1997. By completely outclassing prized Colorado quarterback John Hessler in a sparkling 21-of-28, 258-yard, two-touchdown performance as Michigan thrashed No. 8 Colorado 27–3.

Griese made mistakes in 1997, to be sure. But he *always* did something to erase them. He had a tipped ball intercepted early against Colorado. He also led a critical scoring drive in the final 30 seconds of the first half. Nearly everything was even when Michigan played Notre Dame two weeks later—save for one thing: Notre Dame QB Ron Powlus turned the ball over. Griese did not. Against Iowa in October, Griese had his worst first half of the season, resulting in a 21–7 Michigan deficit. He calmly walked into the locker room, took blame for his mistakes, and told the team there wouldn't be another. Griese threw three interceptions that day. He also scored four touchdowns. And kept his promise, as Michigan stayed unbeaten. Five weeks later, he walked out of Michigan Stadium with a third straight win over Ohio State and a Rose Bowl bid.

Griese's 1997 season at Michigan was arguably the toughest and most mentally disciplined stretch of football by a quarterback in Michigan history. The stats only tell some of the story: 193 of 307 for 2,293 yards, 17 touchdowns, and six interceptions. He also led the team to a 12–0 record with wins over seven ranked opponents, *four* inside the top 10. He saved his best for last, going 18 of 30 for 251 yards and three touchdowns in a Rose Bowl win over Ryan Leaf and Washington State, giving Michigan its first national championship in 50 years.

Griese left Michigan with several records. Some, like the 193 completions he had that year, have been broken. One that never will be, though?

Brian Griese was the last quarterback in the history of football to beat Thomas Edward Patrick Brady Jr.—Tommy to some,

THE PROGRAM: MICHIGAN

Tom to others, Mr. Brady to the Pro Football Hall of Fame—in a true quarterback competition.

Tom Brady's time at Michigan has been well-documented for the struggles he overcame to win the starting job and how it shaped him into the most successful pro quarterback of all time. And while Brady's college successes were small by comparison, his time in Michigan's cauldron of a quarterback room proved as critical as anything else he'd ever experience in football.

Not unlike Griese, Brady entered the program beneath the bottom of the depth chart. Originally planning to attend Cal out of Junipero Serra High School in San Mateo, California, Brady got a late offer from Michigan when the No. 1 passer on U-M's board for 1995, Bobby Sabelhaus (Tom Lemming's No. 1–ranked QB for '95), committed to Florida late in the process. When he got to Michigan in 1995, there were *eight* quarterbacks on the roster. He was no higher than sixth when the year began.

Still, his first year was memorable. Nearly 30 years later, Carr could still recall the first padded practice Brady went through as scout team quarterback against Michigan's starting defense, a group that featured future NFL players at every level. Teams allowed hits on the QB back then. Carr watched Brady get drilled on every drop-back. He couldn't remember if he completed a single throw.

"But he got up every time," Carr recalled.

The competition, however, confounded Brady. He spent endless amounts of time trying to find an edge, routinely asking anyone he could find—even team managers—to dissect tapes of his throwing motion in search of improvement. He saw how deep the line was and it was all he thought about. How he stacked up, where he fit in, when his time might—or might not—come. The entire idea behind the QB system Moeller and Cameron built was to surround talent with more talent, pushing the absolute best to the top every time. It took Griese four years to get his shot.

After Michigan's Outback Bowl loss vs. Alabama to close out 1996, Brady went to Carr and told him he was transferring. Carr responded with a few thoughts. He wanted him to stay, and he wanted him to quit worrying about what others were doing. Carr's final advice to Brady was he believed the QB should stay and compete, to see what he was made of—just as he'd discussed when he signed.

But, if Brady wasn't built for that, Carr added, then he'd gladly sign transfer papers.

The next day, Brady returned to the same office chair, looked his coach in the eyes, and told him he was staying. To prove to Carr, and everyone else, that he was, indeed, built for this. A new player emerged. Brady went from afterthought to actually jumping Dreisbach for the job of Griese's backup in 1997. In fact, there were days in camp when Brady—per observers and even some of Carr's personal notes—was better. Carr's decision that year was harder than people realized, though the choice to go with the experienced Griese was impossible to debate. As were the results.

Michigan brought back nine starters on defense, most of its offensive line, and its top two pass catchers from the national title team in 1998. Pollsters, however, were not impressed. *Sports Illustrated* ranked Michigan No. 8 to start the year—as Brady had never started a game and Woodson was absent. In its blurb about Brady, *Sports Illustrated* also mentioned Michigan's newest quarterback: prized freshman Drew Henson.

Henson was the top-rated high school quarterback in American throughout 1997, sitting in the front row at every home game. From nearby Brighton, Michigan, Henson had one of the greatest prep careers in the history of the state—throwing for more than 5,600 yards and 50 touchdowns while setting the national high school baseball record for home runs (70), RBIs (290), and grand slams (10). He was drafted by the New York Yankees out of high school and given a $2 million signing bonus. Florida State's sales pitch was to show him videos of Deion Sanders playing football and baseball. Henson could have attended any school in America, but grew up a Michigan fan and wanted a chance to be the starter for the Wolverines. Carr called him the "most talented quarterback I've ever been around" heading into 1998. Contrary to rumor, Carr never promised Henson anything by way of playing time in order to get his commitment. Per both Henson and Carr, the coach merely promised him a chance to compete for the job.

Brady indeed won the job out of camp and was named Michigan's starter ahead of a highly anticipated season opener at Notre Dame on September 5, 1998. However, the Henson situation lingered. Fans were obsessed with the freshman, one of the first true recruiting stars of the early Internet era, completely overlooking Brady. On the day of the opener, the *Detroit Free Press* ran a simple question on its sports front: *Can Tom Brady make U-M fans forget about Drew Henson?*

Also still on the roster was Scott Dreisbach, whose perseverance through injury and demotion had inspired the program. In fact it was Dreisbach, not Henson, who got time with Brady early in the opener against Notre Dame—getting in sporadically as a running quarterback. Still, Brady played well—hitting 10 of his first 13 passes and throwing for nearly 200 yards before halftime. Michigan's problem that day came on Notre Dame's first offensive snap, when Autry Denson cut through a massive hole and sloppy tackling for 58 yards on the first play of the game. Notre Dame, led by speedy new QB Jarious Jackson, rushed for 280 yards while conservative Michigan play-calling failed to take advantage of a 23-of-36, 267-yard day from Brady in a stunning 36–20 loss.

In Brady's first start at Michigan, the Wolverines' defense—after setting records in 1997—had its worst showing since losing 51–31 to top-ranked Florida State in 1991.

"Whether it's Tom Brady, Greg Brady, Peter Brady, or Bobby Brady," ESPN's Chris Fowler said on the pregame show the following week, "the [Michigan] quarterback is going to take some heat after a loss."

It got worse.

Michigan welcomed Syracuse and Donovan McNabb a week later. McNabb, a 6'2", 220-pound dual-threat passer who had played basketball with future NBA star Antoine Walker at Mount Carmel High School in Chicago, breezed Syracuse down the field for a touchdown on the opening possession—silencing an already nervous crowd. On Michigan's opening drive, facing a second-and-17, Brady misfired on a throw down the middle and was intercepted. Three plays later, McNabb hit star fullback Rob Konrad for a 26-yard touchdown to make it 14–0, Orange.

After the Michigan crowd booed conservative play calling on the following three-and-out, Syracuse pushed its lead to 17–0. And when the punt team came onto the field following another empty Michigan possession, ABC cameras pivoted to Henson on the sideline.

"And this young man, Drew Henson, from nearby Brighton, Michigan," play-by-play announcer Brent Musburger remarked, "had better get that right arm ready."

Sure enough, after a Syracuse fumble with 13:37 to go in the second quarter, Carr lifted Brady and inserted Henson. The crowd roared. The freshman responded with one short completion before throwing a ball out of the end zone on third-and-four from the Michigan 16. Brady awkwardly re-entered the game to hold for a Jay Feely field goal attempt, only to roll out on the snap for a fake. Brady tossed the ball across his body toward his kicker, but Syracuse had it read and stopped the play short.

McNabb then led a masterful 14-play touchdown drive, making it 24–0 as a now-shocked crowd of more than 100,000 sat in raged silence.

"For Michigan," Musberger deadpanned, "this is a nightmare."

Brady eventually returned to lead Michigan to its only scoring drive of the half before starting the third quarter, but once the score reached 38–7 Syracuse, Carr gave the rest of the game to Henson. He refused to call the situation a QB controversy afterward, offering something else instead.

"I want to develop a quarterback in case something happens with Tom," Carr said after a 38–28 loss that featured poor play from both passers. "The competition is ongoing."

Henson again entered the following week's game and rotated with Brady in Michigan's week three win over Eastern Michigan. At 1–2 entering Michigan State week, with his team's confidence hanging by a thread, Carr refused to answer whether or not Henson would play vs. the Spartans.

He would not. Brady played the whole game, going 15 of 26 for 208 yards, a touchdown, and one pick, in a hard-fought 29–17 rivalry win. With the Big Ten season underway, the QB rotation stopped—Brady led Michigan unopposed the rest of the season, rattling off eight straight wins to share the Big Ten title with Ohio State and Wisconsin. Brady had thrown for 2,427 yards, 14 touchdowns, and 10 interceptions in his first year as a starter. Henson completed 42.2 percent of his 45 attempts for 233 yards and three touchdowns.

Despite a 10–3 record and a co–Big Ten title in '98, Brady again found himself in rotation with Henson—who was constantly facing pressure to give up football for a lucrative baseball career. However this time, Brady left no doubt—going 17 of 24 for 197 yards to lead Michigan to a 26–22 win against Notre Dame. Henson played in the second quarter, but only went 3 of 8 for 40 yards. Despite the performance, Carr said the rotation would continue.

"We've got a great quarterback position," Brady told the *Detroit News* afterward. "I wish people would leave it at that."

Michigan was 5–0 and ranked No. 3 when it traveled to No. 11 Michigan State on October 9. Brady started, but with Michigan trailing 13–10 at the half, Henson opened the third quarter. The result was a mess. The first two possessions were three-and-outs and the third ended with an interception. By the time Brady went back in the game, it was 27–10 Spartans.

The fourth quarter of that game might be the first true comeback of Tom Brady's football career, though it still wound up in defeat. Brady led Michigan on three fourth-quarter scoring drives, two ending in touchdown passes, pushing MSU to the brink before falling 34–31. The following week, Henson again got brief time in the second quarter but was vastly outplayed by Brady. But Michigan still lost, as the defense fell apart in a stunning 35–29 loss to Illinois.

Carr had hoped the QB rotation would be the best thing for the team at large, but after two straight losses—and with Brady playing well—it was obvious the opposite was true. The rotation stopped in week eight and Michigan did not lose a game the rest of the season—including a thrilling 35–34 overtime win over Alabama in the Orange Bowl. The season ended with 10 wins, but nearly all involved knew it could've (and probably should've) been more. The following fall, with Brady in the NFL, Henson missed the first three games of the year after breaking his foot during practice. He went 7–2 as a starter with a thrilling 38–26 win at Ohio State on November 18. Four months later, the Yankees offered him a six-year, $17 million deal with a condition he quit football. He signed, ending his Michigan career after just 351 pass attempts.

From 1990 to 2000, every one of Michigan's starting quarterbacks played in the NFL—including Henson, whose rights were drafted by the Texans in 2003, *and* Dreisbach, who was talented enough to get shots with three pro teams. Combined, those six quarterbacks played in 591 NFL games, with nine Super Bowls, 16 Pro Bowls, and more than 130,000 passing yards (about 75 miles). Elvis Grbac, Todd Collins, Brian Griese, Drew Henson, and Tom Brady combined to play in 57 NFL seasons.

Quite simply, it's one of the greatest 10-year stretches of quarterback talent by a single program in the history of college football.

Carr's next two quarterbacks took up the rest of his coaching career, as John Navarre started 37 games from 2001 to '03 before Chad Henne served as the program's first four-year starter since Rick Leach, from '04 to '07. Both Navarre and Henne, who played more than any of the quarterbacks in the 1990s, broke the 9,000-yard mark—with Henne still serving as the program's all-time leader in yardage with 9,715.

Denard Robinson, one of the most exciting players the program's ever had—from his untied shoelaces to his ever-present bright smile—served as the lone bright spot during Rich Rodriguez's three-year struggle. Robinson, a truly unique player from south Florida, was recruited by Rodriguez to run Michigan's brand-new spread-option offense. Something he did spectacularly in 2010, to the tune of a program-record 4,272 combined yards. The team, though, was decidedly not spectacular—finishing 7–6 with the worst defense in school history.

PART 3: THE FAMILY

Robinson and Devin Gardner, who was also recruited to run Rodriguez's spread option, were both forced to learn brand-new systems upon Michigan's hiring of Brady Hoke in 2011. The duo combined for more than 17,000 yards of total offense at Michigan, but zero Big Ten titles and just one win over hated Ohio State. As great as the QB position was for Michigan in the '80s and '90s, the drought the program went through after that seemed equally deep.

The person who eventually helped change it, of course, was the one who started it—Jim Harbaugh. Harbaugh not only recruited Cade McNamara, a tough-as-nails and undersized quarterback from Nevada who helped Michigan snap its Big Ten title and Ohio State drought in 2021, but he also signed J.J. McCarthy—one of the most physically gifted passers in program history.

McCarthy's three-year run at Michigan produced 6,873 total yards, but more importantly, it produced three Big Ten championships, a 40–3 record, and a 15–0 national championship season in 2023.

On April 25, 2024, roughly 37 years since his head coach became the first Michigan quarterback to be taken in the first round of the NFL draft, J.J. McCarthy became the second—going No. 10 overall to the Minnesota Vikings.

10

The Runners

JAMIE MORRIS HAD NOT BEEN OFF THE AIRPLANE FOR 48 hours and he demanded to see the boss.

Growing up in Massachusetts in the 1970s, Morris was hooked by how different the Wolverines' helmets looked on television and reeled in by how they rarely lost.

The youngest of Earl Morris' four boys, all of 'em football players, Jamie's oldest brother, Joe Morris, went to Syracuse in 1978 and nearly left with the stadium keys. The 5'7" lightning bolt joined football royalty when he passed Jim Brown, Ernie Davis, Floyd Little, and Larry Csonka to set the school's career rushing record (4,299 yards). By the time Jamie reached high school, Joe was with the New York Giants while his other older brothers, Larry and Mike, were at Syracuse. Larry had actually broken Joe's rushing record at Ayer High School (5,758 yards) before joining the Orange and Mike broke every track record Joe ever set.

PART 3: THE FAMILY

Jamie was exactly like his brothers. He began breaking some of Joe's high school track marks as a freshman. The summer before his senior year, he was clocked at 4.35 seconds in the 40-yard dash. He'd later receive an invitation to the Olympic Trials. The literal only difference between the foursome? Jamie wanted to play for Michigan. Specifically, he wanted to *play running back* for Michigan. Which is why he was storming into Bo Schembechler's office—something not even the most tenured assistant coach did—on his second day in Ann Arbor as an 18-year-old freshman in 1984. On the official roster next to Morris' name read "WR/KR."

"What's this!?" Morris, all 5'7", 154 pounds of him, barked at his head coach.

The next four years featured hundreds of seminal moments that accumulated into greatness. None bigger than this. Morris was hardly the only player Schembechler moved without asking. He might've been the most memorable, though. Because rather than throw him out of the meeting he'd interrupted, an amused Schembechler looked at his new diminutive speedster and saw why he signed him.

"You'll get your chance," the coach retorted before sizing up Morris one more time.

"And when you get your ass smacked and you don't know where you are," he continued, "you'll move to wide receiver."

When he left home that summer, his father supplied him with his own military-grade green duffle bag with the name "Morris" stitched to the front. He even taught him how to pack it properly, just like they do in the military. Earl Morris spent 28 years in the Army. A Green Beret who served in Vietnam before becoming a postmaster in Groton, Massachusetts. He and his wife, Addie, had six kids—four boys and two girls. All four of the boys wound up roughly the same height as their father: around 5'7".

THE PROGRAM: MICHIGAN

What the Morrises lacked in size, they more than made up for in speed and discipline. The boys grew up in a "yes, sir; no, ma'am" household where responsible behavior was the expected minimum. Following his brothers to Syracuse appealed to Morris. Boston College was recruiting him. Ohio State had reached out, as had Wisconsin and nearby Holy Cross. When Morris took his official visit to Syracuse, he made sure it coincided with the Orange's December '83 home game against Michael Jordan and North Carolina. Afterward, Morris and his brothers spoke with Jordan—who told Jamie that the Tar Heels' football staff was well aware of him, too.

Flattery was great. But for Jamie Morris, the idea of being his own man—and chasing a dream—was just better.

Morris' confrontation with Schembechler about his position happened shortly after he got to campus in June of 1984. But the quest of having to prove himself had just begun. That summer, Morris stepped on a scale in the weight room in front of teammates on official weigh-in day and found he'd actually lost weight. Still just 5'7", the would-be next star running back for the mighty Michigan Wolverines weighed just 152 pounds. The other players, knowing the youngster's goal to be a RB, cackled. Morris, who had arrived at Michigan in track shape, was devastated. Already questioning whether he'd made the right decision, Morris stormed out of the room unsure where he was headed next before an arm reached out.

Mike Gittleson, Michigan's longtime strength coach, knew exactly who Morris was. He told him bluntly that the program had not seen a faster player since Anthony Carter. After Gittleson pushed Morris' chin up, equipment manager Jon Falk quietly went out and found smaller shoulder pads to fit Morris' frame until he was ready to fill out the bigger ones.

"Without those two guys," Morris recalls emotionally, "I wouldn't have made it."

When Michigan went through its first full-team scrimmage of 1984, rather than splitting the groups into a first or second team, Schembechler decided to pick his own 11 for both on the spot. And when he called Morris' name for the running back spot, he walked over to the freshman and whispered into his ear.

"This is your opportunity."

Morris took his first carry off tackle and exploded into open grass for an 80-yard run. Somewhere, Gittleson and Falk were smiling. Before Morris crossed the goal line, an incredulous Schembechler blew his whistle and started screaming for everyone to get back to the line of scrimmage. Furious at how his defense had just looked, Schembechler walked over to Morris before addressing the rest of the group.

"This *running back* ...," he shouted, "is only 18 years old, and he just tore right through our starting defense... "

Morris heard nothing after "running back." Schembechler told Morris to get back in the huddle and run it again. He did. Same result. On the third try, Morris cut the ball back upfield for another big gash—only to be leveled by star defensive back Garland Rivers. On the ground, writhing in pain from one of the nastiest hits he'd ever taken, all Morris could hear was the voice of beloved RB coach Tirrel Burton in the distance *screaming* for him to get up.

Morris was quickest player in the program, and he ran even lower to the ground than his 5'7" frame—nobody could see him. Still, he was barely 150 pounds and everyone on the field knew it. Burton's first rule for Morris was to make sure he never stayed on the ground. No matter how bad a hit was, don't let them see you wince. The quarterback position is the most important spot on any football field. However, and especially

171

in the old days at Michigan, the running back serves as the team's soul.

The interpersonal dynamic of the position isn't much different from quarterback. There's only one ball and it's a team's job to find as many talented bodies as possible. Their success and failure depends heavily on the five men in front of them and it is their *duty* to support the offensive line, no matter what the blocking looks like. Running backs gain and lose confidence constantly, but their job is to never let you know it.

Their job, frankly, is to produce.

Billy Taylor—or, more specifically, "Touchdown Billy Taylor"—was the first star runner of the Schembechler era, entering the program just as Ron Johnson ran wild in 1968. Taylor was one of seven Black freshmen on Bump Elliott's final squad—a program high at the time. The following year he ran to national stardom when he led Michigan in rushing during the 1969 upset of Ohio State. He ran for nearly 1,800 yards between 1969 and '70 and exploded for a 1,297-yard season as a senior in '71 to set the program's all-time rushing mark at 3,072 yards.

His final touchdown in Michigan Stadium, a beautiful 21-yard game-winner against Ohio State, would feature an iconic call from legendary announcer Bob Ufer, immortalizing Taylor's name in the ears and minds of Michigan fans for generations.

"Taylor's to the 20, down to the 15, down to the 10, 5, 4, 3, 2, 1," Ufer exclaimed, "Touchdown, Billy Taylor! Touchdown, Billy Taylor! Billy Taylor scored a touchdown from 21 yards out!"

Touchdown Billy Taylor's storybook ride at Michigan turned tragic when he lost his mother to a heart attack shortly after the 1972 Rose Bowl. Heartbroken, Taylor's pro football career fizzled and his life spiraled. He became an addict, even homeless for a stint. As hard a fall as one could have. But Michigan running backs don't stay on the ground. Taylor went from homelessness in his forties to earning a doctorate from UNLV in educational leadership in his fifties.

The consistency of Michigan's offensive lines throughout the 1970s made the average viewer believe any runner could find space in the Wolverines' offense. Not true, however. It took a special breed.

Gordon Bell grew the youngest of five children up in the heart of Ohio, along the Miami River in Troy. His father lived and breathed Ohio State football. So Gordon went to Michigan. And four years later, his dad's house was colored in maize and blue. Despite sharing the backfield, the 5'9", 175-pound Bell became just the third runner in school history (Ron Johnson, Taylor) to crack 1,000 yards in '74. He one-upped himself as a senior in 1975, rushing for more than 1,300 yards and outrushing Archie Griffin in the season finale against Ohio State. The man Bell shared the backfield with? Another Ohioan.

Rob Lytle grew up about two hours north of Bell in Fremont. Lytle was a national recruit and, per his son, Kelly, when he picked Michigan ahead of the 1973 season, Woody Hayes showed up at his house demanding to know why. At 6'1" and nearly 200 pounds, Lytle began his career splitting time with the smaller and quicker Bell. Together, Bell and Lytle combined to form the best rushing duo in college football from 1974 to '75—combining to rush for more than 4,200 yards. In 1976, after Bell's departure, Lytle ran for the Michigan record books with a historic season that featured 1,474 yards (a program record) on 221 carries and 14 touchdowns.

An incredible blend of speed, power, and durability, Lytle was a truly complete back who could line up anywhere and get the job done. Impossibly difficult to tackle, Lytle ran low to the ground and gained speed and he rolled through defenders like a freight train rolling down a track.

"He ran like an arrow through snow," Jim Harbaugh once said.

His senior year against Ohio State, with the game tied 0–0 at the half, Lytle ran the ball 10 times in the third quarter—six on the opening possession—to spark a 22-point Michigan second half and a dominant shutout win. Lytle, who died from a heart attack in 2010, left Michigan with a reputation as the toughest runner the program had ever seen.

The thing about college records, though—especially ones at Michigan—is they rarely last. Lytle's record made it less than five years. Bell and Lytle were a terrific blend of power and speed, but the guy who came next—Butch Woolfolk—was both. As a high school senior in 1978, Woolfolk notched a ridiculous 10.1-second 100-meter sprint and a 20.4-second 200-meter run at a meet in Illinois. He stood around 6'1", 210 pounds, and rushed for nearly 1,700 yards as a high school senior before picking Michigan.

As a sophomore in 1979, Woolfolk took a pitch on a third-and-seven from his own eight-yard line, made one cut back toward the middle of the field, and ran through two tacklers before simply running away from the entire defense for a school-record 92-yard run. As a senior in 1981, he did it to the Badgers again. This time in the season opener, taking a handoff around left tackle and down the sideline for an explosive 89-yard touchdown run.

The beat went on. Three years later, Woolfolk left Michigan as the all-time leading rusher with 3,861 yards and a Rose Bowl MVP award in his back pocket.

Jamie Morris' career, of course, topped them all. Not only because he'd run for more yards, but he'd done so out of nowhere. Apart from Bell, the other stars on the Michigan running back list were gigantic. Morris' body was small—but his passion was enormous. He dedicated himself to Gittleson's weight room and added more than 30 pounds to his frame, becoming chiseled speed with vision and relentless energy.

As a sophomore in 1985, playing in a crowded and talented backfield that featured the likes of Gerald White, Bob Perryman, and Thomas Wilcher, Morris distanced himself. Unranked in a season opener for the first time since 1969, Michigan got 119 yards on 23 carries from Morris as the Wolverines controlled the clock long enough to outlast No. 13 Notre Dame 20–12. Morris outrushed Notre Dame Heisman hopeful Allen Pickett by more than 30 yards.

"Guess we're not the dog people think we are," Schembechler said afterward.

Morris' work behind Jim Harbaugh was critical as Michigan's offense found enough ways to support one of its greatest defenses in 1985, culminating in a 10–1–1 season and a 1,054-yard year for Morris. His greatest game as a Wolverine came at the end of another 1,000-yard year in 1986, the week Jim Harbaugh guaranteed Michigan would beat Ohio State and play in the Rose Bowl. Harbaugh got all the attention entering that game, but it was Morris who couldn't be stopped. With Michigan trailing 14–6 at halftime, the Wolverines gave Morris the ball five times on the opening drive of the third quarter inside a raucous Ohio Stadium. His final came on an option pitch from the OSU four-yard line, where Morris darted right before juking Ohio State's Sonny Gordon for a touchdown that silenced the crowd. It was the first touchdown a Big Ten team had scored in the Horseshoe all year. Minutes later, Morris took an inside handoff eight yards up the middle, and through two defenders, for the go-ahead score. When the game ended, Morris had run for 210 yards and two touchdowns on 29 attempts—easily the difference-maker for the Wolverines.

From 1985 to '86, Morris gained more than 2,000 yards and helped the Wolverines to a 21–3–1 record with a Big Ten title and a Rose Bowl trip. The two-year run helped silence any remaining national doubt about Schembechler's ability to make it through the 1980s and helped launch the program into a new era offensively. And when Michigan needed to reload in 1987, it was Morris—serving as team captain—who kept the train on the tracks. A young football team scraped its way to an 8–4 mark in '87. The running back room that season featured a trio of talented sophomores who'd all go on to play in the NFL—Tony Boles, Jarrod Bunch, and Leroy Hoard. Each one of them was bigger than Morris. But each watched and learned that season as Morris went over the 100-yard mark a whopping eight times to establish a new rushing standard at Michigan that would last more than a decade. In 1987, Morris rushed for a program-record 1,703 yards and 14 touchdowns. In his final game as a Wolverine, Morris went out with a bang to the tune of 234 yards and three touchdowns as Michigan ran away from Alabama in the Hall of Fame Bowl—a victory Michigan made without Schembechler, who missed the game due to quadruple bypass surgery.

"We had Bo in our back pockets," said Morris, who heard from Schembechler after the game—who said he "looked like a bull out there."

When he left Michigan, no one in the history of the program had run harder or for more yards than 5'7" Jamie Morris: 4,393 yards. A record that made it the rest of the century.

Around that time, one of the country's most gifted athletes looked like Michigan's next record-breaker. Born in Detroit in 1972, Tyrone Wheatley lost his father when he was just two.

PART 3: THE FAMILY

As a kid, Wheatley looked out for his siblings and younger cousins as if they were his own. He was their superhero. The same was true on any athletic surface. At Dearborn Heights Robichaud, Wheatley blossomed into a legendary track, basketball, and football star. An elite leaper and sprinter, Wheatley won four state championships as a junior at the state track meet: the 100 meter (10.81), the 200 (21.9), the long jump (23 feet, 10 inches), and the 110 high hurdles (14.85). As a senior, he repeated in the long jump, the 100 meter, and the 110 hurdles.

He did all this at nearly 6'2" and a solid 205 pounds. In football, Wheatley could do anything. He played quarterback for a stint, could play receiver, and became a star running back—running for 2,010 yards and 33 touchdowns as a senior in 1991. Wheatley was hands-down the No. 1 prospect in the state of Michigan and one of the top-rated recruits nationally. Wheatley once told the *Free Press* he grew up a Michigan State fan, but wound up preferring Michigan for academic reasons—the same reasons that would keep him in school the full four years, even when he could've left early for the NFL.

Once Wheatley entered Mike Gittleson's weight room, another dimension opened. By his sophomore year, he was 6'2", 225 pounds, and *still* just as fast. Sharing time with four other backs, Wheatley rushed for better than six yards per attempt as a freshman before exploding as a sophomore, rushing for 1,122 yards on just 170 carries in only 10 games. Wheatley missed three games with injury as a junior, shared time with veterans Ed Davis and Ricky Powers, and still broke the 1,000-yard barrier, leading most outside observers to believe he'd turn pro ahead of 1994. Those inside the program, though, knew different.

And this is where the talent overload begins.

Surprising the football world, Wheatley remained at Michigan, joining promising second-year back Tshimanga Biakabutuka for 1994. One of 11 children, Biakabutuka was born in the former Zaire before his family settled near Montreal in Quebec, Canada, in the late 1970s. After first seeing an American football game at 15, Biakabutuka—who was called "Tim" by other kids—transitioned to Canadian vocational college after 11th grade. In the fall of 1992 during his first game as a running back, now 6'1", 200 pounds, he rushed for 239 yards and three touchdowns on just 17 carries. After that one, they called him "Touchdown Tim."

Around this time, Biakabutuka attended Michigan's summer prospect camp. He entered as a complete unknown and left as a player Michigan wanted.

Ahead of the '94 season, Michigan's backfield featured a Heisman candidate in Wheatley, Canada's best prospect in Biakabutuka, and *two* of the best freshmen in America—Chris Howard and Chris Floyd. Floyd was one of the top prospects in the country for 1994, a Detroit product who was all set for Colorado before Lloyd Carr persuaded his mother otherwise. Howard was arguably the top runner in Louisiana, starring for national powerhouse John Curtis Christian.

When training camp began in 1994, Wheatley was the consensus Heisman favorite nationally. That all changed during a Tuesday practice in late August, when Wheatley went down after a nasty hit to the same shoulder he'd hurt the year prior. Biakabutuka came off the bench in the season opener, but didn't need long to steal the show—rushing for 128 yards on just 12 attempts, including a dazzling 36-yard juke fest. A week later at No. 3 Notre Dame, Biakabutuka came off the bench again—this time on the first drive of the game. And Michigan found another star.

As runners, Wheatley and Biakabutuka had much in common—even if Wheatley was nearly 40 pounds heavier (226 to

190). Both were great long sprinters, and each ran with tremendous acceleration. The other thing was power. They never seemed to get tired. On his first carry against Notre Dame in '94, Biakabutuka took a counter 10 yards for a touchdown—running through two tacklers near the goal line to finish it off. On his third carry in the second quarter, he went off tackle again only to be leveled by *five* Irish tacklers just beyond the first-down marker. His offensive line ran over to help him up—but he didn't need it, springing to his feet as if he'd been bitten by a fly. Wheatley would finish the year with 1,064 yards to Biakabutuka's 713, as the duo combined for 21 touchdowns in just 10 combined appearances. That uber-talented '94 team, however, would not get over the Colorado Hail Mary loss. Resulting in an 8–4 year.

Michigan had another four-loss year in '95, but Biakabutuka provided the ultimate pain ointment on November 25, 1995, in front of more than 106,000 at Michigan Stadium. Hosting eventual Heisman winner Eddie George and No. 2 Ohio State (11–0), the junior put on the second-greatest rushing performance in modern Michigan history. Dealing with a calf injury, Biakabutuka had 45 rushing yards after Michigan's first drive. Two carries later, he cut an outside zone back inside and exploded through four tacklers before taking two more out of bounds. He was at 104 yards. On just five attempts, midway through the *first quarter.* By halftime, he'd run the ball 18 times for a ridiculous 195 yards.

The second half was all Touchdown Tim. Michigan's offense sputtered around him and opened the second half—clinging to a 10–9 lead—with six straight handoffs to Biakabutuka. He had gashes in this game, but many of his runs were four- and five-yard chunks—smashing his body through multiple linebackers and defensive backs, gaining speed as the game wore on. He carried the ball 13 times for 108 yards...in the third quarter. At one point in the second half, with Biakabutuka now approaching 300 yards and Michigan needing every one of them, freshmen Aaron Shea and Tai Streets watched the powerhouse jog off the field after a carry before stretching his exhausted body out on the team bench. Seconds later, strength coach Mike Gittleson walked by and—without breaking stride—simply told Biakabutuka to get up. He did. Right back into the game to rip off another run with the same effort he showed on his first. Shea could barely survive a workout at that stage of his career. He looked at Streets, both men who'd play in the NFL one day, with only a few words.

"We've got a long way to go."

In the end, Tshimanga Biakabutuka ran the ball 37 times for 313 yards as Michigan scored the 31–23 upset win. His day ranked No. 2 on the school's all-time list behind only Ron Johnson's 347 versus Wisconsin in 1968. He also broke Jamie Morris' single-season rushing record of 1,703 that day.

Biakabutuka and Wheatley would both leave the program as first-round NFL draft picks, setting a new standard for the position at the school. By 1997, Michigan had signed Anthony Thomas, a 220-pound Louisiana prep legend who ran for nearly 8,000 yards and a state-record 106 touchdowns. The appeal of rushing behind Michigan's powerful offensive lines annually put Michigan in discussion with the country's top running back prospects. Thomas was the No. 2–ranked running back nationally when he signed in '97. Justin Fargas, son of '70s TV star Antonio Fargas, was No. 1 when he signed the following year. When Chris Perry signed with Michigan out of Fork Union (Virginia) Military Academy in 2000, his prep coach told the *Free Press* he was the best back he'd ever had at that age—which included Eddie George.

PART 3: THE FAMILY

Between 1997 and 2003, Anthony Thomas and Chris Perry—two big, powerful backs with speed—combined to rush for 8,168 yards and 94 touchdowns. As a senior in 2000, Thomas rushed for 120 or more yards in eight games, racking up 228 at Illinois, 199 in a loss at Northwestern, and 182 in his final game—a Citrus Bowl win over Auburn. On one attempt in the first half, Thomas broke three Michigan records—becoming the all-time leading rusher (passing Morris with 4,472 yards), all-time leading touchdown man (56), and all-time leading scorer (336).

After splitting time his first two years, Perry opened the 2002 season with a 120-yard, three-touchdown day vs. Washington and never looked back—eclipsing 1,100 yards as a junior before challenging Thomas' single-season mark as a senior in 2003. In the first three games of the season, Perry 549 yards. But it would be his record-setting 51-carry, 219-yard day in the mud during a 27–20 win over rival Michigan State that stamped him as a program legend.

"Perry has the heart of a champion," Carr said of his running back, who'd finish 2003 fourth in the Heisman voting with 1,674 yards and 18 touchdowns (along with 44 receptions). "He's going to punish you."

The evolution in size at running back for Michigan merely ran alongside trendlines nationally. The note Carr made about Perry after giving him the ball 51 times against a hated rival, though, was the throughline dating back to Ron Johnson's big day and Jamie Morris' storybook career: Every running back who made a significant carry for Michigan in the '70s, '80s, '90s, and first half of the 2000s ran with more heart than their bodies could hold. It's not only poetic, therefore, that the man who'd break Morris' all-time rushing record would also share his lack of size—but also that his last name was, in fact, Hart.

THE PROGRAM: MICHIGAN

Leon Michael Hart grew up outside Syracuse in the late 1980s with toughness oozing from his pores. The son of a Black father and a white mother in a predominantly white area of New York, Hart—who once told *The Ann Arbor News* he'd been to nearly 10 elementary schools as a kid—grew up with racism in his family's face on a daily basis while his two young parents battled life's challenges. His folks split when he was a kid; his dad battled addiction; the family lost Mike's youngest sister, Kaitlyn, to a drowning tragedy when she was just two. Mike, just seven, entered adulthood—ready or not—shortly afterward.

He grew up helping his mom with everything, taking care of his siblings—and his mom, too, from time to time. By the time he reached tiny Onondaga Central High School just outside Syracuse, he spoke and acted like a man twice his age. And despite barely standing 5'9", he ran the football like one, too.

The odds of a short running back from a Class D school in a town of around 2,000 people making it anywhere in football are beyond small. Especially in the early 2000s, when the Internet's impact on recruiting was barely beginning. Players in Hart's situation had to get attention by literally turning heads. Which is all Hart ever did in high school. By the end of his *junior season* in 2002 Hart was just 25 yards shy of the state record with more than 7,500 for his career. He'd already rushed for 134 touchdowns, including 60 as a junior. As a senior, he'd only one-up himself—pushing his single-season touchdown record to an absurd 67 in 2003 as he set the national high school career touchdown record with 204 in four years. An incredibly balanced runner with terrific knee-bend—the same trait that made the famously short Barry Sanders impossible to tackle—Hart's cuts and ability to run with explosion so low to the ground made him nearly impossible for small-school teams to tackle. During a playoff game as a senior in 2003, Hart ripped off a

65-yard touchdown run where he broke 10 tackles—one from nearly every member of the opposing team.

"Our kids saw Mike Hart," an opposing coach once told the *Post-Star* after an Ondonaga game. "We got a good look at the numbers on the back of his jersey."

Not unlike Jamie Morris, Hart grew up falling in love with Michigan's winged helmets on TV. His recruitment, like so many during this era, was over before it started. His arrival in Ann Arbor came at a time of uncertainty, as the graduations of Perry and veteran QB John Navarre had left Michigan at another start-over spot in the backfield. Head coach Lloyd Carr's original plan was to transition veteran backup QB Matt Gutierrez into the starting role with a by-committee situation at running back, led by veterans David Underwood and Jerome Jackson.

The week before the 2004 season opener against Miami-Ohio, however, things changed. Specifically, Gutierrez's shoulder was killing him. Unable to practice the week of the game with what would eventually be revealed as a labrum injury, Gutierrez was removed from the lineup for true freshman super-recruit Chad Henne—a prep All-American from West Lawn, Pennsylvania, with a bright future—one that wasn't supposed to begin immediately.

Henne's debut, while very rocky early, was smoother than many feared—though hardly stellar as the freshman went 14 of 24 for 142 yards, two touchdowns (both to All-American senior WR Braylon Edwards), and an interception. The Wolverines routed Miami-Ohio 43–10 on the back of *seven* Redhawks turnovers (including five interceptions), but the bigger problem was at running back. Underwood and Jackson combined to make 29 carries for just 86 yards against a team from the Mid-American Conference. The following week at unranked Notre Dame, a theme repeated itself. Henne continued to improve, the defense did whatever it wanted—but Michigan, suddenly, couldn't run the ball.

Inside Notre Dame Stadium on September 11, 2004, Henne threw for 240 yards, Edwards had 12 catches for 129, and the Michigan defense picked off Notre Dame starter Brady Quinn three times. In literally any other era of Michigan football, this not only likely results in a win—but a dominant one. On that day, though, it was a 28–20 loss—as the Wolverine run game, hurt worse when Underwood suffered a concussion, produced 30 carries for just 56 yards in one of the worst big-game rushing days the program had seen in years.

"We can't run the football," Carr said bluntly afterward. "You can't win on field goals."

Now 1–1 with a true freshman at quarterback and no run game to speak of, Carr and Michigan were in crisis mode the following week when San Diego State's Matt Dlugolecki converted a Michigan fumble into a TD pass to put the Aztecs up 21–17—sending the home crowd into a panic. The offense, once again, was a mess—but with a slight wrinkle. Carr had started to let Hart, a true freshman, carry the ball. By the first drive of the second half, Hart—who found yards on plays where other backs weren't—was the feature back. Michigan scratched out a touchdown drive early in the third quarter and Hart carried the ball eight times on Michigan's final two possessions. The Wolverines won 24–21 but, more importantly, they'd found an answer next to their true freshman QB—a true freshman RB.

Hart surprised everyone with 25 attempts for 121 yards, earning more of position coach Fred Jackson's trust with each carry. He grinded out 99 on 26 the next week in a hard-fought Big Ten–opening win over Iowa. His breakout came two weeks later at home against Minnesota. Michigan was 4–1 by the skin of its teeth, and Carr was now fully on board the true freshman train. On a day when the defense finally met its match in the form of Minnesota's dynamic backfield duo of Laurence Maroney and Marion Barber, Michigan got 328 passing yards from its freshman quarterback (Henne also threw the game-winning touchdown pass in the final seconds), and Carr found out just how tough Leon Michael Hart really was when he gave the 18-year-old the ball 35 times for a freshman-record 160 rushing yards and a touchdown.

Henne's freshman season would go in the books as a historic one. He tied Michigan's single-season touchdown pass mark with 25 and wound up with more than 2,700 passing yards. He also threw 12 interceptions, took a lot of bad sacks, and was bailed out by Edwards' brilliance on more than one occasion. Hart's freshman year would also go in the history books. But without any of the rockiness. After his big day alongside Henne against Minnesota, Hart put Michigan on top of his 5'9" shoulders the following week against Illinois. With Henne struggling to find Edwards in the face of 35-mile-per-hour wind gusts, Michigan's offense more or less turned into what the Onondaga Tigers used to run. Hart right, left, and up the middle. The freshman ran the ball 40 times for 234 yards, both Michigan records for a first-year player.

The performance was classic Mike Hart. His longest rush was 32 yards. Most of his damage came in traffic, bouncing off bodies for six yards when a play was only blocked for three. On an eight-yard run into a horrific wind in the second half, Hart broke five tackles—including three in the backfield.

"He's a kid!" Michigan radio broadcaster Jim Brandstatter joked on his and Carr's *Michigan Replay* TV show the following morning. "What're ya doin!?"

"Well," Carr replied in his signature dry tone. "He likes the ball."

THE PROGRAM: MICHIGAN

The Illinois game was the start of an incredible stretch for Hart, still just 18 years old. Against Purdue the following week, Hart went for 206 yards on 33 carries in a comeback 16–14 win. During Michigan's thrilling three-overtime win over Michigan State the week after that (the Braylon Edwards game), Hart *again* topped the 200-yard mark (33 carries for 224 yards) and became the first true freshman in school history to rush for 1,000 yards in a season. In a five-game stretch from October 9 to November 13, Hart carried the ball 164 times (32.8 per game) for 975 yards. Michigan would lose at Ohio State to close the 2004 regular season, but it still wound up with a share of the Big Ten title—Carr's fifth—and earned a Rose Bowl appearance. Henne's poise gave Michigan a chance, Edwards' brilliance saved the day more than once—but Hart's grit, toughness, and production was the most consistent thing the team had.

The team would find this out the hard way a year later, when Hart's 1,400-yard rookie year was followed by an injury-plagued sophomore season that forced him to miss four games and parts of three others. The Wolverines went 7–5, their worst year in two decades. And while Hart was severely limited, he still managed to crank out three straight 100-yard games in the middle of the year—including a tougher-than-hell 218-yard day on a bad wheel at Michigan State in a 34–31 overtime win.

The 2006 campaign would be the finest of Hart's career. Finally healthy and the full-time starter, Hart topped 100 yards in nine games—including 124 in a massive 47–21 revenge victory at No. 2 Notre Dame in Week 3. Together, Hart and Henne put together the finest offensive season in modern Michigan history—Hart ran for 1,562 yards and 14 touchdowns and Henne threw for 2,508 yards and 22 scores as the Wolverines pushed all the way to 11–0 before falling to Ohio State in the famed No. 1 vs. No. 2 game to close the year. The duo's senior year was supposed to be Michigan's finest hour in a decade—as both Henne and Hart returned, along with star tackle Jake Long, giving Michigan national title hopes ahead of the year. Those lasted four quarters, as Appalachian State's historic 34–32 upset (Hart ran for 188 yards and three touchdowns that day) ruined everything. After Michigan's disastrous start worsened to 0–2 a week later, Hart—now playing without Henne, who was injured—guaranteed Michigan would beat Notre Dame the following week. Behind 187 yards on 35 carries (two touchdowns), Michigan did exactly that—overwhelming the Irish 38–0 to spark a string of eight straight victories (with Hart famously referring to Michigan State as Michigan's "Little Brother" along the way) that got Michigan back into the Big Ten title picture. On an unseasonably hot 84-degree October day against Eastern Michigan, Hart took a first-quarter handoff from Henne, broke three tackles, and scampered for 14 yards. That run put Hart's career total at 4,481 yards—passing Thomas for the school's all-time record.

The year, Lloyd Carr's last as head coach, was filled with bittersweet moments. Henne's shoulder injury and the slow start to the season robbed an ultra-talented team and one of its best players (Hart) of a special season. Instead, Michigan went 9–4—sending Carr out with a 41–35 win over Tim Tebow, Urban Meyer, and Florida in the Citrus Bowl on January 1. Hart would finish the season as an All-American for the second straight year, finishing fifth in the Heisman Trophy race. At Michigan, he set standards that still exist today.

As of this book's publication, Hart was still the school's all-time leading rusher (5,040 yards) and attempts leader (1,015). He still has the school records for the most 100-, 150-, and 200-yard rushing days, with 28, 12, and five, respectively.

It's fair to suggest Hart's career record for carries may never be broken. It took more than 15 years before Michigan found another running back capable of breathing the same air. And, ironically enough, Blake Corum—a team captain on Michigan's 2023 national championship squad—set the program records for both rushing touchdowns in a season (27) and in a career (58) with Mike Hart on the sideline as his position coach.

Corum was a critical pillar in a Michigan resurgence from 2021 to '23 who ended Ohio State's nearly two-decade vice grip on the rivalry. And while Hart never beat Ohio State during his career as a player, he celebrated with his players as if he was still one of them in November of 2021 when the Wolverines gave Jim Harbaugh his first win over the Buckeyes and Michigan just its second since 2003. Corum would break the touchdown record with the game-winning touchdown in the Rose Bowl over Alabama in the national semifinals.

Hart was on the sideline waiting for Corum when he got back. In the stands, beaming with pride some 40 years after he showed up in Ann Arbor with nothing but a green army bag and desire, sat Jamie Morris.

Michigan's running backs—the Family inside the Family—were back on top once again.

11

The Pass Catchers

LIKE MANY OF COLLEGE FOOTBALL'S PROUDEST PROGRAMS, Michigan has its own share of special jersey numbers. Perhaps none more visible than the No. 1, a look and style that was put into Michigan legend by the best athlete the program had seen since, perhaps, Tom Harmon—Anthony Carter.

And the legend of Anthony Carter began before he was old enough to drive.

Built with size you couldn't see and blessed with speed you could hear, the youngest of Manita Carter's five sons—and one of 12 siblings—Anthony had a nickname growing up in south Florida: Little Gnat. He was a freshman the first time he touched a football for Suncoast High School. He took that first touch 78 yards for a touchdown. As a sophomore, after shocking the Florida prep basketball scene by nearly leading his so-so basketball team to a state title, Carter scored *six* touchdowns (four in the first half) in a win over Okeechobee.

"He's so fast," *Miami Herald* sportswriter Barry Bearak wrote during Carter's sophomore season in 1976, "he watches *60 Minutes* in half an hour."

He got his first recruiting letter as a 14-year-old: a basketball offer, per the *Palm Beach Post*, from Florida coach John Lotz. By the time Carter turned 16, he was a national name—blossoming into a true super-recruit before turning into college football's original No. 1. He set the Florida high school receiving record with 3,641 yards—averaging 22.6 yards per catch. Carter scored 54 touchdowns in four years—including five on an eight-catch, 261-yard night during his final regular season game. He was hit after the whistle constantly as teams attempted to wear down his speed, even when he was playing safety on defense. By Carter's senior year, one opposing coach declared there wasn't a defensive back in Florida capable of covering him 1-on-1. Another coach compared defending Carter to a game of "Russian roulette with three cylinders loaded."

Carter was truly blessed. He was also truly cursed.

Carter had world-class speed, reportedly routinely testing at 4.35 seconds in the 40-yard dash. He starred in every sport he played almost from the second he started. He was also quiet, skinny, and relentlessly challenged by peers. His junior high days were filled with schoolyard fights. The *Miami Herald* reported that Carter was forced to repeat eighth grade after being involved in a fight during a school assembly that resulted in the student "bloodying the face" of a teacher. Some of his fights spilled onto the field, resulting in at least one ejection from a Pee Wee game.

He'd developed the reputation of a "bad kid." In reality, though, Anthony Carter was merely a quiet kid trying to get by like everybody else. That's what administrators Gus Bohne and Shirley Burgess, two advisors who would help guide Carter

PART 3: THE FAMILY

through both high school and his whirlwind recruitment, saw when he arrived at Suncoast. The *Herald* reported Burgess was not opposed to starting fist fights with strangers who gossiped nasty rumors about the uber-talented Carter.

Burgess, Bohne, and the rest of the faculty at Suncoast discovered Carter had fallen behind in school due to the learning environment that surrounded him. Once that changed, Carter's grades rose. And while that was a positive, it also only worsened the recruiting onslaught.

As a high school senior in south Florida, Carter was basically a celebrity. Every major college football coach in America had been drooling over him since his freshman year. Miami, Florida, and Florida State basically lived outside his high school. The SEC was interested. USC and UCLA wanted him. So did Notre Dame, Texas, Michigan, Ohio State, and everyone else worth a salt. Prior to his final decision, an NCAA investigator met with Carter for a confidential and seemingly off-the-record discussion about whether schools had committed violations trying to sign him.

In the 1970s, players could sign regional and national letters of intent. The regional letters were essentially state-only commitments. So while Carter initially signed a regional letter with Bobby Bowden's Florida State program as a senior in 1978, the rest of the college football world—including Bo Schembechler's Michigan—still had the final push into February of 1979.

Carter favored Florida State. Along the way, reports surfaced that the Seminoles had discussed giving a scholarship to a female student (purportedly Carter's girlfriend) if Carter enrolled at FSU. This angered Manita and, as a result, Anthony too. Which gave Schembechler an in. Michigan's head coach ensured Manita Carter the only thing the school from Ann Arbor would be putting in her son's pocket was a diploma in four years. He also told

Anthony he could play basketball at Michigan if he wanted to. Moreover—Michigan, Schembechler said, was *evolving*—and if Carter signed, he'd see more than his share of passes.

And just like that, Anthony Carter, a Parade All-American and a five-star recruit before there was such a thing, would be a Michigan Wolverine. It was arguably the biggest recruiting victory of Schembechler's coaching career—as the coach would later declare Carter as the greatest athlete he ever coached.

The first offensive player to wear No. 1 under Schembechler at Michigan, Carter was a beautiful contradiction on a football field. More than halfway through the 1979 season, with the Wolverines pushing the pass offense forward under QB John Wangler, Schembechler, a coach famous for his conservatism, told the press he worried he wasn't playing Carter (a true freshman) enough. A week later, the spindly-legged dynamo made the most famous catch in Michigan Stadium history— the last-second game-winner from Wangler to beat Indiana on homecoming.

Whether it was that first punt return or the famous catch against the Hoosiers, everything Carter did on a football field looked artistic and became the center of attention. From the way everything around him seemed to blur while that No. 1 jersey stayed perfectly visible—albeit shrinking in size as he ran away from the crowd. Off the field, Carter could be painfully quiet. Teammates changed his nickname from "Little Gnat" to "the Hermit." During his pro career, teammates had a phrase for anyone who was able to get dressed and skip the locker room before the media entered to talk: the Anthony Carter Shower.

Including the bowl game, Carter's freshman season featured just 16 receptions. Those catches, however, went for 452 yards and seven touchdowns. An average of 28.3 per catch. In the regular season finale against unbeaten Ohio State, Carter made two spectacular catches: one 59-yard go route down the sideline for a touchdown and another 66-yard post down the middle of the field over three defenders. In the Gator Bowl against North Carolina, he caught another bomb down the sideline—this time for 47 yards—before taking another post 53 yards for a touchdown and finishing with a beautiful 30-yard over-the-shoulder fade catch for a second touchdown.

Carter finished his freshman year with two 100-yard games. The program record was five in a *career*. In total, Carter had six catches for 266 yards and three touchdowns in Michigan's last two games of 1979.

"We've got Anthony Carter," veteran running back Stanley Edwards told the *Detroit Free Press* that year. "A.C. is something like God's gift to football. I've never seen anybody with moves like him."

There was a problem, though. Both those big games Carter turned in were Wolverines losses. Michigan's offense found ways to get Carter the ball, but often as a last resort or in moments of desperation. Schembechler had insisted Michigan would pass the ball more when he signed Carter. He talked about it all summer. But when the season started, conservatism followed. Michigan started the year a nightmarish 1–2 start that shook the foundation of the program. But not because of A.C. He had 14 catches for 208 yards and four touchdowns, despite playing against everyone's best DB, in those three games. By midseason, Michigan had settled in on Wangler at quarterback and the "when" had finally arrived.

Michigan wasn't the only team in the Big Ten trying to modernize its pass game at this time. But it was the only team who had a player like Anthony Carter. It's not just that Carter made more plays than any other receiver—it's that he was open nearly every time he ran a route. If Michigan called a pass play, the only question was whether or not the offensive line would be able to protect Wangler long enough to find an inevitably wide-open Carter.

During a game against Minnesota in 1980, Carter put the full arsenal on display. He made a beautiful acrobatic catch on a poor throw near the sideline to keep the game-opening touchdown drive alive. When Minnesota started doubling him later in the first half, he found ways through that, too. He destroyed a corner at the line of scrimmage and simply outran the deep safety for a 35-yard catch to set up a field goal before doing the same thing on a 20-yard corner route to set up another first-half score. By the third quarter, the Gophers had dedicated two defenders to Carter on nearly every play.

It did not matter.

On a third and long from the Gopher 23, Michigan sent Carter—again facing double coverage—on a fade to the pylon. Wangler released the ball before Carter had reached the 15-yard line. The throw was not accurate, pushing the route back toward the middle of the field right into Minnesota's second defender.

It did not matter.

Carter tracked the ball before either defender, swiftly contorted his body without losing any speed, then perfectly timed a jump to snag the throw in midair before either defender knew what was happening. Carter was so quick to catch the ball and land, his toss to the official after the play almost caught the ref—who had barely had time to start his touchdown signal—right in the face. If you blinked, you missed him. Minnesota blinked a lot that day. Despite doubling Carter all afternoon, the Michigan superstar racked up nine catches for 142 yards and two scores in a dominant 37–14 win.

"Did you people enjoy Anthony today?" a beaming Schembechler boasted afterward.

PART 3: THE FAMILY

The outburst against Minnesota was only the beginning. Carter had five catches for 121 yards and a score the following week in a romp over Illinois. Three weeks later against pass-happy Purdue, Carter had eight grabs for 133 yards and two more touchdowns in a 26–0 win. He caught the only touchdown in Michigan's 9–3 upset win at Ohio State—Michigan's fourth in five years over the Buckeyes. In the Rose Bowl, he added five catches for 68 yards and a score (all in the second half) as Schembechler scored his first career victory in the postseason classic. At halftime, with Carter catchless, Schembechler—famous for his "run, run, run" mantra—told Wangler to start forcing the ball to No. 1. Even if he looked covered. It worked. And after years of banging its head against the Rose Bowl walls, Michigan was finally victorious in Pasadena. Carter's sophomore season went in the books as one of Michigan's finest—51 catches for 818 yards and a school-record 14 touchdowns.

Carter entered his junior season of 1981 as decidedly the best wide receiver in college football and, despite the fact Wangler had graduated, excitement overflowed. Michigan had signed Carter out of high school in 1979. In 1980, Schembechler followed that up by inking Grand Blanc (Michigan) quarterback Steve Smith, ranked as the No. 2 prospect nationally—behind only Georgia running back Herschel Walker—on noted recruiting analyst Charley Holland's top-100 list. With a highly touted young quarterback and an offense that featured arguably the best player in America (Carter), a stellar offensive line, and the dual-threat backfield of Butch Woolfolk and Stan Edwards, Michigan entered its season opener against Wisconsin ranked No. 1.

The Badgers had not beaten Michigan since 1962 and in the previous four meetings, the Wolverines had outscored Wisconsin 176–0. On this day, however, things went differently.

THE PROGRAM: MICHIGAN

With a new quarterback and an experienced backfield, Michigan attempted to bully Wisconsin at the line of scrimmage throughout the first half—only getting the ball to Carter once for 11 yards. It didn't work. The Badgers bottled Michigan up enough that when Michigan was forced to pass, Smith's inexperience showed, resulting in a disastrous day—3 of 18 for 39 yards and three interceptions. Carter caught one pass and Michigan's 1981 run at No. 1 was over.

Carter's run with No. 1, however, was not. The following week against top-ranked Notre Dame, Carter helped settle down a shaky Smith with a 71-yard touchdown catch in the second quarter to spark a 25–7 upset. The first-year starting quarterback completed four passes on the day. Three of them went to Carter. Two were touchdowns. Michigan's new QB settled in from there, developing a great deep connection with Carter—who put up 14 catches for 308 yards and three touchdowns during a two-week span against Minnesota and Illinois before finishing Michigan's 9–3 season with 50 grabs for 952 yards and eight scores.

The only thing about Carter's run at Michigan that wasn't perfect, frankly, was timing. If he'd gotten to play longer with Wangler, or had more time to build a rapport with Steve Smith—or had he come around a few years later, when Michigan's offense was humming with Jim Harbaugh... The "ifs" are part of what makes college football special, though, and the fact Carter shattered Michigan's receiving records anyway was what made him a program icon. Carter, who played in a time when Michigan still ran the option more than it probably wanted to, finished his four-year run with 161 catches for 3,076 yards and 37 touchdowns. Even during a time when the forward pass was starting to blossom, those numbers appeared potentially unbreakable.

PART 3: THE FAMILY

In some ways, they were. It took 20 years for a Michigan receiver to pass Carter's yardage number. That 3,076 *still* ranks No. 2 all-time at the school. The tradition of the No. 1 jersey at Michigan isn't something that's been around forever. It didn't start because Carter asked for it. It started because Bo Schembechler decided to put No. 1 on the front and back of the best athlete he'd ever coached. And in time, the number would come to represent everything Carter stood for at Michigan: modesty, reliability, and electricity.

It would also become a recruiting tool. In 1986, Michigan signed Parade All-American WR/DB Greg McMurtry, an outstanding 6'2" football/baseball prospect from Brockton, Massachusetts, who—like Carter—had offers from every major program in America. The *Boston Globe* reported Schembechler made two in-home visits and had Michigan's staff sweating until the night before signing day. Shortly after announcing McMurtry's signature the following morning, Schembechler revealed an ace up his sleeve. McMurtry would wear No. 1.

Four months after he signed, the country found out why Michigan was so high on this teenager when the Boston Red Sox drafted him in the first round and offered him a six-figure signing bonus to skip college. McMurtry turned it down, citing a desire to get a degree and star inside Michigan Stadium. As a true freshman in 1986, McMurtry started five games (catching 22 passes for 508 yards) and proved a missing piece for Harbaugh and the offense during Michigan's 11–1 Big Ten championship season.

McMurtry went on to lead Michigan in receptions and yards in each of the next three seasons before being drafted in the third round by the New England Patriots in 1990. He wasn't the only Michigan receiver drafted that year, either, as Chicago native Chris Calloway—a perfect 5'10", 186-pound complement opposite McMurtry—went in the fourth round to the Steelers. By 1990, Michigan had three high-level wide receivers playing NFL football: Anthony Carter with the Minnesota Vikings (who snagged him out of the USFL after watching him destroy the Golden Gophers in the early '80s), McMurtry, and Calloway.

If Michigan used the No. 1 to reel in McMurtry, it used the number to motivate Derrick Alexander. Alexander, a big and powerful 6'3" wide receiver with 4.4 speed, was a local product. He starred at Benedictine High School in Detroit as a running back/wide receiver in the fall while averaging nearly 20 points per game as a smoother-than-silk forward in the winter.

By McMurtry's senior year in 1989, the offense was firmly in Gary Moeller's hands. The would-be Michigan head coach was now roughly a decade into Michigan's offensive transformation and saw the duo of Alexander and Cleveland's Desmond Howard as the final puzzle pieces. Howard always wanted to be his own man. The title of his biography is *I Wore 21*, an ode to the fact he made his own way without Michigan's signature jersey.

Alexander was Howard's opposite. Instead of short and loud, he was tall and quiet. He also wanted that No. 1 jersey. And Michigan knew it. Which is why he spent his freshman season wearing No. 40. And after a year of grinding, one of Moeller's first orders of business as new head coach was to give Alexander the No. 1 ahead of the 1990 campaign. By the fall of 1991, Moeller's grand plan appeared ready to launch. Howard had Heisman buzz, Elvis Grbac was seasoned, and Alexander looked ready for a breakout of his own. Two-thirds of the plan worked. Howard won the Heisman, Grbac set records...and Alexander blew out his knee on a kickoff return during the season opener. He sobbed in the recovery room after surgery. Offensive assistant Cam Cameron would later tell the *Free Press*

PART 3: THE FAMILY

he wasn't sure if Alexander would ever leave the hospital, as he was so down on himself.

Alexander's story could've easily been one of Michigan's great what-ifs, especially considering that by the time he returned to health in 1992, Moeller had brought in Amani Toomer—the No. 1–ranked high school receiver—and Mercury Hayes—the No. 4–ranked receiver.

After spending so much time watching others have their moment, Alexander finally started to have his at the beginning of 1992. Unlike Howard's big year, though, many of Alexander's big moments seemed to be overshadowed by something else. He had a spectacular 30-yard touchdown catch in the season opener at Notre Dame to put the Wolverines up 10 in the fourth quarter—but the Irish stormed back late to salvage a 17–17 tie. The following week against Oklahoma State, Alexander had his best day as a Wolverine, hauling in seven passes for 103 yards and two touchdowns. The big headlines the next morning, though, were about how backup quarterback Todd Collins had set a program completion record (29) in his first start subbing for an injured Elvis Grbac.

Truth was, Michigan's 1992 squad was arguably the most talented team the program had seen by that stage. Especially on offense. Sophomore running back Tyrone Wheatley, a kid Alexander knew from Detroit, returned the opening kickoff 99 yards for a touchdown in week three against Houston. Hayes and Toomer were incredibly quick studies. Tony McGee, who caught a touchdown in week four against Iowa, was a revelation as a senior. In total, 11 offensive players on that 1992 roster became NFL draft picks. Alexander's big moment would have to be shared.

He never complained for a second. Which is exactly why Moeller gave him No. 1 in the first place. And by the time

Michigan welcomed rival Michigan State on October 10, Alexander was finally ready for his moment on center stage. Up 14–0 in the first half, Alexander settled under a punt right on the Michigan 20-yard line. The in-state kid playing against the in-state rival made two hard cuts to his right before exploding through a crease and showing the world his knee was just fine. When he crossed the goal line after an 80-yard return score, the normally reserved Alexander jumped high into the air and let out a scream. Michigan coaches had only seen Alexander that emotional once before—emotionally devastated after tearing up his knee. Now, there was only joy.

"When Derrick begins twisting and throwing himself around like that," Moeller told the *Free Press* after Alexander added a 70-yard punt return touchdown later in October against Indiana. "You know he's either very happy or very sad."

Alexander's run with the No. 1 was as much about perseverance and quiet consistency as anything else. He overcame a devastating setback and, rather than running from competition upon return, he stayed to help foster the next generation of Michigan receivers. Alexander had 1,361 receiving yards from 1992 to '93 (and four punt return touchdowns), adding a ridiculous seven-catch, 188-yard day (including a program-record 90-yard TD catch) against Illinois as a senior. Before Alexander's knee injury, he looked like a first-round NFL draft pick. And while he didn't leave Michigan with a Heisman Trophy, upon his recovery, his college career concluded with his name being called in the first round to the Cleveland Browns in 1994.

Eventually, as is the case with any tradition, pressure builds. Tyrone Butterfield came to Michigan from south Florida in 1993 hoping to become the next Desmond Howard. A 5'8", 165-pound receiver/quarterback/kick returner/do-everything Miami Central lightning bug, Butterfield originally committed

PART 3: THE FAMILY

to Florida but wound up convinced he could be a star for Gary Moeller and Cam Cameron wearing the No. 1 for Michigan. By the time he arrived in 1994, though, Cameron was on his way to the Washington Redskins. A year later, Moeller was out as head coach. Butterfield's fit with Lloyd Carr never really materialized and he finished his career at Tennessee State in 1997—the year the Wolverines won a national title.

The 20-year run of the No. 1 at Michigan to close out the 1900s was something that took on a life of its own. It represented a succession plan of sorts. Success begetting success. One generation of receivers teaching the next how it's supposed to be done at Michigan: humbly with consistency. By the time Carr's coaching staff first broke out the No. 1 jersey as a recruiting tool, times had changed. David Terrell had no problem with consistency.

But, quite frankly, he was too good to be humble.

Terrell was raised by his mother, Barbara, in a Jackson Ward housing project in Richmond, Virginia. The streets and neighborhoods Terrell and his siblings walked each day were tough. They were also a stroll in the park compared with what might happen if you stepped out of line under Barbara Terrell's roof. His mother was no-nonsense. With her own kids, the neighbor kids, anybody who entered. David father wasn't around, but he'd later find the type of male direction that mimicked Barbara's when he landed at Huguenot High School to play for Richard McFee—a coach so tough he reportedly once kicked his own kid off the team for breaking a rule.

Mentally tough with energy for days, Terrell blossomed into a powerful, explosive 6'3", 210-pound athlete who was a dominant two-way player in football (some believed he was a better corner than receiver) as well as a do-everything swingman on the basketball team. McFee once told a reporter he believed

Terrell's first love was hoops. But football was where he shined the most. In high school, a reporter from the *Richmond Times-Dispatch* asked Terrell who would win in a 1-on-1—David the DB or David the WR? His answer went a long way toward explaining why there was so much more behind his dominant athletic exterior.

"Receiver wins," he said. "There are so many things to throw a defensive back off balance. That's why it's so hard to be a defensive back. You don't know what the receiver is going to do.... There are so many tactics he can use to get open."

His high school teachers said he could've been a straight-A student if he wanted to. He could've played for any ACC basketball program in America. When the *Roanoke Times* ranked the state's top 50 players ahead of Terrell's senior season in 1997, the kid from Jackson Ward was No. 2 overall—two slots ahead of Hampton quarterback Michael Vick. Terrell would top 1,000 yards and catch 19 touchdown passes as a senior, landing as Tom Lemming's No. 1 overall receiver for 1998.

Terrell originally committed to Bob Davie and Notre Dame, but continued to answer phone calls from soon-to-be Michigan quarterback Drew Henson—the country's top-ranked prospect. Henson had been hounding Terrell and 6'2", 210-pound receiver Marquise Walker out of upstate New York. Walker was more or less Terrell's athletic clone. Also a dominant basketball player who opted to focus more on football, Walker combined power and athletic grace to be a dominant two-way receiver/cornerback at Henninger High School in Syracuse. Terrell was the No. 1–ranked WR for 1998; Walker was No. 2. During a December recruiting weekend in Ann Arbor, with Michigan ranked No. 1 nationally and about to play for a national title, Henson, Walker, and Terrell all spent time together. Not long after, all three had decided to play for Michigan. Carr left the

1998 recruiting cycle with the No. 1–ranked recruiting class in America. And David Terrell arrived in Ann Arbor as the newest member of the No. 1 jersey club.

The trio was supposed to deliver Michigan *another* national championship. In reality, it only really got one season together—as Henson was Michigan's full-time starter (despite missing time early in the year with a foot injury) in 2000. Terrell and Walker combined to catch more than 100 passes for nearly 1,600 yards and 17 touchdowns during a 9–3 year that ended with a win over Auburn in the Citrus Bowl. All three had eligibility to play and chase that national title in 2001, and had Henson not signed with the New York Yankees, it might've happened. Alas, not unlike the case of awkward timing with Anthony Carter, David Terrell had incredible moments at Michigan—but not nearly as many as most believed possible. Terrell wound up a first-round pick of the Chicago Bears in 2001. Decades later, his son, David Jr., lined up at wide receiver for Howard University—studying law. Walker stayed at Michigan alone in 2001, finishing his career with a first-year quarterback in John Navarre—and still setting school records in catches (86) and yards (1,143). Walker, true to his versatile rep, also blocked four punts.

The next and ultimately most successful wearer of the No. 1 was on the roster when Walker graduated in 2001. A 6'3", 200-pound true freshman from Detroit with a familiar last name…was wearing No. 80. Like so many things inside Michigan's football program, the tale of the No. 1 jersey was about to go full circle.

Braylon Edwards, son of former Michigan running back Stanley Edwards—he who once declared Anthony Carter "God's gift to football" long before the world knew it—came to Michigan hoping to be the next Anthony Carter. Also, the next Greg McMurtry. And Chris Calloway. Amani Toomer, Mercury Hayes, Walter Smith, Desmond Howard, Derrick Alexander,

Marquise Walker, and David Terrell. He wanted to be all of them. More specifically, he wanted to be better than all of them. And he was never bashful about letting people know it.

Braylon was still a preschooler when his parents, Stan and Malesa, split up. Divorce, however, never impacted the duo's ability to raise their son. In fact, after the duo remarried (Stan to Carolyn and Malesa to Chuck), Braylon simply added a second set of equally supportive—and strict—parents.

Stan declared Braylon would be a first-round pick seconds after first holding him in the delivery room. By 18 months, he started tossing pillows at his son's feet as he pranced around the family home—hoping to develop balance. Before he was three, Malesa had taught him how to shake an adult's hand and look them in the eye upon greeting them. He loved math. He dressed like he was going to church every day. Braylon's favorite band as a kid in the 1990s? The Temptations.

"He was an old soul," Malesa once told the *Cleveland Plain Dealer*.

Growing up with an active NFL player for a father, and one who was a local star in Michigan, also allowed Braylon to spend parts of his childhood around sporting royalty. By the time he'd enrolled at King High School in Detroit he'd already met and gotten to know multiple Hall of Fame athletes in multiple sports—from Magic Johnson to Archie Manning. Athletically, Braylon was a late bloomer. At Detroit King, Edwards was a 5'8" receiver on a run-heavy team. After a leg injury his junior year, Edwards transferred to Bishop Gallagher—and grew to 6'2". As a senior, everything changed. Now bigger than his dad in his playing days, with all the same physical gifts (and more), Edwards made plays at receiver, quarterback, and running back his senior season—finally drawing the attention of major college programs. Stan and Malesa had been so infuriated no one saw in their son what they did that by the time Michigan finally called to offer Braylon a scholarship, Malesa hung up the phone and made them call again.

Add all of this together and it's easy to see why Braylon Jamel Edwards entered Michigan in 2001 as one of the most unique freshmen the school had seen. Overflowing with confidence, charisma, a mouth that never slowed down, and a mind that always found a way to back it up, Edwards was a handful early. He ran routes the way he wanted to run them. He said whatever was on his mind. He didn't care about the consequences. The 2001 team had capable veteran receivers in Marquise Walker and Ron Bellamy. Edwards, who clearly thought he was better, struggled with the adjustment to life on the bench as a freshman. If Edwards was great at letting everyone around him know when he was upset (which he did throughout the 2001 season), he was even better at changing his situation by simply becoming undeniable.

By the start of his sophomore year, Edwards now looked like a grown man at 6'3", 200 pounds—with the foot speed and body control of a man 50 pounds lighter. His first target of the season should've been a touchdown, as he beat two Washington defenders to the end zone on a post only to be overthrown. His second, the first play of the second quarter, was in fact a touchdown—as Edwards again got behind the defense on a post route before plucking the ball away from a defender at the goal line for a 45-yard touchdown catch. Edwards added two more against Western Michigan in a week two romp and after back-to-back 100-yard games against Utah and Illinois, the sophomore standout was up to 26 catches for 478 yards and five scores in the first five weeks of the season.

Edwards wore No. 80 that year as an ode to Jerry Rice. He'd met Rice as a 12-year-old before a 49ers–Lions game and tried to mimic everything about his game. The honor, while genuine, was only temporary. As Braylon Edwards was meant for something bigger. And he knew it. He wasn't afraid to talk with reporters about his aspirations. He didn't make any secret about nearly transferring during his freshman season. Or that he'd asked for the No. 1 jersey upon arrival, only to be told by Carr that number had to be earned. Edwards' sophomore year had its roller-coaster moments—there were focus drops and he was still focused more on individual improvement—but it was more spectacular than anything else. He finished with 67 catches for 1,035 yards and 10 touchdowns in one of the greatest individual seasons by a Michigan receiver ever. And he did it as a true sophomore. His catch number was only 10 away from setting a school record and his yardage total was less than 100 yards from the best year David Terrell ever had. When Edwards asked for the No. 1 again entering the spring of his junior year, Carr had no choice but to give it to him. Carr had been an assistant coach at Michigan during Anthony Carter's run and held the No. 1 jersey in higher regard than anyone inside the program. Even if there might've been reticence about whether or not Edwards was firmly all-in for the team above himself, his play had undoubtedly earned the honor.

That reticence turned public by the start of the 2003 season as Edwards, now wearing Carter's number, came off the bench in the season opener against Central Michigan. And while Edwards still caught five balls for 78 yards and two scores, his extended sideline time was long enough for reporters to notice.

"Braylon Edwards and I are not on the same page," Carr told reporters after the game. "Braylon is a very good reader, so what he needs to do is find what page I'm on and get there. That's all I'm going to say."

In reality, Edwards' opening-game punishment was the result of being late to a team meeting. Hardly Anthony Carter–level behavior. Neither were the drops Edwards spread around his otherwise brilliant season opener against CMU. This was the contradiction of Braylon Edwards. For long stretches he looked like the best wide receiver the program had ever seen. Then, out of nowhere, he'd drop an easy first down. Or he'd do something small and immature to irk Carr.

Carr never had problems with players speaking their mind and Edwards was hardly an exception. In fact, the coach encouraged such behavior. Outside his office in Schembechler Hall was a gigantic dictionary. If a player wanted to come in, he simply had to spell and define whatever complicated Word of the Day the coach selected.

His grief with Edwards wasn't born from dislike but from fear.

Carr saw how talented Edwards was and knew how easy it'd be for him to knock himself off track with immature behavior. The idea of a player not realizing his potential—especially one this good—over foolish self-control issues was the very thing that kept Carr up at night. He believed it was his duty as a coach, and an educator, to maximize the ability of every person in his care. And with the young and incredibly talented Edwards, Carr went through stretches when he questioned that on a near-daily basis. The fact he'd said anything to the media at all spoke to how concerned Carr was about Edwards' attitude entering a critical season. And while it angered the receiver (and his parents—something Carr was prepared for), the message did what it was supposed to.

Not unlike the time he told Tom Brady "sure, kid, go ahead and transfer—but I guarantee you'll regret it" or when he held his ground after Charles Woodson threatened to quit before

THE PROGRAM: MICHIGAN

the Ohio State game, Carr's superpower with players was his ability to know *exactly* where their ignition switch was. Carr played to Brady's insecurity and competitive tenacity. He was back the next day. Carr played to Woodson's soft spot (he called his mom), but also earned the player's eternal respect *because* he stood his ground against an immature youngster who needed the lesson. Edwards carried a similar mindset. He saw everything, he heard everything, he forgot nothing—and he answered every challenge, no matter what.

By mid-October, Michigan was a disappointing 4–2 and headed for a date with 17th-ranked Minnesota at the Metrodome in Minneapolis. The first three quarters were a nightmare, as the Wolverines failed to stop the run and did nothing offensively—falling behind 28–7 to start the fourth quarter. Even after two touchdowns in less than a minute—a John Navarre pass to Chris Perry and a Jacob Stewart pick-six—Michigan still found itself in deep trouble after Gophers quarterback Asad Abdul-Khaliq scored on a 52-yard touchdown run that nearly took the roof off the dome to push Minnesota's lead back to 14 with just 11 minutes left.

The jubilation lasted about 50 seconds. Edwards ran right by his man and down the Michigan sideline before Navarre lofted a beauty into his arms for a 52-yard touchdown response that quieted the crowd. Michigan would score the game's final 10 points, including a last-second field goal from Garrett Rivas, completing a 31-point fourth quarter and the largest comeback win in program history. The 2003 team, a quarter away from 4–3, would rattle off six straight to close the year—including a dominant 35–21 win over No. 4 Ohio State—to win the Big Ten title and clinch a Rose Bowl bid. Edwards had 100-yard days in each of Michigan's final four games that year, including 130 and two touchdowns against the Buckeyes, to finish with a school-record 85 catches for 1,138 yards and 14 touchdowns.

Edwards flirted with the idea of leaving for the NFL after that season, but returned to finish his degree and fulfill Stan's prophecy he'd be a first-round pick. He cut his trademark Afro and vowed to lead what would be a very young offense, led by a freshman quarterback, as a senior. He'd learned why Carr was hesitant about giving him the No. 1 ahead of his junior season. And now knew why the coach was proud to have him wear it as a senior in 2004.

"I learned to wear the number," Edwards told *Free Press* columnist Drew Sharp that summer, "not let the number wear me."

As a senior, Edwards put together the greatest single season by a wide receiver that Michigan's ever seen. Playing with a true freshman quarterback (Chad Henne), a new-look offensive line, and a true freshman running back (Mike Hart), Edwards carried the load constantly as the Wolverines struggled to find their flow early on. He also happily stepped back and supported the improved rush attack during a quiet midseason stretch. Edwards had seven games of 100 yards or more that season—one fewer than Desmond Howard had for his career. His titanic 11-catch, 189-yard, three-touchdown showing during a thrilling 42–34 three-overtime win over Michigan State simply became known to fans on both sides of the rivalry as "the Braylon Game." His 172 yards in a loss to Ohio State were the most by a Michigan receiver against the Buckeyes in the history of the rivalry. He finished his career as the school's all-time leader in catches (252), yards (3,541), and touchdowns (39). All of those records remain as of this book's publishing, with his career yardage total appearing nearly unbreakable. With three touchdowns in the 2005 Rose Bowl against Texas, his final game at Michigan, Edwards set a new Big Ten record for career touchdown catches.

The man he passed?

Anthony Carter.

12
The Protectors

"From this day to the ending of the world,
But we in it shall be remember'd;
We few, we happy few, we band of brothers."

THE STORY OF CRISPIN AND CRISPINIAN, THE TWIN SAINTS who inspired Shakespeare's iconic "St. Crispin's Day" speech from *Henry V*, revolves around cohesive toughness. Per legend, the brothers stood calmly and together as they were executed for spreading their religious beliefs around the year 285 AD. The twins funded their gospel by crafting shoes. They became known as the Christian saints of cobblers, tanners, and anyone who worked with leather, a material known for the tightly woven fibers that make it difficult to soften.

If Crispin and Crispinian are the patron saints of leather, then those in winged helmets along the offensive line have forever served as the patron saints of Michigan football.

THE PROGRAM: MICHIGAN

Michigan's offensive-line traditions date back to the start of the program. And while much changed during the first half of the 1900s, Michigan's national championship season of 2023 *still* featured some base concepts Bo Schembechler ran in 1969. Fielding Yost, one of the first humans to master American football, built the original hurry-up offense around his line's ability to work faster than the opponent. The early era of Michigan football produced a gaggle of top-tier linemen when sizes were more modest. Germany Schulz, a College Football Hall of Famer credited with inventing the spiral snap, starred at Michigan in the early 1900s. He stood 6'2" and weighed 215 pounds. Francis Wistert, the eldest of Michigan's famed Wistert brothers (with Albert and Alvin) was roughly 210 pounds when he played his last game at Michigan in 1933. By the time Alvin wrapped up his All-American career in 1949, he weighed 223 pounds.

The physical evolution of the offensive lineman was gradual, though if there was a boom it came in the 1960s. And while this decade is hardly known as the greatest in Michigan's football history, it did produce arguably its greatest offensive lineman.

Dan Dierdorf was destined for football glory before he even knew it. Growing up in Canton, Ohio, Dierdorf grew up near legendary League Field—home of America's first pro football team, the Canton Bulldogs. In middle school, Dierdorf watched the construction of the Pro Football Hall of Fame on a site about three miles from where he slept. He weighed 240 pounds as a sophomore and smashed a city discus record as a junior. A heavyweight wrestler, Dierdorf was also a three-year starting tackle at Glenwood High School—an enormous, agile athlete with power everywhere. A special prospect.

Not everyone agreed, though. Specifically, Ohio State coach Woody Hayes. Despite his size, Dierdorf didn't play youth football and only went out for the seventh-grade team *because* he was so big. Once describing himself as a "just happy to be there guy," Dierdorf was still discovering his passion for the game. Perhaps it came across to Hayes, famous for his football-or-nothing mindset and constantly in search of players who'd rather lose a limb than miss a game. Dierdorf originally thought he was destined for a school in the Mid-American Conference, so long as it wasn't with incandescent Hayes disciple Bo Schembechler at Miami-Ohio.

Jim Reichenbach, Dierdorf's prep coach in Canton, knew Michigan assistant coach Don James from their own playing days back in Ohio. James relayed Reichenbach's information about a hidden gem in northeast Ohio that neither Ohio State nor Michigan State wanted. Not long after, the mild-mannered Elliott was in Dierdorf's living room offering him a scholarship up north in Ann Arbor. He basically committed on the spot.

"I don't think he got out of the driveway," Dierdorf recalls.

Dierdorf spent large chunks of 1967 at Michigan in the university wrestling room. Dave Porter, the defending NCAA heavyweight wrestling champion, was also a defensive tackle on the football team. His size and power made it relatively impossible for anyone on the actual wrestling team to spar with him. Dierdorf, also playing on the freshman football team, took the job and Porter won the title again in 1968. Also around this time, Dierdorf served as recruiting host for a football/wrestling prospect from Minnesota with a loud mouth and a penchant for booze. The Minnesotan's trip to Michigan was brief, consisting of beers with Dierdorf and tight end Jim Mandich before he ventured into a new professional direction that required a name change and an expensive wardrobe.

You and I know him as Ric Flair. The Nature Boy.

The 1968 season would be a critical one for Bump Elliott. It would also be a successful one by any standard save for one: Michigan's. The young Wolverines had a true superstar in running back Ron Johnson, but the supporting cast had its issues. The Oosterbaan–Elliott era still featured great offensive-line talent. Tom Mack was a tight end from Cleveland Heights before Elliott turned him into a tackle in 1964, resulting in an All-American season in '65 before embarking on an NFL career that featured 11 Pro Bowls and a trip to the Hall of Fame. Mack was outstanding. He could've used more help, though.

By '68, Elliott had solved that problem—sort of. He had talent up front with Dierdorf, Bob Penska, Dick Caldarazzo, Dave Denzin, and Stan Broadnax. That fivesome paved the way for Johnson's iconic 347-yard masterpiece against Wisconsin on November 16, 1968—a game in which Johnson scored on runs of 67, 60, 49, 35, and 1 yard(s).

The only problem? The stadium was half full. As great as the run game was that day, youthful mistakes kept expectations low.

Johnson's historic day came one week before Michigan's finale with Ohio State. The 1968 Buckeyes were unbeaten and had national title aspirations, as usual. Moreover, it was arguably the best Ohio State team Woody Hayes ever had. Michigan was a surprising 8–1, with a chance to shock the world and go to the Rose Bowl. Dierdorf hurt his knee on the first offensive series and Michigan's offense never recovered. Playing with one hand tied behind its back against a generational Ohio State team, Michigan watched Hayes run the ball 79 times for 421 yards in a 50–14 laugher.

By the time Dierdorf's knee had fully recovered in 1969, he and Michigan had a new coach. Bo Schembechler, the one guy Dierdorf *didn't* want to play for out of high school. But that was then. By the fall of 1969, Dierdorf was no longer just happy to be there. And while there were *many* days during Schembechler's famous first training camp when Dierdorf wanted to throw in the towel, it was during these stressful times—as had been the case when Reichenbach pushed him in high school—that he discovered his love of football. The harder it got, the better it felt. The hard, truly, is what makes football great. Dierdorf *loved* how challenging the game was to master both mentally and physically, and how great it made him feel to move another man five yards against his will.

The team Schembechler took over in 1969 was, indeed, in need of mental adjustment. At the same time, anyone claiming he arrived at Michigan with a bare cupboard is simply lying. Dierdorf, Mandich, and defensive back Tom Curtis were some of the finest young talents in the country; all three would eventually earn passage to the College Football Hall of Fame. Not unlike Yost's focus on the little moments between the big moments that inspired football's first hurry-up offense, Schembechler's focus on being consistent with all the small details that happened between the tackles on both sides of the ball—the stuff no one else saw—was the difference for not just the team, but every individual.

Especially Dan Dierdorf. He'd improved as a first-year starter in 1968, but gradually. Even during Johnson's romp versus Wisconsin, Dierdorf showed signs of an elite player who was unsure of himself. His talent flashed, but not every snap. He fell off too many blocks and while his superior balance allowed him to consistently recover, he was on his back foot more than he'd like. He had a good year. But, to Schembechler's point from the moment he walked in the door, Dierdorf could've had a great one.

In 1969, he'd do just that.

It took Michigan's offense about two months to truly show consistency during Schembechler's first season. But Dierdorf proved to be a different person almost from the first snap against Vanderbilt. No longer unsure of himself, the hulking junior tackle was now routinely the first man off the snap on every play. He wasn't falling off blocks, he was finishing them.

At Minnesota on October 25, 1969—Saint Crispin's Day—the exhausted but changed Wolverines sat in a halftime locker room with a 3–2 record, trailing the Golden Gophers despite having outgained them for two quarters. If Schembechler's most famous team was ever going to quit, it'd have been right there—on the chilly banks of the Mississippi, with the sport's oldest trophy on the line.

"This day is called the feast of Crispian: He that outlives this day, and comes safe home, will stand a tip-toe when this day is nam'd," Shakespeare wrote, probably not (but maybe?) about offensive linemen. "And rouse him at the name of Crispian. He that shall live this day, and see old age, will yearly on the vigil feast his neighbors, and say 'tomorrow is Saint Crispian!'"

Michigan's patron saints did not quit that day. On the team's opening possession of the third quarter, Dierdorf (who played right and left tackle) pancaked his man to spring Billy Taylor on a 19-yard run into Minnesota territory. Behind Dierdorf, Caldarazzo, Jack Harpring, Bob Baumgartner, and Guy Murdock, Michigan ran the ball seven straight times after that—culminating with a three-yard scoring plunge. There was no dust cloud. Just mud, sweat, and blood.

Michigan scored 28 unanswered points in the second half on Saint Crispin's Day of 1969, all touchdown runs, ripping off 193 of its 304 yards *after* halftime in a dominant 35–9 win that Schembechler famously called the group's greatest triumph to date. During a four-game stretch from October to November, Michigan's offensive line produced 1,419 rushing yards—including a school-record 524 at Iowa on November 15, the week before Ohio State. On what proved to be Michigan's game-winning scoring drive in the first half against the Buckeyes, Dierdorf threw one of two critical blocks on the left side that sprung Taylor for a terrific 28-yard run to set up a score. The other came from the honorary lineman that year: Jim Mandich.

Writers started comparing Mandich to iconic tight end Ron Kramer before Schembechler took the job. At least 20 years ahead of his time as a player, Mandich was an elite pass catcher who played with the after-catch ability of a running back at 6'3", 220. He caught 43 passes for 576 yards as a junior and was the unquestioned leader, the only captain, of the '69 team. One of the greatest 1-on-1 competitors to ever play at Michigan, "Mad Dog" earned 12 prep letters at Solon High School in Ohio as a football, basketball, and track star. In trying to compare the two during the '68 season, Bennie Oosterbaan told the *Toledo Blade* that Kramer's ability to make the big-time catch was slightly better than Mandich's—but even then, as a sophomore, Mandich was Kramer's equal as a blocker. Throughout history, coaches at Michigan have talked about a standard of performance at each position. In 1969, Jim Mandich and Dan Dierdorf set respective Michigan standards for their positions that wouldn't be topped for at least the remainder of the century.

In Mandich's case, perhaps longer.

His 50 catches in 1969 stood as a Michigan record by a tight end until 2002, and his 662 receiving yards held through 2013. As of this writing, no Michigan tight end has served as a better two-way player in terms of receiving and blocking than Jim Mandich. As of 2024, Michigan's had 18 tight ends selected in the NFL draft since Mandich went in the second round of 1970. It's my contention that Mandich's skill set *still* remains a notch above the rest. The one who might top him, ironically enough, was on the roster as of this book's publishing: All-American

Colston Loveland. Mandich was that good and is one of only a handful of skill players from the 1960s whose talent, in my estimation, would translate to today's game. A three-time Super Bowl winner with the Miami Dolphins, Mandich died after a bout with cancer in 2011. He was just 62.

Like Dierdorf, Mandich was a Hall of Fame talent the day he walked in the door at Michigan. Once his consistency sharpened, confidence followed, and talent did the rest. Schembechler's first coaching staff, notably longtime assistant Jerry Hanlon, get plenty of credit for that. Hanlon, a squat and fiery former running back for Ara Parseghian at Miami, was a day-one addition for Schembechler and spent the next 23 years with the program—18 as offensive line coach. Even outlasting Schembechler himself. After his retirement in 1991, Hanlon's attention to detail was still around the football building. The day after the season-opening win against Colorado in 1997, first-year offensive line coach Terry Malone got to his office before the morning dew faded. He found Hanlon waiting in his office, notes in hand and ready to inform the new assistant of all the stuff he'd messed up during an otherwise dominant performance. Malone simply smiled and took the seat next to the old teacher.

The talent Hanlon and Schembechler inherited in 1969 would've been enviable by any standard. However, their ability to replenish and continue developing similar players for the next two decades would set Michigan apart nationally.

Reggie McKenzie's childhood in Highland Park, Michigan, was an education in mental toughness. His parents, Henry and Hazel, made sure their eight children were fully aware of what *not* to do outside their home. McKenzie once told a *Free Press* reporter the closest he came to trouble was during a field trip to a prison with the Boy Scouts. Henry, who grew up working

PART 3: THE FAMILY

farms in Georgia, was a model of hard work. Hazel was even tougher. In Frank Lieberman's book *Bo's Warriors*, McKenzie recalled a childhood lesson from his mother on discipline.

"Son, you're not going to embarrass me," she'd say. "I'll kill you first."

He got his first job delivering newspapers at 12. By eighth grade, McKenzie was wearing a size 14 shoe. Much like Dierdorf, McKenzie was an athletic kid whose quickness survived his growth spurt before landing at Michigan out of Highland Park in 1968. Dierdorf wowed Michigan's coaching staff with how light his feet were at nearly 280 pounds. McKenzie was lighter, topping out around 255. His feet, however, were electric. McKenzie ran like a tight end. As a pulling guard, his explosion off the ball and natural balance allowed him to pull and trap with power and grace. Michigan's offense could bore its own fan base to tears with how simplistic things were, the same handful of plays over and over and over. The Michigan offense got booed by the home crowd twice in the first three weeks of 1970. By the time Michigan was 9–0 later that fall, though, things changed.

Michigan's offensive lines had been talented during the Bump Elliott years. But this was different.

Michigan changed a lot in 1971. Record-setting quarterback Don Moorhead was gone. Defensive stars Henry Hill and Marty Huff graduated and Dierdorf was in the NFL with the St. Louis Cardinals. The strength of the team was right over the ball—center Guy Murdock, left guard Reggie McKenzie, right guard Tom Coyle. Murdock was part of Elliott's final recruiting class and an early standout alongside Dierdorf on the '69 team and Coyle, a sophomore from Chicago, had won the team's most promising freshman award in 1970. The offensive line also had an honorary member that year in the form of tight end Paul Seymour. A product of Shrine Catholic in Royal Oak, the massive 6'5" Seymour came to Michigan as a wide receiver and grew into a terrific blocking tight end (eventually a tackle). Jim Coode, an Ohioan built a lot like McKenzie, took over at left tackle. Replacing Dierdorf on the right side was his good friend from East Lansing: Jim Brandstatter.

Michigan's program is historically littered with players born from enemy territory in Ohio. Brandstatter came from a different, albeit equally intense, type of enemy territory. The son of former Michigan State All-American Art Brandstatter Sr. and younger brother of ex–Michigan State football *and* basketball standout Art Brandstatter Jr., Jim Brandstatter (his mom also went to MSU) might've followed along—had he received an offer from Duffy Daugherty. Instead, Bump Elliott drove the hour north to his family home and held court with Art Sr. for hours—reminiscing about the old days and all the great Wolverines–Spartans battles over the years, as the two (both military men) had great respect for each other.

By the '71 season, Brandstatter had blossomed from the big, nervous sophomore whom Schembechler kicked out of practice for *correctly* covering a punt back to a dependable, powerful bookend for arguably the best OL in college football. Moorhead's absence did, as everyone predicted, impact Michigan's ability to throw that year. It also didn't matter.

In the first four games of 1971, Michigan quarterbacks completed just 25 passes (6.3 per game). The retooled offensive line, meantime, paved the way for 1,225 yards (306.3 per game) and 17 touchdowns. Michigan went 4–0 and entered East Lansing's Spartan Stadium in week five ranked No. 2. The previous 20 years of the Paul Bunyan Rivalry went against history, as Michigan State more or less dominated the series from 1950 through the end of Elliott's run in 1968—going 13–4–2

PART 3: THE FAMILY

during that span. Daugherty's first game versus Schembechler in 1969 featured a 348–176 Spartans rushing advantage, notching another win for Michigan State. By the time the two teams returned to Spartan Stadium in '71, the game was the most anticipated chapter East Lansing had seen in years. More than 80,000, a Spartan Stadium record, came to see if Daugherty's squad could fight back the rising Michigan tide and extend the golden era of Spartan football for just a bit longer. Instead, they watched Michigan's offensive line—featuring an MSU legacy their team didn't want in Brandstatter—officially put that era to bed.

On the sixth play of the game, Billy Taylor took a sweep to the left and found a massive rush lane after Brandstatter's seal took out three Spartans. Taylor's 38-yard touchdown silenced the massive crowd and, for Michigan State, it got no better from there. Michigan outrushed once-mighty Michigan State 322–59 in a supremely physical 24–13 Michigan win.

"Michigan is the finest football team we've played all year," Daugherty, who stepped down a year later, said afterward. "Everything that is said about their excellence is correct." After two decades of being on the wrong end of the in-state rivalry, Michigan would go on to own the next 40ish years in the series.

The game was also the best Brandstatter played. After helping push Michigan to a perfect 11–0 season, including another win over Ohio State, which ended with a one-point loss in the Rose Bowl, Brandstatter started a broadcasting career that stretched the rest of the century as an in-game voice for both Michigan and Detroit Lions football, serving as a radio color analyst (with some play-by-play at U-M) for both as well as a longtime television host for his beloved alma mater. After more than 40 years as the voice of Michigan football, Jim Brandstatter called his final game inside Michigan Stadium on November 27,

2021, when the Wolverines—paced by their best offensive line in a generation—snapped an eight-game losing streak against Ohio State, paving the way for Jim Harbaugh's first Big Ten championship. Brandstatter's broadcast partner that day? Dan Dierdorf. The duo would retire, together, following that season.

The No. 1 reason why the Schembechler era got off to the start it did was because of how efficiently Michigan owned the line of scrimmage. Dierdorf, McKenzie, Murdock, Harpring, Coode, and Seymour were all draft picks. Standards for each position were set and one of the greatest offensive-line factories in history followed.

In 1974 Michigan welcomed a trio of talented freshmen: Mark Donahue from Brother Rice in Chicago (where U-M found Tom Coyle); Mike Kenn, a gigantic tackle who was also a standout hockey player in Illinois; and Walt Downing, a football, track, and wrestling standout from Coatesville, Pennsylvania. The trio started together in 1975 and helped pave the way for both Gordie Bell and Rob Lytle's respective 1,000-yard seasons. Downing moved inside to center in '76 and things got even better. Together with tackle Bill Dufek, Downing and Donahue gave Michigan an iron wall on the right side as Lytle set the new school rushing record. Dufek and Donahue were All-Americans, and Downing would join Donahue as an All-American again a year later in 1977.

It's tough to pinpoint *exactly* when traditions begin. But from 1970 to 1980, Michigan's offensive-line room had produced eight All-Americans and 14 NFL draft picks. In 1978, Michigan hired Mike Gittleston as its strength and conditioning coach. That year, Jon Giesler and John Arbeznik helped Michigan rush for nearly 300 yards *per game*. From 1978 to 2007, no coach at Michigan appreciated and taught the program's history harder than Gittleson. Recruits were brought in

PART 3: THE FAMILY

and shown, exactly, how to push themselves to become the next Dan Dierdorf or Mark Donahue. George Lilja, Ed Muransky, Bubba Paris, Kurt Becker, Tom Dixon, Stefan Humphries, John "Jumbo" Elliott, and John Vitale would all go on to follow those directions, each earning All-America honors throughout the 1980s—getting their pictures forever planted on the wall inside Michigan's football building.

The better Michigan's OL reputation got, the easier it became to recruit nationally. Paris—a hulking 6'6" tackle—came to Michigan from Kentucky. Humphries, a standout guard, came to Michigan from Florida powerhouse St. Thomas Aquinas. Elliott, a massive 6'7" tackle, came from a small town on Long Island.

Elliott's story particularly illustrates just how good Michigan's entire operation—from head coach to every offensive assistant on down to the strength staff—was with the development of offensive linemen in this era. Before he was Jumbo, John Elliott was a nice, quiet, gigantic kid from Lake Ronkonkoma, New York, who—like Dierdorf 20 years earlier—was just happy to be somewhere. Also—he was too nice.

For every person who's ever played football, two questions must be answered. How much pain can you take and are you capable of inflicting as much or more on another person? The first one is easier than most think and the second is often harder. Unleashing yourself at another human without fear of consequence is hardly stepping on ants. Coaches refer to a player's correct answer to either question as their "light switch." Some guys show up with their switch naturally on, their anxieties buried deep. Others need more time. Some, no matter their talent, never get there.

Elliott was heavily recruited along the East Coast by solid programs, but no serious powers. That changed when Elliott's high school coach, Fred Fusaro, showed Gary Moeller film of Elliott making 19 tackles and four sacks in a playoff game. He watched the tape for five minutes before offering Elliott a scholarship for 1983. Everything about his body screamed future All-American, future NFL star, future millionaire. Everything else about him was overwhelmed and tentative. His nickname "Jumbo," he once told *The Detroit News*, came after Schembechler hollered "come on, Jum-Bo, pick it up!" as the massive Elliott lagged a good 20 yards behind the entire team during a warm-up drill in his first Michigan practice.

His light switch was firmly in the off position.

At one point during Elliott's freshman year, the coaching staff took him aside for a conversation. They were about to pull the oldest of football coaching tricks: They were going to lie to him. The coaches told Elliott, in blunt terms, that this wasn't working out. His gentle demeanor, timid personality, and awkwardness just wouldn't cut it at a place like Michigan. They'd call the smaller schools back east to help find him a new home and that would be that. Unless, of course…something changed, like, right now.

It's a bold move to challenge a player as talented as Elliott like that during his *first* year on campus. But football is a bold game. Elliott returned to the practice field and finished every block he found. Not to the ground, but *through* the ground. If he had to block two guys at once, he did. If he had to get into a fight protecting a smaller player, he did. His switch flipped. Elliott became perhaps *the* critical cog in Jamie Morris' run through Michigan's record book. Morris and Elliott developed a bond that remains today. In fact, when Elliott found out about his College Football Hall of Fame election in 2020, he was literally on the other line chatting with Morris.

PART 3: THE FAMILY

The collegiate success certainly helped develop Michigan's reputation with OL recruits. But the pro football success had become an even bigger bonus. Dierdorf's legend as one of the toughest players to ever wear a helmet—he once played through an NFL season with a broken jaw—helped Michigan's rep even more when he became a *Monday Night Football* broadcaster in 1987. McKenzie and Seymour both blocked for O.J. Simpson in Buffalo. Downing, Elliott, Humphries, and Becker all won Super Bowl rings. Paris won three of them.

As the '70s turned into the '80s, Gittleston's influence over Schembechler was critical as Michigan began to recruit bigger linemen. As the '80s shifted into the '90s and size became the rage, Gittleson was careful not to get carried away. He personally weighed every player who ever made a dress list the day of every game from 1978 to 2007. And with rare exceptions, every one of those players weighed 299 pounds or less on game day. Big enough to maul someone, small enough to do it on the move. When one star linemen left, Michigan always seemed to have another waiting. Dean Dingman, a 280-pound guard from Wisconsin, started as a true freshman in 1987. Wilkes-Barre, Pennsylvania, tackle Greg Skrepenak became the first Michigan lineman to make Jumbo Elliott look smallish—as the 6'8" 320-pounder was one of the few exceptions to Gittleson's 300-pound rule as he became a unanimous All-American in 1991. Wild and powerful south Floridian Steve Everitt became one of the best interior linemen in college football, starring alongside All-American Joe Cocozzo on Michigan's unbeaten 9–0–3 squad in 1992. All 6'8", 330 pounds of Jon Runyan showed up in 1993 and raised the size bar once more.

By the time Jon Jansen showed up to Michigan in the spring of 1994, Michigan's offensive line had more or less become its own fraternity inside the larger fraternity that was Michigan football. Jansen played at Clawson High School as a gigantic 6'6" tight end/linebacker who doubled as a basketball star. He came to spring ball in 1994 as a 240-pound tight end but quickly asked Moeller what his fastest path to the field would be.

"Right tackle," he answered.

And so it was. The number of times a Michigan coach has had to convince a talented high school prospect he'd be better at another position is too high to count. In *many* of those situations, the player resisted—privately, publicly, or both. Jansen had zero hesitation, immediately dedicating himself to his new life as a member of Michigan's offensive-line fraternity. Gittleson changed his body, adding 50 pounds of muscle while keeping the quickness that made him such a unique player.

When Jansen signed with Michigan, the program looked incredibly healthy from the outside. A year later, with Moeller suddenly ousted, it looked anything but from any angle. Four-loss seasons in 1994, 1995, and 1996 damaged everything about Michigan's program—including the assembly line inside its OL factory.

Sort of.

In late 1996, just ahead of the team's Outback Bowl loss to Alabama, Lloyd Carr and offensive line coach Mike DeBord—already struggling to find depth up front due to health concerns and general on-field struggles—asked a true freshman from south Florida to switch from defensive tackle to offensive guard. Steve Hutchinson had come to Michigan to be a defensive tackle. There was a problem, though. He was bad at it. Michigan signed Hutchinson out of Coral Springs knowing he was one of Florida's top prep offensive linemen, but also knowing he wanted to play defense. So, Carr let him. Against seasoned offensive linemen, Hutchinson was a fish out of water. Nothing worked. By the end of the regular season, with

PART 3: THE FAMILY

dwindling numbers, Carr went back to a frustrated Hutchinson and asked if he'd like to try offensive guard.

After *one* drill, Carr nearly swallowed his whistle. Hutchinson's explosion and body control off the snap was better than some of the starters. His power—aided by his massive hands—was off the charts and he moved as well as any big man on the team. In the film room later that night, a group of assistants sat in awe—replaying Hutchinson's practice clips, mouths agape, as if they'd just witnessed a miracle.

"He is literally a bear," Jansen said in *Mountaintop*. "And if you can find a bear to play offensive guard, you've got yourself a Hall of Famer."

Entering 1997, Carr and DeBord (now offensive coordinator) had moved Hutchinson and fellow defensive lineman Chris Ziemann to the offensive line. Jeff Backus, who lost 50 pounds after an emergency appendectomy in January, had somehow made it back to full strength ahead of his redshirt freshman season. All–Big Ten guard Zach Adami moved to center, a spot he'd never played.

Bonded together as a sort of uber-talented island of misfits, Jansen, Hutchinson, Backus, Adami, Ziemann, Steve Frazier, and David Brandt came together under first-year OL coach Terry Malone and, as one, protected and pushed Michigan's offense to a national title. More or less reigniting, and saving, the school's famed OL tradition in the process. Jansen, Backus, and Hutchinson would all enjoy decade-long pro careers. As predicted by Jansen, Hutchinson indeed earned passage to the Pro Football Hall of Fame in 2020. And while the tradition continued through the remainder of Carr's head coaching tenure with the likes of No. 1 overall pick Jake Long and Rimington Trophy winner David Baas, the drastic shift of the Rich Rodriguez era changed everything.

THE PROGRAM: MICHIGAN

Rodriguez, who took over in 2008 from the retiring Carr, retained just one assistant coach. He also got rid of Gittleson and, with him, any chance he had of keeping the fires of those Michigan traditions lit. Rodriguez recruited talented linemen, to be sure. David Molk won the Rimington in 2011; Taylor Lewan would go on to be a first-round pick. Even his strength coach, Mike Barwis, was terrific. But the consistency was gone, as were the depth and general recruiting appeal. Neither Rodriguez nor Brady Hoke nor even Jim Harbaugh was able to compete with the top schools in the country for the best-of-the-best when it came to prep OL prospects.

Not even Harbaugh, whose hiring in 2015 brought the school a whirlwind of attention, turned this tide. Michigan's offensive lines improved after he arrived, but not enough. Over time, Harbaugh's process changed. In 2018 he hired former Ohio State offensive line coach Ed Warinner and Sherrone Moore, a 32-year-old former college guard turned tight ends coach. Warinner and Moore totally changed Michigan's approach to recruiting linemen. Instead of targeting five-stars and missing, they began signing overlooked—but supremely athletic—project athletes.

Ryan Hayes, a 6'7" high school tight end who might've weighed 250 pounds upon his signing. Trevor Keegan was an athletic 6'6", 300-pounder from Illinois whose enthusiasm and talent far outweighed his polish or know-how. They welcomed Andrew Vastardis, who turned down a scholarship at Old Dominion for a chance to walk on and compete in Ann Arbor. Zak Zinter was highly recruited, and the guard had plenty of chances to leave after a dreadful 2020 season. But he didn't. Michigan stopped rushing young line talent, allowing it to develop physically and mentally, while trusting savvy veterans like Ben Bredeson and Grant Newsome to have their voices heard.

PART 3: THE FAMILY

One thing Harbaugh did fix immediately upon his return was the restoration of the tight end position. Harbaugh played with some of the best TEs Michigan ever had in Craig Dunaway and Eric Kattus. The difference between Michigan tight ends and tight ends from a lot of other schools? The Michigan guys catch *and* block. It's always both. Derrick Walker and Tony McGee in the late '80s and early '90s; Jay Riemersma, Jerame Tuman, Mark Campbell, and Aaron Shea—all draft picks, all guys who *first* made their money as blockers. Harbaugh inherited record-setting pass catcher Jake Butt, arguably the school's most complete two-way tight end since Jim Mandich.

In 2016, Butt led one of the deepest tight end groups Michigan's ever had—and one of the best group's any school ever had—as *seven* tight ends on the roster (Butt, Sean McKeon, Zach Gentry, Devin Asiasi, Ian Bunting, Nick Eubanks, and Tyrone Wheatley Jr.) would play in the NFL. Butt's career took an unfortunate turn in the 2016 Orange Bowl, his final college game, when he tore an ACL. Still, his impact at Michigan lives on. Every team Harbaugh coached at Michigan had top-end tight end play—including the last one, as Colston Loveland, perhaps the best yet, and AJ Barner (a draft pick in 2024) were two of the team's top performers.

It didn't happen overnight and there were struggles, but—almost because of those struggles—Michigan's culture began to change. Linemen got tougher mentally and by the time Moore took over as position coach ahead of the 2021 season, former players—for the first time in two decades—started talking to each other about how, suddenly, it was starting to feel like the old days again. Hayes put on more than 60 pounds and lost zero speed, Keegan got all the polish he needed, and Vastardis simply outworked and outstudied every player on the roster to the point of becoming an extra coach on the field. Dubbed

"Gramps" by his teammates, the former walk-on brought everything together and for the first time in a long time Michigan's front five began to play as one.

Much like the 1997 line, perhaps even more so, Michigan's 2021 group of Zinter, Vastardis, Hayes, Keegan, and Andrew Stueber literally changed the program. Michigan's offense topped 3,000 yards rushing—without a running quarterback—for the first time since 1992 and that fivesome gave the school its first ever Joe Moore Award, given annually to the nation's top offensive lineman. Zinter, Keegan, and Hayes returned in 2022, joined by center Olu Oluwatimi and a combination of Karsen Barnhart and Trente Jones at right tackle to win both the Joe Moore trophy and the Big Ten title again. Zinter, Keegan, Barnhart, and Jones were all critical pieces of Harbaugh's final team, the 2023 national champions.

And while he wasn't on the field that day, "Gramps" best summed up the offensive line shift that had changed the program two years prior.

"We want our guys to see the whole picture," Vastardis told me in 2021, often citing the group's "brotherhood" as he spoke. "So, not only do you know your role, but you know the goal of the scheme. What we're trying to accomplish."

The other thing he and his teammates wanted, he said, was a chance to set things right again at one of the places that invented what it means to play offensive line at a high level. He spoke of the old guys, the faces on the wall. How he and his teammates thought about guys like Dierdorf and McKenzie. Jumbo Elliott and Bubba Paris. Jim Brandstatter, Steve Everitt, Jon Jansen, and anyone who'd ever paid the price in the trenches for the Maize and Blue.

"I know that they know," he said, "that we're doing this for everybody who's ever put on a winged helmet."

PART 3: THE FAMILY

A week after Michigan secured the 2023 national title, in his final public address as head coach at a trophy celebration in Ann Arbor, Harbaugh concluded his speech by reciting—most of it from memory—a passage from an old play called *Henry V*.

"From this day to the ending of the world, but we in it shall be remembered," Harbaugh said. "We few, we happy few, we band of brothers. For he today that sheds his blood with me shall be my brother. And gentlemen in England now a-bed shall think themselves accursed they were not here. And hold their manhoods cheap, while any speaks, that fought with us, upon Saint Crispin's Day."

13

Front Seven Belief

WHEN MICHIGAN'S FOOTBALL TEAM REPORTED FOR TRAINING camp in 1985, *many* believed the program was nearing collapse. A 6–6 record in 1984 shook supporters, created unrest, and left the program's vibe in a foreign state.

When defenders picked up their playbooks that summer, they could turn to page 11 and read the following:

"If you think you are beaten, you are; if you think you dare not, you don't," the passage began. "If you like to win but think you can't it's a cinch you won't…. Life's battles don't always go to the stronger or faster man; but sooner or later the man who wins is the man who thinks he can."

The poem was "Thinking," written by Walter Wintle in the early 1900s. If Michigan's historic brand of defensive football has a mantra, it's that passage. The belief, no matter what anyone says or does, that you're good enough to stop whatever's

PART 3: THE FAMILY

coming. The ability to truly give the game you've got, for as long as you've got it. Nothing more, nothing less.

The list of players who lived this mantra is gigantic. There was only one Henry Hill, though.

The youngest of seven children, Hill was a 5'10", 200-pound tight end and shot-putter at Eastern (now Martin Luther King) High School in Detroit. Lightly recruited with great grades, Hill took an Opportunity Grant scholarship to Michigan to study law. Later, Hill participated in Michigan's Black Action Movement class strike of 1970. The strike demanded Michigan change enrollment standards to help increase the number of Black students coming from underfunded schools. Students with the intelligence who, due to a broken educational system, were given zero resources or shot to get into a college.

Football was the furthest thing from his mind until a few familiar faces changed it.

Bill Yearby was one of the original defensive stars at Michigan in the 1960s, a consensus All-American in 1965. John Rowser was another Michigan man from Eastern, earning All–Big Ten honors as a defensive back in '66 before starting a decade-long pro career in Green Bay. Rowser and Yearby both knew Hill. By the time he got to college, Hill weighed around 220 pounds and was running the 40-yard dash in 4.6 seconds. He had the hand speed of a champion boxer and the power to go with it. In the spring of 1967, Yearby and Rowser persuaded Michigan to offer Hill a tryout. He ran one route and the ball bounced off his face mask. Everything after that was exceptional.

Michigan took a chance and put Hill, still just 5'10" and 220 pounds, with the defensive linemen on the freshmen team. A year later, with Michigan trailing Cal 14–0 in the 1968 season opener, opportunity knocked when starter Tom Goss got hurt.

THE PROGRAM: MICHIGAN

Michigan inserted Hill for the first time on a third-down play. Impossible to ignore because of how small he was in comparison to those blocking him, Hill's speed was even more eye-opening. He fired off the ball before every Cal lineman, knifing behind a guard's pull for a tackle-for-loss that forced a punt. Hill finished with five tackles, two for a loss—and barely played. He was in the starting lineup the following week and by game nine, with Michigan suddenly 8–1, Hill led the team with more than a dozen TFL. He joined a defensive front that featured Cecil Pryor, a big and fast kid from Corpus Christi who'd agreed to leave Texas not only because most of the state schools had racist recruiting policies, but also because Bump Elliott's staff agreed to let him play quarterback. Per Jim Cnockaert's *Michigan: Where Have You Gone?*, Pryor was one of several former quarterbacks turned defensive standouts, as he and Michigan's *entire* secondary that year actually had come to Ann Arbor to play QB. Pryor and Schembechler instantly clashed, with the coach reportedly throwing the big man off the team twice during the summer of '69. Once the year began and the coach realized how explosive Pryor was, a rocky relationship smoothed. And remained that way for decades.

Centers trying to block Henry Hill in the late '60s and early '70s did so with one hand tied behind their back. Hill's explosion was so good that by the time the center snapped and recoiled, Hill was often already in the backfield. If he slanted into a guard, his punch could dislodge players 50 pounds heavier. He played low and only carried muscle. He confused opponents as much as he infuriated them. He started seeing double teams, eventually triple teams—and still made plays. Fearless, tenacious, relentless, and almost always the smallest person in the tackle box. He never cared about the last part. Asked by the *Ann Arbor*

PART 3: THE FAMILY

News in 1969 if Michigan had given him a football scholarship yet, Hill said he didn't want one and wouldn't ask. He already had his educational grant; his school was paid for.

"Why take a [football] scholarship from someone else?" Hill added.

When he tried out for the team, it wasn't to see if he could make it. He wanted to know if he still loved the game. He did. His belief and effort, not his height and weight, became his—and Michigan's—signature. Together with standout junior linebacker Marty Huff, an athletic Texan by way of Toledo who came to Michigan as a fullback before racking up 250 tackles his final two years, Hill and the Wolverines were able to take the middle of the field away in an era when winning the matchup directly over the ball was everything. In the locker room after Michigan's 50–6 thrashing over Iowa, its fourth in a row, a week ahead of its famed 1969 date with Ohio State, a *Free Press* reporter asked Hill if Michigan had a chance against what many believed to be the greatest college team ever assembled.

"Be out there Saturday," he replied. "We aren't going to run and hide."

The Buckeyes faced a fourth-and-1 from the Michigan 11 on their first possession and challenged the one guy they were told not to challenge. Before Jim Otis reached the line of scrimmage, Hill had spun off two blocks, reset himself, and grabbed the fullback for a wrestling tackle short of the marker. Ohio State's first big shot had been fired and Henry Hill basically caught the bullet with his bare hands. Everything after that was downhill.

The blueprint for modern defensive football at Michigan was drawn by guys like Henry Hill, Marty Huff, and Cecil Pryor. Their belief in their own talent, and the team's plan, was almost usually stronger than that of their opponent.

"Give me a place to stand" is an old Michigan defensive mantra. Hall of Fame head coach Lloyd Carr, a defensive assistant by trade, used the phrase to sum up Michigan's general philosophy during his run. The belief was simple: If given "a place to stand" anywhere on the field, even if it's the 1-yard line, the defense is getting a stop. If the ball is short of our opponent's goal line, then there's still a chance. Carr used to preach that if Michigan's defense had a place to stand, the belief in the huddle had to be as strong on first-and-goal as it was on third-and-30.

Many call this delusion. Those who've rushed the passer at Michigan call it playing defense.

Dave Gallagher came to Michigan from small Piqua, Ohio, in 1970 as the 6'4", 220-pound son of a doctor. A bruising and agile prep fullback and a double-double machine in basketball, Gallagher had offers for both sports. Gary Moeller, who grew up about 45 miles north of Piqua in Lima, Ohio, was in his first year as a Michigan assistant when he recruited Gallagher as a positionless defender who could study to become a doctor.

The NCAA changed its freshman ineligibility rule in 1972, meaning Gallagher was one of the final players forced to sit his first season. He watched an elite defense that featured standouts like Henry Hill, Pete Newell, Tom Beckman, Jim Betts, Mike Keller, and so many more. By the start of his sophomore season, Gallagher (who had served as a captain on the freshman team), had earned a starting spot for the opener against Virginia. On the first defensive snap of the game, the sophomore from Piqua spun off a block and made a tackle for a short gain. One play, one stop. A week later against UCLA, Gallagher made one of the most athletic plays by a defensive lineman Michigan had ever seen. On a third-and-6 midway through the first quarter, UCLA called a screen and Gallagher read it immediately. Rather than continue blindly rushing the passer, Gallagher stopped himself mid-sprint and peeled back toward the back before camping out and waiting for an errant throw. His leaping interception gave Michigan the ball inside UCLA's 20, sparking a dominant 38–0 win.

The '71 team was uniquely Michigan. The offense leaned heavily on Reggie McKenzie, Billy Taylor, and the ground game and the defense was just a wall.

Safety Thom Darden picked off four passes, linebacker Mike Taylor—following in Bill Yearby, John Rowser, and Henry Hill's footsteps from Detroit—made a then-record 132 tackles. Butch Carpenter and Tom Beckman each had 10 tackles for loss. The defensive captain that year was mild-mannered and quiet safety Frank Gusich. Along with Thom Darden, Gusich was one of college football's original hybrid safety/linebackers (Michigan called his spot its "wolf" position). His ability to flip a switch from gentleman to bat out of hell the second his chin strap snapped amazed teammates and coaches. Michigan sports information director Bill Cusumano compared him to Clark Kent in an interview with *Sports Illustrated*. Gallagher, meanwhile, was a revelation as a first-year defensive lineman—having zero trouble adjusting to the physicality of the Big Ten as he produced 36 tackles (two for a loss) to go along with the interception and another pass breakup.

Michigan's 1971 defense is arguably the greatest in school history. In modern history, it's absolutely the greatest.

Since Michigan started recording defensive stats in 1936, the '71 defense is the only one that held opponents to fewer than 200 yards per game. They yielded just 2,360 yards (196.7 per game) and 6.9 points per game—posting three straight shutouts and holding nine of 12 opponents to seven points or less. Gallagher, Gusich, Taylor, and company willed Schembechler's third team to an 11–0 start and fell one point short of a national championship by way of the 13–12 Rose Bowl loss to Stanford.

Gallagher raised his own bar as a junior, posting 56 tackles (four TFL) and two more pass breakups on another Big Ten title team that finished 10–1. The 1973 season would go down as one of the most bittersweet in the history of the program, as the Wolverines rode another powerful rush offense and punishing defense to a 10–0–1 record, the lone blemish being the infamous 10–10 tie with Ohio State to close the year. Gallagher's final game at Michigan was the 10–10 tie and he finished the year with one of the most productive seasons by a defensive lineman in program history, making 83 total tackles and adding another interception. He became a first-round pick of the Chicago Bears in 1974 and wound up attending medical school at Michigan while he continued his pro career in New York and Detroit before—as promised—becoming a doctor.

As the Wolverines were rolling through their '73 season, a Detroit Western High School sophomore named Ron Simpkins began making waves as a running back/basketball standout—who never got anything worse than an A-. Most of the midwest wanted Simpkins. Moreover, he was a scholastic All-American—and had interest from Yale, Harvard, and Princeton, all schools offering him a chance to study psychology. A unicorn of a prospect, the 6'1", 223-pound Simpkins was in the stands at Michigan Stadium in 1975 to watch Woody Hayes and company stretch their unbeaten mark against Michigan to four years with a 21–14 win. Ohio State won the game, but linebacker Calvin O'Neal (who set a school record with 151 tackles that year) and Michigan's defense kept Archie Griffin under 60 yards rushing. Shortly afterward, Simpkins announced he'd be a Wolverine. O'Neal returned for the '76 season to complete the most decorated run by a linebacker at Michigan to date—378 career tackles. A tackling machine who earned a captain nod that season, O'Neal raised the standard—and answered every question—before passing the torch to the supposed next great one in Simpkins. In the 1977 opener against Illinois, Simpkins—now playing with fellow standout linebacker John Anderson—led the team with 11 tackles and a fumble recovery.

There was nothing "supposed" about Ron Simpkins.

An incredibly instinctual player with a great first step and even better core strength, Simpkins was a crate of dynamite on wheels. Early in the Illinois game, the Illini tried to run an option play to Simpkins' side. The play-side tackle and tight end came down to wall Simpkins off. Upon arrival, the guard got two fists in the chest and went flying before Simpkins made the tackle for no gain. His first step was never wrong and almost always faster than his opponent. His hand speed was reminiscent of Henry Hill's. Only he was bigger, faster, longer, and more explosive. Michigan's fourth game of '77 would be its first major test when No. 5 Texas A&M, winners of 10 straight, brought bruising fullback George Woodard and do-it-all halfback Curtis Dickey to Michigan Stadium. On the game's first play, A&M ran Dickey right at Simpkins. The Michigan linebacker beat the guard and center to the hole, tossed the fullback, and speared Dickey for a booming hit before he and his teammates celebrated as if to let the Aggies know there would be more coming. A&M opened its next possession with a trap play at Simpkins, who once again split a double and leveled Dickey. Up next, on second down, was a pitch to Dickey. That didn't work either, as Simpkins beat him to the sideline and knocked him into the team bench. Simpkins went sideline to sideline and knocked guards around all day, making 15 tackles as Michigan limited Dickey to just 45 yards on 15 attempts. Woodard had 153 rushing yards, but needed 39 carries to get there. Michigan destroyed A&M 41–3, sending notice to the country the Wolverines were for real.

By the end of the fifth game, a 10-point win over Michigan State, the Wolverines were 5–0 and Simpkins was on a record-breaking tackle pace with a staggering 64 stops by himself. Things slowed down a bit for Simpkins during October, but he entered the Ohio State game after back-to-back double-digit-tackle days versus Northwestern and Purdue. With a lot left in the tank. In what would be Woody Hayes' final trip to Michigan Stadium, Ohio State trailed 7–3 at halftime before forcing a punt on the opening drive of the third quarter hoping to begin a drive and take the lead. On first down, two Michigan defenders crashed into Ohio State running back Ron Springs (father of future corner Shawn Springs), dislodging the ball and sending it into the air. Simpkins, fighting off a block some three yards away, saw the ball and dove into the air for a spectacular fumble recovery that set Michigan up with a short field. Three plays later, it was 14–6, and the Wolverines were on their way to the Rose Bowl. Simpkins finished that game with a career-high 20 tackles. The brilliant sophomore from Detroit added 16 more tackles in the Rose Bowl to finish his first year as a starter in the record books—174 total tackles, nearly 15 per game, and a new Michigan standard.

Simpkins nearly matched his own record as a junior, racking up 168 more tackles and putting him just behind O'Neal's career total in just two seasons as a starter. In fact, Simpson got off to a relatively non-superhuman start as a senior in 1979, causing fans to wonder if something was wrong. Nothing was wrong, Michigan's defense had simply improved—and Simpkins wasn't needed *quite* as much. He still finished with 150 tackles—shattering the career record. Simpkins made 29 tackles for loss, seven fumble recoveries, and 11 pass breakups—leaving the program as its greatest linebacker of all time.

PART 3: THE FAMILY

A title Simpkins arguably still holds today.

Among the few Michigan football records that may last forever, Simpkins has two—tackles in a season (174) and career tackles (516). In today's era of massive substitutions, both records—especially the career mark (the next closest is Jarrett Irons at only 440)—should be safe for a long time. For context, Junior Colson—a three-year starter who won three Big Ten titles and a national title from 2021 to '23—got 42 games in those three seasons (at an All-American level) and made 245 career tackles. Devin Bush Jr. got 38 games in his three seasons, two of which were All-America campaigns—193 career tackles. It's hard to argue against Simpkins being the greatest LB Michigan's ever had.

Simpkins' final season was also a challenging year for the program, as the Wolverines dropped three straight games by just eight total points to end 8–4. And after the infamous 1–2 start in 1980, the program was desperate for a true believer.

Like so many unsuspecting Michigan legends, Andy Cannavino grew up in the heart of Buckeyes country with Ohio State blood in his body. His father, Joe, was an All-American halfback who played with Hopalong Cassady for Woody Hayes. Andy grew up in Cleveland, football-obsessed and hell-bent on being a Buckeye. Like his father, he was a running back in high school. Cannavino ran over people at St. Joseph's in Cleveland, the same school that'd later produce Desmond Howard. His style might've worked if he'd had speed with the power, but he didn't. Ohio State didn't want him. Neither did Notre Dame. Even Indiana, who had gone just 2–8 a year prior in Lee Corso's third season, turned Cannavino down.

So, to recap: a salty, football-crazed Ohioan who loved to hit and had a chip on his shoulder the size of Cincinnati. If that's not a perfect candidate to play football at the University of Michigan, the sky's not blue.

Cannavino was a freshman in 1977, the year Simpkins set the school tackling record. Simpkins and then-senior John Anderson, an eventual member of the Green Bay Packers Hall of Fame, were All-Americans that year and never afraid to share knowledge—just as O'Neal had done. Cannavino spent the early portion of his time at Michigan getting pummeled daily on the scout team—but also showing enough savvy as a quick, smart, and tough linebacker to impress the staff. Cannavino could be a coach's dream. He listened to everything, absorbed information, and emptied his tank on every rep he took.

Mike Trgovac also grew up Buckeye-obsessed in the state of Ohio. And unlike Cannavino, Woody Hayes absolutely wanted him. An all-state defensive tackle/champion wrestler at Austintown Fitch High School near Youngstown, Trgovac had offers from both Michigan and Ohio State. In 1976, Michigan snapped its four-game skid against the Buckeyes with a dominant 22–0 win in Columbus. Trgovac was on an official visit at the Horseshoe that day.

"I left my mom and dad, walked over to the Michigan sideline," he wrote in Kevin Allen's *What It Means to Be a Wolverine*. "It was obvious Michigan was kicking their butt that day." Not long after, Trgovac joined Cannavino in Ann Arbor.

By the third game of 1980, though, Michigan sat with a 1–2 record with just one win in its last six games. It was the worst stretch of Schembechler's career. At some point after the second loss, an assistant asked Cannavino—now a starting linebacker and team captain—to survey the situation. He'd remembered watching Ohio State's 1979 team. Hayes' tyranny had finally grown old and new coach Earle Bruce offered a fresh perspective. Cannavino recalled how loose and free Ohio State had played a year prior, when the Buckeyes had beaten Michigan. The staff was grinding the team too hard, Cannavino said.

PART 3: THE FAMILY

The response was volcanic. Schembechler called Cannavino into his office the next day.

"How dare you tell us we're working too hard!" Cannavino recalled the coach screaming in Jim Brandstatter's *Tales from Michigan Stadium*. "You're my captain! You've got to be me on the field! You want me to call up Reggie McKenzie and Dan Dierdorf and tell them I'm working *you* too hard!"

Cannavino left the meeting in tears. But responded exactly the way his coach wanted—even if it meant calling out his friends and peers in front of everyone. Michigan won its next seven games, including three straight shutouts in November, before heading to Columbus on November 22. Cannavino was so emotionally intense pregame that teammates wondered if he'd be able to make calls on the field. Early in the game, after a sweep went out of bounds toward Ohio State's sideline, an in-the-moment Cannavino crossed paths with Bruce, the new coach who represented the program that never wanted him. All he saw was red. He flipped him the middle finger and ran back onto the field to finish a 9–3 Michigan win in the Horseshoe. Cannavino finished with a game-high 11 tackles and, a little more than a month later, he and Trgovac helped Schembechler win his first Rose Bowl on his sixth try.

Left for dead in September, historic champions by January. True believers indeed.

But if the start of Cannavino's senior year had been the worst point of Schembechler's coaching career, the end of Mike Hammerstein's junior year passed it by a strong margin. Michigan entered 1985 on the back of a dreadful 6–6 season and opened the year unranked for the first time since 1969. Public questions about whether or not Schembechler needed to retire existed.

THE PROGRAM: MICHIGAN

The '84 season was the best of Hammerstein's career. With his younger brother, Mark, playing offensive line, Mike made 55 tackles (10 tackles for loss) and five sacks and, if it weren't for Michigan's poor record, he'd have probably earned postseason honors for it. Mark and Mike grew up in a big, strong, and competitive family as the oldest of retired Air Force pilot John Hammerstein's four boys. All of them went on to become collegiate athletes. All of them went on to be high achievers in their chosen fields. The group is perhaps best exemplified by the resume of the youngest, John—he went to Indiana to play football and wrestle, the latter as a heavyweight. He's now a doctor, who married another doctor.

In so many ways, Mike Hammerstein played football like a cornered animal. *Relentless* doesn't really do it justice, as Hammerstein often made plays in the opponent's backfield simply by driving his feet harder and longer than the multiple players trying to stop him. He'd develop moves over time, he became versatile enough to rush from just about any spot along Michigan's front, he ran down ball carriers out of his area and ate double teams in the run game over and over again. Michigan's 1985 defense was filled with this type of belief. Senior defensive back Brad Cochran—one of the most versatile defensive backs Michigan's ever had, also a player who suffered from depression and wound up briefly leaving the program earlier in his career. Mike and Doug Mallory, brothers and sons of Bill Mallory—the coach who took over for Schembechler at Miami-Ohio in 1969. Andy Moeller, the son of top Michigan assistant Gary Moeller and, like good friend Jim Harbaugh, a kid who'd grown up watching Michigan. Garland Rivers was a junior corner in '85 who'd been good enough to play big reps as a true freshman two years prior. There were pieces, to be sure. Just about enough to make a champion.

PART 3: THE FAMILY

The missing piece was already on the roster, though he'd spent the previous year as a true freshman on the scout team.

Before Mark Messner finished his decorated run at Detroit Catholic Central, legendary coach Tom Mach had already told the *Free Press* he was "the best lineman I've ever seen." He was a national recruit. He nearly went to UCLA before deciding to play at Michigan so his ailing stepfather could watch him in person. When Messner came back from his UCLA visit, per Kevin Allen's book, he found what looked like an unfamiliar Oldsmobile parked in his driveway. Before he could figure out the owner, Bo Schembechler—who'd been there waiting for him—popped out with a Michigan highlight tape in his hand. He gave the tape to Messner, told him *firmly* that he belonged at Michigan and not a beach in California, got back in the car, and drove off.

Schembechler never went inside.

He had Messner the minute that old car door shut.

Though mostly raised by his mother and stepfather, Messner's biological father was Max Messner, an ex-NFL linebacker. In high school, he played directly over the center as a 6'4", 230-pound nose tackle who could do anything. Mostly rushing on the outside at Michigan, Messner's power and athleticism was almost a mirror of what Hammerstein brought inside. Ferocious off the snap with an endless motor, Messner was too quick for opposing linemen and generally as fast (or sometimes faster) than the opposing quarterbacks. On his first series as a starter in the 1985 opener at Notre Dame, Messner was so nervous he puked on an opposing lineman before a third-down snap—and still made a tackle that forced a punt.

The addition of Messner allowed the '85 defense to completely embrace exactly who it was: an undersized group who'd been counted out, but also one of the fastest Michigan had ever seen. The worrying stopped and guys started to believe. They beat people their way, with effort and pursuit and enthusiasm. Unranked in the home opener against No. 12 Notre Dame, inside linebackers Andy Moeller and Mike Mallory hung in against everything the Irish run game had, combining to make 35 tackles as Michigan held Notre Dame to just 2.4 yards per attempt on 39 carries—in South Bend. The biggest difference that day, though, was along the line. Messner and Hammerstein combined to make a ridiculous 20 tackles and four sacks as Notre Dame's offense—which had more depth, polish, and proven ability than Michigan's—was forced into four field goals during a hard-fought 20–12 Wolverines upset.

Michigan faced three straight ranked foes to open the '85 season. It outscored those opponents 74–15. The entire defense, top to bottom, had spent the entire summer working to slay every demon that 1984 presented. By the time Michigan went to Michigan State on October 12, it was ready for a party. The previous season had been rough across the board, but things collapsed when Harbaugh got hurt in the ugly 19–7 home loss to the Spartans. After spending a year thinking about it, Michigan's defense entered a raucous Spartan Stadium and never let the home team breathe. MSU made just six first downs the entire game, ran the ball 35 times for only 83 yards, and managed just 2.6 per play as the Wolverines put on a 31–0 thrashing in front of Michigan State's largest home crowd in six years. It was Michigan's second shutout of the year and through five games, the defense had not allowed a point in the fourth quarter.

That streak ended the following week in a brutally tough 12–10 loss in the famed No. 1 versus No. 2 game at Iowa, even though Michigan's defense was valiant in defeat. The thing that makes Michigan's 1985 defense unique, though, is what came next. They played well enough to beat Chuck Long and Iowa;

PART 3: THE FAMILY

the offense couldn't say the same. Those types of frustrating days can break a defense's spirit.

Nothing broke in 1985, though.

A week later they were nearly perfect in the second half against Indiana. Two weeks later, when Jamie Morris got hurt and nothing worked offensively at Illinois, Michigan's defense forced four fumbles and made three sacks and Andy Moeller—Gary's son, who'd watched his dad get fired by the very school standing across from him as a kid—gave Michigan everything his 225-pound body had for 60 minutes. He made 19 tackles, 15 of them by himself, and Michigan's defense kept the dam plugged the whole way, refusing to allow a touchdown. On the game's final possession, the score tied 3–3, Illinois had the ball on the U-M 20 with four seconds left and a chance to score one of its greatest wins ever. Not on Andy Moeller's watch. Gary Moeller's kid helped create penetration on the game-winning field goal attempt, helping senior DB Dieter Heren get a fingernail on a 37-yard attempt that hit the bottom crossbar and popped out, preserving the tie—robbing Illinois and preserving an unbeaten year for Michigan.

"You take a vote and 99 percent of the people say you're gonna lose a game like that," Andy Moeller told the *Free Press* later that season. "But we never give up."

Michigan's 1985 defense is not remembered as one of the best in program history because it was perfect, though it came close a few times. It's remembered as one of the greats because it never stopped believing in each other.

Messner, Hammerstein, Moeller, the Mallorys, Rivers, Cochran, Ivan Hicks, Billy Harris, Jeff Akers, and Tony Gant were all true believers who helped pull Michigan's program out of the ditch and back on the right track with a spectacular 10–1–1 Fiesta Bowl championship season from nowhere.

Moreover, the core of that unit—including Moeller and Messner—came back and did it again in 1986. Their legacy is all over Michigan's record book. Mike Mallory and Andy Moeller both finished their careers with more than 300 tackles. When Mike Hammerstein left, his 37 tackles for loss was a program record. It did not take his young buddy Mark Messner long to shatter it, as he picked up a whopping 70 tackles for loss and 36 sacks during his four years as a starter; both numbers are still Michigan records. More than anything, though, the 1985 defense set a new standard for what it meant to play on that side of the ball at Michigan. Almost all of it was rooted in passion and the belief you can do more than the average person.

And while that new standard was set before he arrived, there may not be another player in Michigan football history that exemplifies it more than Chris Hutchinson. A Texan by way of Illinois with family roots in Michigan, Hutchinson was a pint-sized 6'1", 220-pound defensive tackle from Houston's Cypress Creek with no chance to play near his family home, as the bulk of the Southwest Conference deemed him too small. As a boy, Chris was fond of time spent at his grandparents' house in Marshall, Michigan. So when Michigan showed interest, he jumped.

When he walked in the door of Mike Gittleson's weight room during the summer of 1988, Chris Hutchinson was exactly what those southern coaches said he was: too small and not strong enough to play defensive line with the big boys. What he did over the course of the next year—and, really, the next four—would become stuff of legend inside the program.

Hutchinson attacked every workout as if it were the last thing he'd ever do with breath in his body. He exhausted himself mentally and physically on Monday only to show up Tuesday and do it again. Same for every other day that ended in 'y.' Gittleson was famous for his ability to wring out talent prospects didn't know they had. If a particular lift became too easy for a player, Gittleson banned him from it—forcing him to level-up somewhere else. Hutchinson never found a piece of iron he couldn't conquer. He gained 30 pounds of twitched-up muscle in a year and took that focus onto the football field. Hutchinson never played bigger than 250 pounds. He never got any taller or longer. But perhaps no player in the history of the program got more out of his body on a day-to-day basis than Michigan's original "Hutch." He made an instant impact as a redshirt freshman in 1989 and was a key part of Michigan's Big Ten title teams in 1990 and 1991. As a senior in 1992, Hutchinson tied Messner's single-season sack record with 11 as the Wolverines went unbeaten at 9–0–3. The day after a week two win over Oklahoma State, a game that put him in crutches and a walking boot for a bit, Hutchinson hobbled into a University of Michigan classroom and spent six hours acing his medical board exam. Nothing—not even the hypoglycemic student who annoyed the entire room by nervously fiddling their sandwich the entire day—fazed him. When he left Michigan, Chris Hutchinson owned *five* Big Ten championship rings and was on his way to becoming a doctor.

"For me, it was just: I'm not gonna have *any* regrets," Hutchinson once told me. "A lot of people say that, right? But when push comes to shove and that voice in the back of your head tells you it's OK to pull up a little bit, you don't listen to it.

"You hear it. And then you tell it: 'This is not what we're going to do today.'"

Hutchinson and linebackers Erick Anderson, Steve Morrison, and Jarrett Irons carried on this type of stoic, consistent, relentless approach throughout the first half of the 1990s. And while the Moeller–Carr transition impacted every part of the team, and stopped progress briefly, no group was more affected by the switch than Michigan's defense.

Carr had been Michigan's defensive coordinator since 1987 and once of the program's most trusted defensive voices since 1980. No individual on-field coach did more to instill the idea of belief and togetherness into his players than Carr, the former schoolteacher/quarterback who used to show up to college team meetings in a full suit and tie—confusing some younger teammates about whether or not he was a coach. He was as buttoned-up as it got when it came to business, but Carr's personal touch—his ability to understand what made people special and different—was his true Hall of Fame trait.

And by 1997, with nothing to lose, Carr began heaping more and more practice time onto a walk-on linebacker who used to sleep in his car outside the weight room waiting for it to open in the morning. Eric Mayes had watched Michigan's Hail Mary loss to Kordell Stewart and Colorado from the stands as a student in 1994. Mayes' mother picked cotton in Mississippi as a girl. His father worked fields in Missouri before eventually joining the Air Force. He was a free spirit who spoke his mind and had the unique ability to hold a deep and honest conversation with anyone. Black, white, walk-on, superstar, whatever.

When Mayes made the team in 1995, he didn't have an official number. Technically, he was 16-R, for reserve—as tight end Jay Riemersma was the actual No. 16. He dressed in the freshman locker room with a stall between two youngsters named Tom Brady and Charles Woodson. He talked to both, and everyone else in there that year, about life, music, football, and literally anything else that came to mind. He first caught Carr's attention during a scrimmage when backup quarterback Colby Keefer rolled out on a bootleg pass and appeared ready to scramble. Mayes was playing deep safety in cover 2 at the time, supposed to be responsible for his deep half of the field. However, once he saw Keefer turn the corner he exploded toward the ball. He'd completely ignored his assignment, but he also made a sack. Not long after, Mayes was moved to linebacker and by the spring of 1997, he'd earned reps with the first team. Off the field, his ability to get along with anyone—no matter where they came from—rubbed off on others. The team grew closer than ever that summer and, while Mayes suffered a season-ending injury early in the Wolverines' run to a national title that year, his name lives on as a co-captain of that club and a critical cog in the wheel.

Mayes, Sam Sword, Glen Steele, Rob Renes, Rob Swett, Andre Weathers, Marcus Ray, James Hall, and so many others joined Charles Woodson that season to build arguably the greatest defense in school history—completely changing schemes to a more blitz-heavy attack and leaning into the idea of letting players be themselves. On the field and off. The other signature that year was about a brotherhood forged in fire. Michigan's 1997 team was—and remains—one of the closest groups in program history. They argued and fought like brothers, they forgave and forgot like brothers. Cried together, bled together, partied together, won together, and celebrated together. Twenty-five years later, the bulk of that roster—and so many of those defensive stalwarts—remains as close as family, a brotherhood within a larger one.

That specific defense went on to inspire a generation of extremely talented pass rushers and tacklers, plenty of Michigan natives. Detroit Pershing prep All-American Larry Foote was a literal perfect fit for Jim Herrmann's blitz-heavy scheme and his passion and enthusiasm for the game far outweighed his lack of size, as Foote came to Michigan at just 6'2", 215 pounds, and left with school records. Foote's run from 2000 to '01 produced 166 tackles (a ridiculous 45 for a loss), seven sacks, 16 pass breakups, and two picks. His 26 tackles for loss in 2001 were a school record. LaMarr Woodley was one of the top prospects in the country, playing alongside fellow super-recruit Charles Rogers on Saginaw High School's behemoth of a team before signing with Michigan in 2003. Woodley, for all intents and purposes, was Michigan's first modern edge player. Athletic enough to drop into coverage against tight ends, backs, and some receivers and powerful enough to put his hand on the ground, stop the run, and sack the quarterback. The 6'2", 270–pound Woodley was one of college football's most dominant players in 2006, racking up 12 sacks (a new school record), 16½ TFL, four forced fumbles, and four recoveries. Foote and Woodley combined to play 22 years in the NFL, winning Super Bowl XLIII together with the Pittsburgh Steelers.

Brandon Graham, essentially Woodley's athletic doppelgänger, was a do-everything football-loving five-star talent from Detroit Crockett. An offensive lineman who also sacked quarterbacks, kicked extra points, and handled punting, Graham ran a 4.43 40 at around 250 pounds as a senior. Graham spent his first two years at Michigan (2006–07) doing a bit of everything and, while the Rich Rodriguez era produced little for Michigan fans to be happy about, Graham's work with new strength coach Mike Barwis was spectacular as he transformed his body and landed all over Michigan's record book, finishing his run with 29½ sacks and 56 tackles for loss, both second all-time to Messner.

Rodriguez's switch to a spread-option completely changed the way Michigan recruited offensive linemen, but his switch to a 3–3–5 defense wound up severely impacting the school's ability to continue pursuing top-end defensive talent—especially at or near the line of scrimmage. Brady Hoke's defenses from 2011 to '14 were far more familiar to Michigan fans, as Hoke and returning

PART 3: THE FAMILY

defensive coordinator Greg Mattison reinstalled an even front and brought back principles the team had used to win a national title in 1997. Hoke, a longtime Carr assistant, and Mattison helped mentor talented players like Mike Martin, Jake Ryan, and Frank Clark. More important: They started to recruit prospects who fit that original mold. Big-time athletes who were doubted due to one arbitrary reason or another like Chris Wormley, Maurice Hurst, Chase Winovich, and Taco Charlton. When Jim Harbaugh took over for Hoke in 2015, that process continued—and while Harbaugh switched defensive coordinators (and philosophies) more than any of his peers, he never changed his recruiting profile.

When Mattison and Harbaugh were finished evaluating a Dearborn Divine Child ahead of 2018, Harbaugh determined he'd found the closest thing to a "perfect recruit" he'd ever seen. A star in the classroom, an elite athlete with a top-notch frame, a player who lived for football and worked harder than anyone in his orbit. It was Chris Hutchinson's son, Aidan—a bigger, longer, faster version of his old man.

When Aidan Hutchinson's Michigan career started, the program was not in a great place. By 2018, the team's Big Ten title drought was nearing 15 years and the struggles against Ohio State (Harbaugh started 0–5) had Michigan football in a chokehold. Hutchinson surprised coaches with how fast he put on weight as a freshman, as a bout of Osgood-Schlatter in his 6'6" frame that hampered him in high school was now long gone. By 2019, just a true sophomore, Hutchinson was Michigan's most explosive defender but also its hardest worker—by a mile. After a humiliating 35–14 loss to Wisconsin that September, a 19-year-old Hutchinson *fumed* outside the locker room afterward. His answers were short; he fidgeted in his chair and did his best not to explode at a room of reporters asking him why Michigan's defense no longer looked like Michigan.

"We have a lot of good guys [here]. You guys aren't in our huddle, you're not on the sideline with us, you don't know what goes on with our defense," he finally relented. "But we're going to fight."

Michigan struggled to another four-loss season in 2019 and things hit rock bottom after Hutchinson broke his ankle and missed most of the pandemic-shortened and nightmarish 2020 season. His play as a freshman and sophomore had been good enough to get him drafted ahead of the 2021 season, but no one knew quite where. Hutchinson didn't really care. Instead, he walked into new strength coach Ben Herbert's weight room that January and told the entire weight staff to "wring me out" on a daily basis from that day until his last hour as an eligible college athlete. He wanted to come back to Michigan to finish all the things he and his dad had talked about, even with—and especially with—the world firmly declaring the once-historic Wolverines firmly dead in the water.

Michigan's 2021 season is one of the football program's most magical years of all time. The Wolverines exorcized two decades' worth of demons in one season, finally beating Ohio State and earning the program's first Big Ten title since 2004. Their best player, from wire to wire, was Aidan Hutchinson. He was outstanding against good teams—and *dominant* against the great ones. In games vs. Washington, Michigan State, Penn State, Iowa, and Ohio State that season, Hutchinson made 10.5 of his program-record 14 sacks. He also finished the year with 16½ tackles for loss and had one of the greatest individual efforts by a Michigan defender against Ohio State with seven tackles, three sacks, and *countless* run blocks destroyed.

Midway through Hutchinson's senior year, I sat down with Eric Mayes. No one defends the legacy of their team harder than the '97 guys. The pride and intensity they played with is not

PART 3: THE FAMILY

something every team or player truly understands. If someone in this country starts talking about the greatest defenses of the last 50 years and doesn't have the Michigan 97s at or near the top, Marcus Ray will find that person and change their mind. If he doesn't, Dr. Eric Mayes will.

We were scheduled to talk about old times, and we did. But when I asked him about what he'd seen from the 2021 team in real time, his smile widened. Aidan Hutchinson, he said, was the first Michigan defender he'd seen in some 20 years who played with the *exact* type of relentless passion his 1997 group trademarked. Aidan Hutchinson, Mayes told me, could've played on his team any day. The fact he wore No. 97 made it even better.

Minutes after securing that historic win over the Buckeyes in 2021, one that would spark a three-year Big Ten title run that culminated in a 2023 national title, Hutchinson—who became the No. 2 overall pick of the Detroit Lions the following spring—told reporters Michigan's bad luck against Ohio State had officially stopped earlier that year. When Hutchinson manifested Michigan's win in the rivalry during a dream.

"Sooner or later," Walter Wintle wrote, "the man who wins is the man who thinks he can."

14

The Wolves

WALK INTO ANY FOOTBALL RECRUITING CAMP IN AMERICA and you'll see the same thing every time. The line for receivers triples the size of the line for defenders covering them. There are two reasons for this. The first is obvious: Wide receivers are cooler. They catch touchdowns, they're on TV more, the whole deal.

The second reason? Fewer truly have what it takes to live like a wolf.

By the time Tom Curtis reached northeast Ohio's Aurora High School in the early 1960s, he was, without exception, the best player on every field, court, or course he touched. Good enough to make you smile with wonder and sick with jealousy all at once. An All-State quarterback who scored 28 points per game in hoops while leading the golf and track teams, Curtis' only young regret was he didn't have enough time for baseball.

He came to Michigan to play quarterback for Bump Elliott in 1966. A lot of other guys did, too. Before football became

PART 3: THE FAMILY

the specialized sport it is today, the best skill players on every college football team (either side of the ball) were high school quarterbacks or basketball stars—or both. When Curtis arrived, he discovered he was one of four quarterbacks—on just the freshman roster.

One type of person stands in a long line and waits for a path to appear.

Wolves cut their own way.

Curtis began to focus on his prep defensive position—safety—as a sophomore in 1967. By midseason, it looked like he'd never left. Curtis picked off a halfback pass against Indiana in week five for his first interception before adding two more a week later at Minnesota. At Illinois on November 11, he broke out—undercutting a post route for a first-quarter interception before adding two more in the fourth quarter, including one on the final drive of the game, to preserve a 21–14 Michigan win. Curtis set a Michigan record with seven interceptions in his first season as a varsity player. A year later, he broke the Big Ten record with nine. In 1969, Curtis finally earned All-America honors and had two picks in Michigan's famed upset over Ohio State, playing his final game in the Rose Bowl.

Curtis' ball tracking was the best of his era. His football IQ wasn't far behind. Impossible to fool, Curtis often ran routes better than the opposing receiver, often beating his man to the ball for a pick. Always on time and never in a hurry, Curtis prowled Michigan's secondary with grace and precision for three years to the tune of a school-record 24 interceptions (Michigan's record book says 25, though media reports and box scores suggest 24). In an era when teams barely threw the ball. Charles Woodson, the only defensive Heisman winner in NCAA history (who played in the late '90s), is second on Michigan's list with 18.

Later in life, Curtis and his wife, Debbie, had three children—including a daughter, Tammi. Tammi eventually married Jason Carr, the son of then Michigan head coach Lloyd Carr—giving the Carr-Curtis tribe *two* College Football Hall of Famers. Tammi and Jason—with Tom and Lloyd in their corners—began the ChadTough Defeat DIPG Foundation in 2015 after tragically losing their five-year-old son, Chad, to an incurable brain tumor (DIPG). The Carr's foundation has raised millions, funding researchers across the United States, in search of a cure for DIPG. Carr kept a framed Hall of Fame photo of Curtis in his office post-retirement and the pair's grandson, C.J. Carr, was a quarterback at Notre Dame as of this book's publishing.

Curtis was a humble superstar who made others better by simply being around them. His career interceptions record shares air with Ron Simpkins' tackle mark. It might last forever. When he went into the College Football Hall of Fame in 2005, Curtis' legacy among players who *didn't* attend Michigan was almost as sparkling.

"Defensive coaches in meetings bring up great players from their era," former Alabama and fellow HOF inductee Cornelius Bennett told the *Free Press*' Mark Snyder at the time. "I always remember [Tom Curtis'] name sticking out."

Thom Darden heard similar from coaches—about how great Curtis was at literally everything he'd ever done. Only not from a distance, but right next to him as an underclassman from 1968 to '69. Of all the traditions that make Michigan great, the one where elite seniors inspire promising youngsters to replace them is easily the most fruitful.

Darden grew up 90 miles west of Curtis in Sandusky, Ohio, and was cut from the same athletic cloth. A natural at everything, Darden—who grew up ambidextrous—was a dominant

PART 3: THE FAMILY

pitcher who once hit nearly .700 while striking out 175 batters in a youth league. Also a basketball star, Darden entered Sandusky High School in 1964 with football on the back burner. He preferred hoops and baseball. Football, however, would be where he truly stood out. Though he couldn't know it as a high schooler, Darden was ahead of his time as a prospect. Perhaps by decades.

A 6'2", 190-pounder with speed, agility, balance, hands, and length, Darden was one of football's original Tweeners—a tag on prospects whose build bucketed them *in-between* positions like linebacker and defensive back. Neither was true for Darden, as his ability to flip between either safety spot while supporting the run gave him skills other DBs in that era just didn't have. Offensively, Darden played quarterback (what'd I tell you?). He also played halfback. And hated both. For Darden, the light didn't come on until he learned safety—where he could hit others before they could hit him.

The defense Schembechler installed at Michigan was rather traditional, but with a twist. He played what was then known as a five-man front with two linebackers and four defensive backs. One of those backs was actually also a roving part-time linebacker—big enough to fit the run, fast enough to cover the pass. Younger Michigan fans may recognize this role as the one Heisman finalist Jabrill Peppers starred in for Jim Harbaugh more than four decades later. Harbaugh's staff referred to their version of this position as a "viper" defender. Schembechler's staff called it a "wolf."

Thus, Darden became Michigan's original "wolfman."

The new role fit Darden better than any traditional spot on the field. It'd be reductive to say that the quickness and efficiency with which Darden learned and mastered Michigan's new role was *the* difference in Schembechler's magical 1969 turnaround season. At the same time—if Darden had been playing basketball somewhere else instead of already on the roster when the new staff arrived in 1969, Bo Schembechler's legacy would've been different. Darden made a whopping 82 tackles (including six for a loss) with two interceptions and was easily the biggest schematic difference, as he let Michigan adapt to an opponent's pass game without substituting.

The 1969 team was able to shave off an average of 20 rush yards allowed per game and by the end of November, it was peaking. By 1970, it began to soar. With Henry Hill and Marty Huff controlling the run game, a confident Darden was joined in the secondary by Frank Gusich, Bruce Elliott, Bo Rather, and Jim Betts—a former backup quarterback from Cleveland who *volunteered* to change from offense to defense. Darden added punt return duties in 1970 (8.5 per return) and upped his interception total to five (with 10 pass breakups and a fumble return for a score). So many of Darden's interceptions (he made 11 and returned two for touchdowns) were the result of a quarterback just not seeing him. While the rest of the defense was in man coverage, Darden was often in a one-man zone, reading the quarterback from his trademark crouch before pouncing on the ball.

The most memorable of his Michigan career came in his final game against Ohio State on November 20, 1971, at Michigan Stadium. Moments after Billy Taylor scored his famous fourth-quarter touchdown to give the Wolverines a 10–7 lead, Darden dropped into coverage when Don Lamka threw the ball to Dick Wakefield on an over route right in front of him. Darden broke on the ball immediately—leaping and catching it above Wakefield's shoulders for the game-sealing interception.

PART 3: THE FAMILY

"I was trying to figure out how to get the ball and finally I just said, 'To heck with it,'" Darden told the *Free Press* afterward. "I'll just jump over his back."

Hayes was livid, arguing Darden had run into Wakefield before the ball arrived. The furious coach stormed the field to confront the lead official, getting directly in his face before drawing a flag and having to be removed by his own players. Once back on his sideline, his outburst continued as Hayes destroyed multiple first-down flags before an NCAA-record crowd of 104,016 (which included Big Ten commissioner Wayne Duke) and a gigantic national television audience.

Darden became a first-round pick of his hometown Cleveland Browns in 1972 and would lead the NFL in interceptions by 1978. Curtis was able to set a standard for the safety position, but Darden was something else. His versatility and the creativity it afforded Michigan began attracting more just like him. Randy Logan was a little-used wingback out of Detroit Northern who followed the lead of Darden and Betts, moving to safety in 1971 before taking over for Darden as the new Wolf in 1972. Just like his predecessor, Logan was a total menace—making eight tackles for loss and adding four interceptions, one he returned for a score, to earn All-America honors. Logan was joined in the secondary by *another* former quarterback that season in sophomore safety Dave Brown.

Brown was plenty familiar with Thom Darden's story by his senior year at Akron Garfield High School in 1970. A standout quarterback/wide receiver who also played deep safety, Brown told *The Michigan Daily* Darden had personally helped recruit him to Michigan. Brown entered the program as a wide receiver as a freshman, but did so with an open mind. With Logan taking over for Darden at the Wolf in '72, Brown began to compete at Curtis' traditional deep safety spot. And within days, Michigan had another natural. An explosive 6'1", 185-pounder, Brown ran and cut like a great receiver. He was also a fearless tackler. By the Minnesota game on October 28, 1972, Brown was on his way to stardom.

On the fourth snap of the game, Brown lined up at deep safety and chased down an option from 30 yards away. This repeated itself, over and over. Brown was everywhere against the Gophers' option, chasing down pitch men, hammering quarterbacks, and helping out with the fullback. He finished the game with 13 tackles, two punt returns, and two interceptions. The second was particularly brilliant, as Minnesota attempted a quick option pass to the tight end in the left flat but was stunned when Brown came screaming into the area for a perfectly timed 68-yard pick-six that had its own vapor trail. Afterward, Schembechler told reporters it was the greatest safety performance he'd seen against an option team.

Brown was 19 years old.

Eventually, teams stopped trying Michigan through the air. The Wolverines saw 274 passes in 1968. Five years later, during Brown's spectacular sophomore campaign, that number dipped to 200. His punt return ability also became a weapon, as Brown returned three (one each season) for a touchdown. The final, against Colorado in 1974, was a brilliant 88-yard jolt where Brown caught the ball on his own 12, immediately shook a tackler, ran through four more, and juked the kicker on his way to the paydirt. It was an electrifying display of everything Brown had: speed, hands, vision, power, and agility.

"There isn't anything Dave Brown can't do," Schembechler told the *Akron Beacon-Journal* ahead of Brown's senior season, a year in which he earned unanimous All-America honors while playing alongside talented Wolf Don Dufek Jr. Dufek, the son of legendary Michigan fullback Don Dufek Sr. and brother of

PART 3: THE FAMILY

All-American OT Bill Dufek, became an All-American himself as a senior and stood as, perhaps, the greatest example of Schembechler's preferred playmaker: In addition to being drafted by the Seattle Seahawks in the NFL, Dufek was picked by both the Detroit Red Wings (NHL) and the Minnesota Fighting Saints (World Hockey Association) in their respective drafts.

From 1972 to '74, with Dave Brown patrolling the back end for Michigan as the most complete play-making defensive back in America, U-M opponents averaged just *5.8 points per game* with 11 shutouts and 30 wins in 33 attempts. He became just the second Michigan defensive back to be picked in the first round of the NFL draft. Joining, of course, Thom Darden. Michigan's defensive style and success during this era had no equal nationally. It also helped change the game. Many programs entered their pass-happy eras during the early 1970s. Those same programs were afraid to throw against Michigan.

The true beauty of football, of course, is that nothing ever remains the same.

As was the case with Michigan's offensive transition from an option quarterback to a throw-first passer, college football's uptick in passing forced Michigan's defense to change as well. Bill McCartney took over for Gary Moeller as Michigan's defensive coordinator in 1977 and by 1980, he'd become the first major college coach to use the nickel defense. Offenses began taking bigger advantage of the substitution rule, which led to more formations, which led to defenses being forced to adapt. This was a trying stretch for Michigan, as the program went 50–22 from 1979–84.

And as was the case with so many other things, it was the 1985 group that finally smoothed it out. When Moeller returned in 1980, he brought Lloyd Carr with him. Carr, a former quarterback (of course), taught defensive backs how to think about the game like a quarterback—and how to leave a bad play in the past, where it belongs.

Perhaps the biggest piece in 1985 was senior safety Brad Cochran. A touted receiver from Brother Rice High School outside Detroit, Cochran showed up to Michigan even further ahead of his time than Thom Darden. At 6'3" and north of 200 pounds, with 4.5 speed and agility to match, Cochran was nearly a positionless talent. He could cover receivers in press, play deep safety, fit the run, return punts, and catch passes on offense—if you asked nicely.

Cochran moved to DB as a freshman (forced to cover Anthony Carter every day) and, unbeknownst to him at the time, suffered from bouts of severe depression. A loner who was extremely hard on himself as a promising reserve in 1981, Cochran experienced worsening depression in 1982, which led to a blow-up directly at Schembechler inside his office that summer. Cochran quit and transferred to Colorado, where doctors gave him a proper diagnosis. Once Carr discovered this, he reached out to Cochran and eventually, after explanations and apologies, the DB was welcomed back.

Michigan's famed 1985 defense bonded through varying degrees of shared suffering. Cochran had overcome so much personally. Mark Messner's stepfather was battling cancer. Andy Moeller and the Mallory brothers (Mark and Doug) had to prove they weren't just the coach's kids. Garland Rivers had been one of the best young defensive backs in the country in 1984, on one of the worst defenses Michigan had ever seen. If a single piece were missing, it wouldn't have worked. It was a perfectly matched and self-made unit.

Tripp Welborne was also self-made. In that he was born with it. All of it.

PART 3: THE FAMILY

Sullivan Anthony Welborne III, or "Tripp" for short, grew up in North Carolina the son of a PhD and a kindergarten teacher. He was a member of the National Honor Society and nearly became high school class president. A literal Eagle Scout, Welborne was also one of the country's best athletes as a senior at Page High School in Greensboro. In 1987, Welborne was North Carolina's top-ranked wide receiver and its top-ranked defensive back. About a month after he signed with Michigan, he went for 28 in a high school playoff game—including the game-winning jumper at the buzzer. A Parade All-American and a five-star football recruit before that was a thing, Welborne was basically the same thing as a basketball player. North Carolina, less than three years after Michael Jordan's departure, offered him a scholarship as a guard. In the end, Welborne picked Michigan for a few reasons. He told the *Greensboro News & Record* that Michigan was going to let him play receiver and also give him a chance to try out for the baseball team. (He was great at that, too.)

When Welborne got to Michigan in the fall of 1987, even as a true freshman, he was already one of the best athletes in the program. A day-one guy, not unlike what Charles Woodson became a decade later. In fact, Welborne had the goods to be the type of two-way star Woodson was. One might argue part of Carr's inspiration for making sure Woodson got a chance to play both ways came from Welborne. Carr wasn't the head coach in '87, though, and Bo Schembechler wanted no part of a two-way player. He wanted Welborne in the secondary. Welborne, of course, was not the only star receiver who wanted to catch passes in Michigan's offense. By the time he arrived, Moeller's transition was in full force and the roster was overloaded with experienced receivers. Welborne had a clearer path to the field as a DB, so he switched sides—giving Carr the greatest athlete he, or anyone on his defensive staff, had ever coached.

THE PROGRAM: MICHIGAN

Teammates would eventually compare Welborne to Robert Redford's "Roy Hobbs" character from *The Natural*. He set the North Carolina career receptions record and finished with 18 career picks. Not to mention all the basketball stardom. After spending a season on offense, not having done anything defensively since high school, Welborne walked over to the other side ahead of the 1988 season and looked like a guy who'd already been there five years. If a great athlete needed just two reps to master a new drill, Welborne only needed one. His only athletic equal at Michigan at that point in time was Anthony Carter. His talent was that special.

On the third defensive snap of the year in the 1988 opener at Notre Dame, Welborne lined up in the slot (the new version of Michigan's Wolf position) and the Irish ran a power play right at him. Welborne, showing no fear, sprinted to the hole and leveled the back for a gain of one. Next play, same thing: same result. On third down Welborne dropped into coverage and helped take away half the field, forcing a punt. A natural indeed. Welborne's sophomore season produced 72 tackles and five interceptions, as his feel in coverage was just as good as his feel in space offensively.

In 1989, Welborne got to add punt return duties. Trailing in the third quarter during a week two visit to UCLA, Welborne fielded a punt near his own 30-yard line. He drifted right before making one cut and turning on the jets, erupting for a 63-yard return that set up a go-ahead touchdown. He had an 18-yard return that set up the first score against Maryland a week later, 13 tackles (including 2½ for loss) in a physical 10–7 win over Michigan State, another 13 and a fumble recovery in a tie with Iowa, a sack against Purdue, an interception versus Illinois, a 30-yard punt return (and another pick) at Minnesota, and a third interception in the Rose Bowl.

PART 3: THE FAMILY

An All-American as a junior, Welborne started 1990 by outreturning Rocket Ismail in the season opener against No. 1–ranked Notre Dame—adding nine tackles and a sack in a four-point road loss. Keep in mind, at this time, Michigan's roster had other capable returners in Desmond Howard (the '91 Heisman winner) and Derrick Alexander (17-yard career average). But Welborne, who already had a full load defensively, was just that much better and everybody knew it. Including Howard and Alexander. Welborne's effortless athleticism was revered by younger players on the roster and by the middle of his senior season, Welborne looked like he'd be a first-round draft pick in 1991.

Everything changed on November 17, 1990, Michigan's 10th game of the year, against Minnesota. Playing on Michigan Stadium's artificial turf, Welborne fielded a punt on his own 49 at the beginning of the third quarter and exploded down the right sideline, jump-juking one defender before flying into open space. Approaching the Minnesota 20, Welborne began to run out of room with two defenders closing in. Rather than go out of bounds, he attempted to cut and turn himself back upfield, blowing his right knee out in the process. Welborne's knee injury was extensive, shredding multiple ligaments and requiring two surgeries to repair. It was his final play as a Michigan Wolverine. He'd end the season a unanimous All-American, joining Dave Brown on the short list of two-time winners.

As for his punt return that day? It set up another go-ahead Michigan touchdown in another Michigan win. To say teammates were shaken by Welborne's injury would be an understatement. Howard talked about it repeatedly during his Heisman season. Welborne? Standing in front of a downtrodden Michigan locker room, despite the on-field win, Welborne fought back tears as he addressed his brothers as their MVP one final time.

"Everything's going to be alright with me," Welborne said, pushing his chin upward as he attempted to keep his voice from cracking. "I just need you all to win this last game [against Ohio State]. It's my last game. I want everybody to come through for me, OK?"

In Ohio Stadium the following week, Michigan's defense picked off three Buckeyes passes and held star back Robert Smith to just 43 yards in a 16–13 win that included a fourth-down stop in the final minutes.

In the locker room after the win, co-captain John Milligan grabbed a football and declared the following to the rest of the team.

"On defense today we played with a helluva lot of emotion, and one of the reasons we played with a helluva lot of emotion is because we had to come together," he said. "We were missing one of our great players, one of our great friends. This game ball goes to Tripp Welborne."

Welborne would eventually get a shot in the NFL, drafted by the Minnesota Vikings in the seventh round the following spring, but another knee injury in 1992 forced a far-too-early end to one of the most brilliant what-could-have-been careers in modern football history. Some scouts pegged Welborne as a potential top-10 selection prior to his injury and his impact as a high-level defensive back/returner in a 1990s NFL could've been spectacular. Welborne really never sulked, though. He was the son of two brilliant minds and had one of his own, starting a business career before eventually landing in education himself.

As gracefully as Welborne handled his adversity, it wasn't nearly as simple for everyone else.

The transition from Schembechler to Moeller was successful on the field, producing Big Ten titles and a 28–5–3 record through three seasons. Off the field, however, pressure

PART 3: THE FAMILY

began to mount. The five losses and three ties were scrutinized and dissected. Michigan's awkwardly unbeaten 9–0–3 season of 1992 might've been the boilover point. Purely from a pro talent perspective, Michigan's 1992 squad might be the best the program's ever had. A total of 17 players on that roster became NFL draft picks, including five first-rounders, three future Pro Bowlers, and one Pro Football Hall of Famer. The Hall of Famer, by the way, was a true freshman. And he started every game.

Tajuan "Ty" Law grew up outside of Pittsburgh in Aliquippa, Pennsylvania. His mother had him at 16 and, during Law's childhood, his father wasn't around. So his grandfather, Ray, looked after him. It would've been beyond easy for Law to fall off track as an unsupervised youth in a dying old mill town, but he was different. Ray Law knew as much. Ty was a younger cousin of Tony Dorsett, himself an Aliquippa superstar before embarking on his own Hall of Fame career. Athletically, he was a six-foot, 190-pound version of Welborne. He did everything and anything as a high school athlete and had his pick of schools by the end of his senior year in 1991.

If Lloyd Carr was one of the top recruiters in the country at that time, his young pupil Jim Herrmann wasn't far behind. Herrmann recruited with his eye and his gas pedal. An extremely dedicated and hard-working linebacker at Michigan, Herrmann spent the first several years of his post-playing career as an unpaid assistant in Ann Arbor. By '92, he was a 32-year-old full-time assistant who lived for football and recruiting. When he wasn't cutting film or coaching, he was in his car recruiting. He'd drive anywhere to see a player he thought was worth it, never opposed to taking up temporary residence outside the high school if need be. He went after Law with everything he had, eventually landing his signature ahead of the 1992 season—around the same time Herrmann was making stops west of Sandusky to learn about a 14-year-old named Charles Woodson.

The legend of Woodson showing up in 1995 and immediately going toe to toe with Amani Toomer is what people inside the program point to when they want to prove what different looks like. Law, however, basically did the same thing in '92 against Derrick Alexander—*immediately* proving he was different. By week seven, Law became the first true freshman to start at corner at Michigan since first-year players became eligible. He'd start five more games, including 10 tackles in the 13–13 tie with Ohio State. On the same stage as a sophomore in 1993, he'd one-up himself. Law, now a full-time starter and an All-Big ten corner, drew All-American receiver Joey Galloway. On Ohio State's second drive of the game, Bobby Hoying went deep for Galloway on a play pass and Law beat the receiver to the spot, swatting the ball to the ground before giving a finger-wag to the offense. Later in the first half, this time approaching the red zone, Ohio State tried the same thing—going deep on play action to Galloway. Once again, Law beat Galloway to the spot. He found the ball faster, timed his jump better, and just stole the ball from the All-American in midair for a terrific interception near the goal line. Then, trailing 21–0 with a minute left in the half and driving again, Ohio State tried Law—with the same concept—for a third time.

The definition of insanity, they say, is doing the same thing over and over again when you know the result ahead of time. Law leapt into the sky and picked off another deep shot, Michigan's fourth interception of the half. Galloway finished the game with just three catches, none of them against Law—who grabbed two picks and made two PBUs in Michigan's 28–0 romp. Law was the best player on a field that included Galloway, Eddie George,

PART 3: THE FAMILY

Terry Glenn, and Chris Sanders—all future NFL weapons. A year later, Carr would tell *Sports Illustrated* it was the single greatest performance by a cornerback he'd seen at Michigan.

Indeed, Law was Michigan's most purely talented corner—in all areas—since Tom Curtis graduated in 1969. He wasn't the fastest player on every field he saw, but he was plenty fast enough and, like Curtis, he was just impossible to fool. Teams eventually stopped trying Law, who wound up with eight career interceptions and 19 pass breakups in just three seasons. His only blemish: not being able to knock the ball down in the end zone during the nightmarish Colorado loss in 1994. Law, who helped Herrmann and Michigan recruit and land Woodson, left before his senior season for the NFL—later claiming the move displeased Carr, creating a rift between the player and the program. Law eventually returned to Michigan as an honorary captain during a game (coached by Jim Harbaugh) in 2019 before being enshrined into the Pro Football Hall of Fame in 2019. Both Law's mother and father were in attendance, seated next to two empty seats held for his late grandparents. Especially Ray "Pap" Law.

"[They] believed in me more than I believed in myself," Law said. "That's how I got here."

Woodson was in Canton that night, too, supporting the teammate he never got to have. Woodson arrived in 1995, just after the iceberg that was Moeller's spring firing. His original plan was to start as a freshman opposite Ty Law, making one half of the best cornerback duo in America. Instead, he got to Michigan and found a bunch of nervous, angry, and frustrated kids who weren't sure where to go.

One of those kids was Marcus Ray, a talkative and extremely bright linebacker turned safety who'd grown up as a Michigan fan in Columbus, Ohio, simply because it pissed people off.

Ray had a habit of doing that, as truth-seekers often do. He also didn't really care, either. Combine all this with the fact his football IQ was at least a decade ahead of his age by the time he enrolled and it's easy to see why Ray began 1995 in the coaching staff's doghouse. Much, though not quite all, of that changed mid-year after Carr took over and hired Oklahoma State's Vance Bedford as his coaching replacement in the secondary. It was exactly what Ray needed.

Bedford was the type of coach who prided himself on his ability to teach football to anyone. A genius, someone who speaks a different language, a five-star corner, a zero-star corner, whatever. "If you can count to three, you can play for me," he often quipped. He worked tirelessly to simplify the game in ways that allowed defenders to play faster, which meant hours on hours of film study. Which was right up Ray's alley. Ray and Bedford spent what basically amounted to days together in the film room. No longer disinterested or bored, Ray found himself consumed by learning the ins and outs of both offensive *and* defensive football. Some players thrived in the "do-your-job" environment, worrying about nothing but their assignment. Ray thrived in knowing everyone's job, often better than they did. Including the guy he was covering.

By the middle of 1995, Ray had gone from ignored to the starting lineup—a spot he never left. A hard-hitting, trash-talking, quick-thinking strong safety, Ray blossomed into a type of physical, table-setting safety the program hadn't really had. Multiple teammates have called him the smartest player they've ever played with. Woodson, a close friend and roommate, routinely leaned on Ray for insight into both what Michigan was running *and* scouting reports on opponents.

When Eric Mayes went down as the on-field voice of Michigan's defense in 1997, Marcus Ray picked up the rope and

PART 3: THE FAMILY

ran it across the finish line. So much so that he may have been the biggest All-America snub in the country during Michigan's national title run that year, as Ray finished 1997 with 71 tackles, (four tackles for loss), five interceptions, and four pass break-ups on one of the greatest defenses of all time. In an era when teams were starting to throw the ball all over the place, Ray and Co. kept 12 opponents to an average of just 133.8 pass yards per game—still Michigan's best number over the last 40 years (as is its number of 9.5 points per game allowed). In 1996 and 1997, Michigan's defense gave up just 10 touchdown passes—fewer than some of the program's best groups have allowed in one year. That secondary—coached by Bedford and led by Woodson, Ray, Andre Weathers, Tommy Hendricks, and Daydrion Taylor—goes in this book as the greatest defensive backfield in the history of Michigan football.

The program would spend the next 25 years comparing literally every defense assembled to the 1997 group. Every great corner prospect—be it Marlin Jackson, Leon Hall, Jourdan Lewis, or Jabrill Peppers—was compared to Woodson in some way, shape, or form. Great safety prospects like Ernest Shazor and Marlin Jackson were compared to Ray. Linebackers to Dhani Jones and Ian Gold, linemen to Steele and Renes. No one stacked up. A yearslong drought turned into a decades-long drought. Culminating in a new rock bottom: a 2–4 record during the COVID-19–shortened 2020 season.

Mike Sainristil arrived at Michigan two years before that. Things around Jim Harbaugh's program weren't as rocky during Sainristil's freshman year of 2019. But after giving up 62 at Ohio State the season before, things weren't much better either. Born in Haiti shortly after the country's 2000 election, Sainristil and his family fled civil unrest and relocated near Boston. Growing up, he quickly took to football—carving out a niche as a short, fast kid who'd line up anywhere and hit anything, no matter how much it outweighed him. Running back, receiver, corner, safety, whatever. Sainristil was a dynamic two-way prospect at Everett High School who doubled as a musician (piano, drums, and violin). Completely overlooked due to the fact he was small (5'9", 170ish) and didn't have a true position, Sainristil was *exactly* the type of player Harbaugh was looking for at the time—a tough, smart, hard-working kid who loved football and didn't care about anything but winning.

Sainristil came to Michigan as a receiver, but wound up flip-flopping back and forth from wide receiver to defensive back during his first three seasons—basically whenever the staff needed him. Harbaugh referred to him as a "three-way player." In an era of specialization, Sainristil was a breath of fresh air—a utility piece who was willing to do whatever it took to put the team ahead of himself. During Michigan's historic Big Ten title year of 2021, Sainristil—now a confident and trusted voice—said he and a few teammates put a new twist on the old Schembechler phrase.

Instead of "Those who stay will be champions," Sainristil said Michigan's team talked about it as "Those who stay...will stay," and be remembered as people who gave everything they had for Michigan's football program. He took the word "champions" out of the sentence, and proceeded to win three straight Big Ten titles. By 2022, Sainristil moved from receiver to safety and immediately became an All–Big Ten performer with eight pass breakups (including a terrific day at Ohio State) and 58 tackles before turning into an All-American nickel for the 2023 national championship squad, racking up 44 tackles, 12 pass breakups, and six interceptions to finish his career as a three-time Big Ten champion, a two-time captain, and a one-time national champ.

PART 3: THE FAMILY

A second-round pick in 2024, Sainristil was born with all the athletic traits that his secondary peers boasted in their day. Speed, agility, explosion, and strength. However, the *other* thing he was born with is something even rarer—the ability to lead. Michigan football captains have long declared that honor, awarded to them by their brothers during the most formative time of their lives, the greatest of their career. From Tom Brady to Aidan Hutchinson and all stops in between.

During Michigan's run to the 2023 national title, while writing this book, I had a former Michigan captain (who also played in the NFL) sum up his observations on Sainristil's two-year run with the badge—one that, not unlike 1997, saved the program.

"He's the best we've ever had," the captain declared of Sainristil. "The best."

Sources

Books
Kryk, John. *Stagg vs. Yost: The Birth of Cutthroat Football.* Rowman & Littlefield Publishers, 2015.

Newspapers and Periodicals
Akron Beacon-Journal
Ann Arbor News
Argus-Press
Boston Globe
Cleveland Plain Dealer
Detroit Free Press
Detroit Tribune
Greensboro News & Record
Miami Herald
The Michigan Daily
Richmond Times-Dispatch
Roanoke Times
Sports Illustrated
Toledo Blade